*To my niece, Hannah,
and to my nephews, Justin and Nicklas*

Serving Older Teens

Libraries Unlimited
Professional Guides for Young Adult Librarians

Teen Library Events: A Month-by-Month Guide
Kirsten Edwards

Merchandising Library Materials to Young Adults
Mary Anne Nichols

Library Materials and Services for Teen Girls
Katie O'Dell

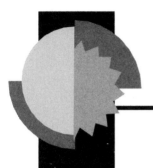

Serving Older Teens

Edited by
Sheila B. Anderson

Libraries Unlimited Professional Guides for Young Adult Librarians
C. Allen Nichols and Mary Ann Nichols

A Member of the Greenwood Publishing Group

Westport, Connecticut • London

Library of Congress Cataloging-in-Publication Data

Serving older teens / edited by Sheila B. Anderson
    p. cm.—(Libraries Unlimited professional guides for young adult librarians, ISSN 1532–5571)
    Includes bibliographical references and index.
    ISBN 0–313–31762–3 (alk. paper)
    1. Libraries and teenagers—United States. 2. Young adults' libraries—Activity
programs—United States. 3. Young adults' libraries—Collection development—United
States. 4. Teenagers—Books and reading—United States. 5. Young adult
literature—Bibliography. I. Anderson, Sheila B. II. Series.
Z718.5.S48 2004
027.62'6—dc22   2003061053

British Library Cataloguing in Publication Data is available.

Library of Congress Catalog Number: 2003061053
ISBN: 0–313–31762–3
ISSN: 1532–5571

First published in 2004

Libraries Unlimited, 88 Post Road West, Westport, CT 06881
A Member of the Greenwood Publishing Group, Inc.
www.lu.com

Printed in the United States of America

The paper used in this book complies with the
Permanent Paper Standard issued by the National
Information Standards Organization (Z39.48-1984).

10   9   8   7   6   5   4   3   2   1

Contents

Series Foreword

We firmly believe in young adult library services and advocate for teens whenever we can. We are proud of our association with Greenwood Publishing Group and grateful for their acknowledgment of the need for additional resources for teen-serving librarians. We intend for this series to fill those needs, providing useful and practical handbooks for library staff. Readers will find some theory and philosophical musings, but for the most part this series will focus on real-life library issues, with answers and suggestions for frontline librarians.

Our passion for young adult librarian services continues to reach new peaks. As we travel to present workshops on the various facets of working with teens in public libraries, we are encouraged by the desire of librarians everywhere to learn what they can do in their libraries to make teens welcome. This is a positive sign, since too often libraries choose to ignore this underserved group of patrons. We hope you find this series to be a useful tool in fostering your own enthusiasm for teens.

C. Allen Nichols
Mary Ann Nichols
Series Editors

# Acknowledgments

I am extremely grateful to Amy Alessio, Patrick Jones, Robyn Lupa, and Kristine Mahood for contributing their vast experiences and broad knowledge to this book. Information and advice from these contributors with various backgrounds, who reside in different parts of the United States (and some who have lived in multiple locations), have broadened the perspective of this book and made this a richer resource for readers.

# Introduction

Imagine a children's librarian suggesting that a toddler read a book in the Junie B. Jones series. It is unlikely this would happen, especially since most toddlers cannot read. How about directing an average eleven-year-old child to attend a library program geared for preschool children? Again, the thought is preposterous, since the majority of eleven-year-old children have very different interests and cognitive abilities than younger children. Now suppose the focus were on teenagers rather than children. Children's librarians ensure that their clientele are served in libraries based on their ages and developmental stages. Librarians serving young adults, however, are not as inclined to offer specialized programs and services for teens in different developmental stages—even though the needs of teens of various ages fluctuate tremendously. The fact is, most libraries do little to differentiate between services to twelve- and thirteen-year-old middle schoolers and eighteen-year-old high school students.

Throughout life, people are categorized differently, and often by age. Around age thirty, people start to refer to themselves, and others, as in a certain decade. "Oh, he's probably in his thirties," or "She's got to be in her fifties by now," you might hear someone say. When referring to infants, adults are more likely to be more specific, especially since babies grow so much in the first year. Parents will tell you how much the baby has changed in the past three months, including everything from formula to facial expressions. Young children are also categorized by age, such as the "terrible twos" and the milestone of five, when a child finally enters kindergarten. Between kindergarten and late child-hood, there are still a lot of celebrated milestones. Parents, and even aunts and uncles, will measure heights and weights of children, celebrating as they go by putting hash marks on walls and refrigerators.

As children enter adolescence, we lose focus on and celebration of age milestones. Once a person reaches age thirteen, most adults clump everyone into the category of teenager. This is a huge span of six years, and there are a lot of developmental changes occurring throughout these years. Society typically does not pay as much attention to the diversity of teens in different age groups as it does to children, who are routinely segregated by ages. In schools, there is a defi-nite transition for teens from middle school to high school. Designed specifi-cally to keep people about the same age together, schools intentionally segregate teens of different ages and stages. In doing so, they ensure that what is being taught is practical for the age group, and that exposure to certain societal behaviors is also somewhat appropriate.

There are other milestones for teens that do not directly involve school. Getting a driver's license is one of these milestones, as is purchasing an automo-bile. Another milestone may be attending the prom. Some teens may consider sexual activity a milestone, but since this occurs for the first time at various ages (and sometimes never), it is difficult to pinpoint sexual activity as a generic milestone for everyone—including teens and adults. The largest milestone for most teens is usually graduating from high school and the relief of leaving adolescence behind and entering adulthood.

In American libraries, there is usually little variation in services and pro-grams for teens that is based on their ages. Few libraries offer programming that is specifically for, say, juniors in high school, or have a library section that is only for seniors who are planning to enter the military. This is not the case re-garding services for children in public libraries. Most children's departments, for instance, divide collections based on "easy reader" and "juvenile." Before a child is even born, some libraries have programs and materials for expectant mothers. How often are there programs for parents whose children are about to turn thirteen? There are books available about parenting a teen, but it is hardly celebrated and rarely the focus of any public library program. At many hospitals, when children are born the public library steps in, giving every new parent a book suitable for an infant and information about the public library. Do libraries give pediatricians books that can be given to thirteen-year-olds visiting the doc-tor's office for a physical? Perhaps libraries could celebrate the birthdays of older teens each month. All of the people turning sixteen that month could visit on the sixteenth of January, February, March, etc., and would be provided with information about library services particular to this age group. The service could be repeated on the seventeenth, eighteenth, and nineteenth of each month.

When a child reaches the toddler years, librarians have special story hours just for this age group. As children grow, there are more programs, and most public libraries classify the third stage of childhood as "school-age," providing services for those who are in kindergarten through fifth grade. Many public libraries do have programs for younger teens. This has been traditionally considered the perfect teen audience because young teens who have just left the children's department may feel lost and may have more free time to participate in programs. Besides babysitting, mowing lawns, and delivering newspapers, teens typically cannot have a regular job at this age, and thus they are usually left with a lot of free time. There has also traditionally been concern among youth service workers about how young adolescents spend their time, especially after school hours.

As teens grow older, around ages fourteen through sixteen, there still may be some library programs and services that focus on their needs. In the middle stage of adolescence, teens are typically very busy with their social lives, academics, athletics, and jobs. When they visit the library, they are often rushed, since they are attempting to juggle a lot of tasks simultaneously. However, by the time teens reach late adolescence, they find little specialized support at the library.

PROFESSIONAL RESOURCES

The publishing market for young adult librarianship provides a wealth of valuable resources for librarians who serve teens, but the materials available for public librarians are not targeted to specific age groups. Rather, they tend to group teens into one category, or split them between middle school and high school. Rarely is there a category other than middle and high school. The problem has been discussed at length. For example, in *Managing Young Adult Services: A Self-Help Manual* (Neal-Schuman, 2002), author Renee Vaillancourt addresses this issue, noting that there is a lack of literature within the profession about teens of different ages who are in various developmental stages:

> *The wide variations in maturity that librarians refer to as young adults (Young Adult Library Services Association's [YALSA] defined age range is 12 to 18), is not often acknowledged or addressed in the professional literature. However, the needs and interests of a sixth grader are vastly different from those of a senior in high school. Although there are benefits to grouping junior high or middle school students with high school students (particularly in the public library, where staff to serve each individual group are usually nonexistent), there may also be times when it is more appropriate to host programs that target a particular subset of "young adults" only. Some libraries even separate their*

> *YA collections into "middle school" and "high school" sec-*
> *tions or target older teens in the YA area and serve the needs*
> *of younger teens in the children's department. (p. 28)*

Another book that explores the issue of services to older teens is *Young Adults and Public Libraries: A Handbook of Materials and Services* (Greenwood, 1998), edited by Mary Anne Nichols and C. Allen Nichols. In Chapter 1, "Adolescent Development: An Emotional Roller Coaster," Melanie Rapp describes the three different stages of adolescence, describing how library services can be tailored for each stage. In Chapter 3, "Trends in Young Adult Literature," Michael Cart examines the publishing field and literature for older teens. He says that in the early 1990s, George Nicholson of Dell/Delacorte/Doubleday Books for Young Readers suggested that a new type of YA fiction be created with older teen protagonists. Cart states:

> *All of this invites the question, "How Adult is Young Adult?"*
> *which was the title of a program I moderated at ALA's an-*
> *nual conference in New York in July 1996. Appearing were*
> *Nicholson, now a literary agent; editor Marc Aronson; au-*
> *thor Francesca Lia Block, whose YA novels have great ap-*
> *peal to readers in their 20s; and Carla Jenkins, then senior*
> *buyer for the Barnes and Noble chain of superbookstores.*
> *The program's purpose was to explore the possibility of cre-*
> *ating a viable body of literature for readers 16 to 24. This*
> *would refocus attention on the now-neglected older teens*
> *while expanding the definition of 'young adult' to include*
> *18- to 24-year-olds, members of the famous (or notorious,*
> *depending on your point of view) "Generation X." Such a lit-*
> *erature, I proposed in my opening remarks, might be called*
> *"Gen-Y," a cross between Gen-X and YA. (p. 30)*

Differences in adolescent stages are described in *Do It Right! Best Practices for Serving Young Adults in School and Public Libraries* (Neal-Schuman, 2001), by Patrick Jones and Joel Shoemaker. In the introduction, Mary K. Chelton outlines some of the social myths about teens relating to stages and the actual differences in developmental characteristics.

In *Connecting Young Adults and Libraries: A How-to-Do-It Manual*, 2nd ed. (Neal-Schuman, 1998), author Patrick Jones explains the importance of getting to know the teen audience. He provides samples of different milestones in early, middle, and late adolescence as described by Elizabeth Fenwick and Tony Smith, authors of *Adolescence* (DK Publishing, 1996).

However, in spite of heightened awareness of the problem and the need, librarians still have little in the way of practical guidance for working with older teens, particularly in the public library setting. Books written for school media specialists are more likely to specify age groups, since schools segregate students based on ages.

The exception to this rule is materials published about collection development for teens. Generally, they segregate teens by age, but most often the segregation still involves a distinction between middle school and high school instead of early, middle, and late adolescence categories. Although there are some books in print that focus specifically on high school students, many are out of date.

Seniorplots: A Book Talk Guide to Use with Readers Ages 15–18 (Bowker, 1989), by John T. Gillespie and Corinne J. Naden describes the plots of eighty books in twelve different categories that are specifically important to older teens, such as growing up, interpersonal relationships, guidance, and health. The authors specify the challenges that older teens face compared to younger teens. As an example, in the introduction to the section about interpersonal relations, the authors state: "Adolescents as they reach adulthood face new problems in getting along with people, particularly as their relationships are constantly changing and often bringing with them new and different conflicts" (p. 41). Another book focusing on collection development for older teens, *Best Books for Senior High Readers*, edited by John T. Gillespie (Bowker, 1991), is geared for librarians assisting teens who are ages fifteen through eighteen, or in grades ten through twelve. This comprehensive book includes subjects relating to both the recreational and curricular needs of older teens. *Books for You: A Booklist for Senior High Students* (National Council of Teachers of English, 2001), edited by G. Kylene Beers, Teri S. Lesene, and Michael Cart, includes an annotated bibliography of fiction and nonfiction books of interest to high school students. *Arco Reading Lists for College-Bound Students* (Arco, 2000), by Doug Estell and others, although not specifically a publication in the library field, targets older teens in that it includes lists of books that are required reading at colleges and universities throughout the United States.

Similar to Arco's book, *Outstanding Books for the College Bound: Choices for a Generation* (ALA, 1996), edited by Marjorie Lewis, is a compilation of books that have been selected by the Young Adult Library Services Association (YALSA) for students who are preparing to enter college. The selections include fiction, nonfiction, the arts, biographies, poetry, and more. A YALSA committee of librarians continuously updates the list, and in recent years has added the term "lifelong readers" to exemplify that the books are also valuable to those who are not planning to attend college.

The Alex Awards, also a product of YALSA, distinguish nonfiction and fiction books that have been published for adults but that have appeal to teenagers. Although these selections are not specifically for older teens, it can be concluded that older teens may be more likely to read books that have been published for adults.

These resources are certainly noteworthy, and they will provide you with a good start at understanding older teens and better serving their needs. However, there is still plenty of room for concrete suggestions and guidelines for working with this age group.

Most librarians rely on library journals to build collections for teens. Library journals typically categorize reviewed materials by age ranges but not always specifically for older teens ages sixteen through nineteen. For example, reviews of adult materials in *Booklist* include a notation if the book may also be appropriate for young adults, along with a one-line description telling why the book has teen appeal. *Booklist* includes materials reviewed in an age category entitled "Books for Older Readers," but the range is anywhere from sixth through twelfth grade. Another popular journal for young adult librarians, *School Library Journal*, includes two categories that may pertain to the collection needs of older teens. The book review section includes "GRADES 5 & UP," which is a large span, but it also includes a section titled "ADULT BOOKS FOR YOUNG ADULTS." The reviews in this section include both fiction and nonfiction titles. *Voice of Youth Advocates* uses a coding system to determine the appropriate age of various reading materials and does specifically address older teens in one of the categories. The grade level interests include middle school (defined as grades six through eight), junior high (defined as grades seven through nine), senior high (defined as grades ten through twelve), and adult-marketed books recommended for young adults.

ABOUT THIS BOOK

The intention of *Serving Older Teens* is to change the way librarians think about and serve teens—in particular, older teens. Hopefully this book will promote a trend for young adult librarians to consider serving teens based on their developmental stages, just as children's librarians have done for their patrons for many years, and will get them started customizing collections and services for older teens.

Serving Older Teens fills a gap in the young adult library services field by concentrating on many aspects of public library services to teenagers who are in the stage of late adolescence. It explores many ways for public librarians to give older teens individualized attention and meet the special needs of older teens who are preparing for adulthood: through collection development, designing a teen space, booktalking, and more.

Serving Older Teens is intended for a wide audience, including young adult librarians, public library generalists, reference librarians, and children's librarians who may serve older teens in some capacity. Some aspects of the book will be useful to college and university librarians serving freshmen ages seventeen through nineteen, or even slightly younger students who are involved in dual-enrollment programs, attending high school and college simultaneously. Young adult librarians who wish to improve services and collections for older teens are provided with valuable information for expanding services. Public library generalists and reference librarians can learn more about the needs of older teens. Also, other youth service workers, such as social workers, health practitioners, personnel from faith-based organizations, and corrections workers may benefit from some of the features in the book, such as the booklists.

You can better serve older teenagers, first and foremost, by understanding teens and making library services to older teens a priority. Instead of offering a session at the library on research for all teens, for example, why not target older teens who are comparing colleges? As an alternative to visiting a high school and booktalking the same nonfiction book titles to ninth graders as to high school seniors, why not focus on nonfiction topics that are especially pertinent to seniors? By learning about the special needs of older teens, you can begin the process of understanding why older teens differ from children, younger teens, and adults of various ages.

Who Is the Older Teen?

For the purposes of this book, older teens are those who are in the late stage of adolescence. They are typically juniors and seniors in high school or college freshmen. Their ages range from sixteen through nineteen. The characteristics of the older teen are discussed at length in Chapter 1, but keep in mind that it is sometimes unwise to categorize older teenagers simply by their age. This is an extremely diverse population. Some sixteen-year-olds are in college, while there are seventeen–year-olds who are still sophomores in high school. Furthermore, in many cases there is a fine line between late adolescence and adulthood. The age eighteen, for example, can be perplexing. Someone aged eighteen may feel he is both a boy and a man, because he is in the middle. Remember that an eighteen-year-old may be a private in the Army, the father of two children, someone who has been homeless for the past three years, or a criminal who is being released from a juvenile detention center after being incarcerated for many years. The term "older teen" means something different from one person to the next, especially since communities throughout the United States vary.

What This Book Covers

This book offers specific guidance and tips on key services to older teens. Various contributors discuss ways to develop and promote your collection and customize your services to meet the needs of older teen patrons.

Chapter 1, "On the Verge of Adulthood: Older Teens and the Library," explores general issues related to serving older teens in the library. You'll find tips for gathering demographic information about older teens in your community. During the late stage of adolescence, teenagers experience psychological and physiological changes that are common to the age group. These developmental changes and their impact on service to this age group are reviewed in Chapter 1.

Since older teens differ from people of other ages, there are some ethical situations to consider when serving this population, such as truancy, confidentiality, and equal access. Older teens need customer-service oriented, nonjudgmental, and knowledgeable staff to assist them with their informational and recreational needs. Staff must be trained to work with older teens, who are almost adults and who have unique needs compared to younger teens. These are some of the topics discussed in Chapter 1.

What do older teens need from public libraries? Like patrons of any age, older teens need factual, up-to-date, and reliable information. Chapter 2, "Need to Know, Chance to Grow: Nonfiction Resources and Programming Ideas for Older Teens," gives detailed information about nonfiction resources, especially for older teens, as well as suggestions of programs to enhance these library materials. As older teens prepare to enter adulthood, they require library materials that support this transition in their lives. If they plan to leave home, they may need information about college life, opportunities in the military, driving, budgeting, nutrition, and career opportunities. Older teens also need recreational reading materials, just like people of other ages. However, their interests are usually more varied than those of teens in early and middle adolescence. Some teens may only be reading books that were published for adults. Other older teens may have difficulty reading, or they may not be able to read at all. Many teens consider nonfiction, as well as fiction, to be valuable, recreational reading material. Broad library collections include nonfiction materials that cater to people with a variety of interests, viewpoints, and hobbies. To promote the library's collection, staff should consider offering programs for older teens. By including the appropriate library materials in their collections and by offering practical programs that relate to the lives of older teens, librarians can give this specialized population what they need in the public library.

In Chapter 3, "Respect for the Future: Making Space for Older Teens," Amy Alessio, who maintains her own young adult space with a sports theme in Illinois—complete with astro turf and lockers—focuses on how to create and maintain a space in public libraries for older teens. Her practical suggestions for young adult spaces can be used by librarians who are starting from scratch as well as by those who are refining an existing, functional space.

What books are available for older teens, and what are they already reading? Patrick Jones, in Chapter 4, "The Hip and Well-Read: The Reading Interests of Older Teens," chronicles the history of the "problem novel" and provides information about what older teens currently enjoy reading. His comments are enlightening, and you can use his thorough lists of edgy young adult fiction, cult fiction, and cult nonfiction to build your library collection.

In Chapter 5, "Real Books for Real Teens: Realistic Fiction for Older Teens," you'll learn why older teens may be attracted to reading realistic fiction, and why it is important for librarians and other youth service workers to become familiar with this genre. You'll also find a thorough, annotated list of realistic fiction that is particular to older teens. The list is subdivided by topics that are of interest to older teens, such as abuse, family problems, high school life, pregnancy and parenting, and universities and colleges.

Kristine Mahood, booktalker extraordinaire, gives you practical information about how to enthusiastically booktalk to older teens in Chapter 6, "Off the Page and Onto the Stage: Booktalking to Older Teens." She presents dynamic booktalk samples, along with thematic lists of fiction and nonfiction titles that are especially appropriate for older teens.

In Chapter 7, "Thinking Outside the Book: Nonprint Collections for Older Teens," Robyn Lupa opens up to a world of materials with great teen appeal—including videos, DVDs, music, electronic databases, software, games, Internet sites, and recorded books. She also explores the many practical and ethical issues that are of concern when providing nonprint materials to older teens.

CONCLUSION

Older teens are at an important stage in life, and they are important to libraries. Many older teens will soon vote, and many others have already turned eighteen and are able to vote and have a voice in our democratic process. Older teens can be a benefit to your library. In some states, older teens are drafted to speak about the importance of libraries at legislative hearings and finance committee meetings. Some library boards include older teenagers. An example is Harford County, Maryland, as described in "Making a Difference: Harford County Public Library's Teen Board Member," by Audra Caplan (*Young Adult Library Services* [Winter 2003]). Each year a high school junior is selected to serve on the library board during his or her senior year in high school. This process of including teen input has been in existence since 1994. Caplan, who is the Harford County Public Library Director and who was elected as vice president/president-elect of YALSA, states, "I believe that the board and library staff all agree that the addition of a teenager on the board has helped improve service to this population and the teen perspective in discussion is always useful" (p. 10).

By demonstrating to older teens how libraries can serve their needs, you can help ensure that as adults they will continue using the library and to support libraries through voting for politicians who also support libraries.

Furthermore, older teens are contemplating how to enter adulthood, and they are considering future careers. With older teens, librarians have a wonderful opportunity to promote librarianship. The February 2003 issue of *Library Journal* features an article by John N. Berry entitled "Recruit New Librarians at Work," in which he discusses the topic of recruitment into librarianship. Surveys have shown that few current or post-high school students entering college ever consider becoming a librarian. Berry urges librarians to promote their own profession, especially to those who currently work in libraries. There is currently a shortage of librarians in the United States. By offering positive library services to older teens, you can promote librarianship as a career and libraries as a valuable and necessary service to Americans.

Our profession needs more public librarians who are particularly passionate about serving older teenagers. You can help make that happen, as others have already begun. As a librarian at the Cumberland County Public Library & Information Center in Fayetteville, North Carolina, from 1995 until 1999, I worked with many high school students, including a teen named Mary White. Mary writes:

> *In 1996 as a high school senior in Fayetteville, North Carolina, I was at a challenging point. Suddenly I had to think about life after graduation. I wasn't an adult or a kid. Where did I belong? Librarians must consider this question when serving older teens. Teens must remain plugged into the library or face slipping away from this resource. I was fortunate that librarian Claire Fitzgerald (1967–1996) started Teen Read, a summer reading program, and Inform U, a college workshop. Today I'm a library science graduate student at the University of North Carolina—Chapel Hill. During those high school days when I continued to be plugged into the library, I had a place of investigation for school, but also a place for enjoyment of information. Those lessons have continued to impact my life. As a librarian, I hope to serve as this kind of catalyst for others.*

Claire Fitzgerald, sadly, was killed in an automobile accident before age thirty. But during her career as a librarian, Claire obviously had a strong impact on Mary White and her future. Undoubtedly, Claire inspired many other older teens to have a love for libraries and reading.

Remember, your influence on older teens might be crucial and life-changing. Consider Claire. Older teens who are served well in public libraries may be inspired, six years down the road, to serve older teens in library settings as well. Claire Fitzgerald made a difference for Mary White. Allow your zeal for serving this unique age group to make a difference.

1

On the Verge of Adulthood: Older Teens and the Library

Sheila B. Anderson

"**Y**ou're a what? A librarian? You don't look like a librarian!" When is the last time you heard those words? How did you feel, and how did you respond? When I lived in Fayetteville, North Carolina, and worked as a young adult librarian, my colleagues and I often met young Army guys in bars. (Fayetteville is the home of Fort Bragg, one of the largest military installations in the United States.) For a few reasons, we used to tell soldiers that we worked in jobs other than our true profession. We usually told them one of two things: either that we were strippers at one of the many clubs in town, or that we were grocery store employees, working in the frozen food section at Winn-Dixie. Why did we lie? The first reason is that as public servants, we quickly discovered that people could hang out at the library all day in search of us. In one instance, a soldier brought my coworker a stuffed animal on a busy Sunday afternoon and pestered her while she tried to help customers at the reference desk. The second reason we lied about our true profession is because we knew that it was a hassle to respond to the stereotypes. We were tired of explaining that not all librarians are elderly ladies wearing thick eyeglasses and buns in their hair; that we did not stamp books and tell people to be quiet all day; and that yes, indeed, we had to go to college to become librarians.

Now consider the multitude of stereotypes that exist about teenagers. Teens are perceived by many adults to be loud, obnoxious, irresponsible, and even dangerous. Haven't you heard adults make stereotypical comments about teenagers? And when was the last time you made a deprecating remark about a teen? Assuming that all teenagers are the same and that all teens have the same attitudes and interests is unfair and wrong, just as assuming that all librarians are the same is wrong.

For example, regarding ages and physical attributes, do you know a teenager when you see one, and are you sure? What would you guess to be the age of the last teenager that you saw? Since teenagers progress on a physical level at different ages and in different stages, sometimes it is not easy to distinguish age differences. A teen who looks to be about age thirteen may actually be fifteen. On the other end of the spectrum, some fifteen and sixteen year olds look like they are in their early twenties. Their cognitive abilities may not have caught up to their bodies, though, and someone who is sixteen but looks nineteen may still be at the same maturity level as someone who is thirteen. Sometimes adults become frustrated when they see teens whom they perceive to be older acting immaturely, but it is not always behavior that the teenager can control.

Being able to move beyond stereotypes is the first step in serving teenagers. What is your image of today's teens?

In 2000 I served on YALSA's Best of the Best Books for Young Adults Preconference Committee. The preconference at the American Library Association's 2000 Annual Conference in Chicago gave librarians the opportunity to discuss books and to create a list of the top 100 books for teenagers. The list was to be derived from previous Best Books for Young Adults lists. For the first time in YALSA's history, teenagers were invited to participate in the discussions and in the voting process at the 2000 event. I collaborated with YALSA's Local Arrangements Committee to involve three middle school students from the Chicago area—Deana Rutherford, Katie Cobb, and Lauren Tidd—in the discussion and voting process. The day after the event, the teenagers had a chance to explore the exhibits. Inspired by the teens' enthusiasm, I wrote an essay for the *Journal of Youth Services in Libraries*, and in it I stated:

> *On Saturday, the three teens and their moms explored the exhibits. They enjoyed picking up free books, speaking with authors and publishers, and talking with librarians they met. "Librarians are not all old ladies with reading glasses," Katie said. "This proved that the stereotypes are wrong—they're human and easy to connect with." (Anderson 2000, p. 20)*

Katie had come to the realization that librarians are not all alike, and I was especially moved by this comment. I was proud of her for being able to look past the common stereotypes of librarians and to stand up for us, saying that we are, indeed, human like everyone else. At the time, I wondered how many adults, including librarians, were able to have the same open mind about teenagers. If adults were attending a function with many teenagers present, would they reach the conclusion that not all teenagers are the same, and that the stereotypes about teens may not be valid? Would the adults classify the teenagers as "human," and would they determine that teens are approachable and easy to connect with?

Deanna, one of the other participants, continued her involvement with librarianship after the conference. She started subscribing to the mailing list YALSA-BK, where she has entertained librarians with her enlightening comments about young adult literature. In addition, she began contributing as a teen reviewer to the library journal *Voice of Youth Advocates*. Deanna also became an author in the inaugural issue of *Young Adult Library Services*, YALSA's journal that replaced the *Journal of Youth Services in Libraries,* which formerly was published in conjunction with the Association of Library Services to Children (ALSC). In her article, Deanna, a high school junior in the 2003–2004 school year, describes her frustrations when participating in a speech about marketing to teenagers. She writes:

> *By the time a few of the adults had made their speeches, we were hopping mad. Almost everyone that spoke, with a few exceptions, seemed to have reached the conclusion that the only way to get a teenager interested in doing anything is to bribe them with large quantities of food. Pizza doesn't hurt, I guess, but I've always resented the implication that my generation is completely comprised of brainless, hormone-driven, junk food vacuums that only care about parties and members of the opposite sex. The age stereotypes were thick in the air by the time it became my turn to speak. (Rutherford 2002, p. 9)*

Deana's negative feelings were the result of hearing from adults who stereotype teenagers into one large group, and who have determined that all teenagers are exactly the same, similar to how many librarians feel when people assume that those in the library profession are all old ladies with glasses! Just as librarians may vary due to age differences, teens vary as well, and it is dangerous to rely on age or any other stereotypes when describing an entire group of people.

It is also incorrect to believe that all teenagers need the same type of service from public libraries. The youngest of teens may still travel to the library with their parents, and they may still feel more comfortable in the children's section of the library. Teens in the middle stage of adolescence may be struggling to juggle academics, athletics, jobs, and their social lives. They may be less likely to use the library compared to teens of other ages due to a multitude of other priorities. Older teens have their own set of circumstances that have an impact on library use, or in some cases nonuse, of the public library.

AT WHAT AGE DOES A TEENAGER BECOME AN "OLDER" TEENAGER?

"Older teen" is a slippery term. Determining who fits into the category of "older teenager" is not an easy task because teenagers of various ages develop mentally and physically at different times during the long span of adolescence. Age breakdowns and definitions of "older teenager" vary depending on geographical locations, cultural norms, and societal circumstances. Whereas in most of the United States "older teenagers" are considered those in their last years of high school and into their first year of college, this is not always true in other countries or cultures. For the purposes of this book, though, the term "older teen" typically refers to teens between the ages of sixteen and nineteen or those who are in grade ten through freshman year in college.

It is also difficult to conduct and find research specifically on older teenagers. Most of the researchers and statisticians have grouped teenagers into one of three categories: those who are thirteen through eighteen years old, those who are either in middle school or high school, and those who are ages fifteen through nineteen. So what is the problem when trying to separate out information about older teenagers?

The first category, obviously, is entirely too broad, since someone who is thirteen will differ vastly from someone who is nineteen. The second category, middle and high school, assumes that all teenagers are still in school, and this is not always true. The last category, ages fifteen through nineteen, which is typically used by the U.S. Census Bureau, is problematic because those who are fifteen are not yet older teens, and in some cases those who are nineteen may be too old to be categorized as those served by young adult librarians in public libraries. Since the magical age of eighteen is the legal age of adulthood in many states, some libraries do not consider eighteen year olds to be young adults.

In contrast, the Young Adult Library Services Association (YALSA) of the American Library Association (ALA) has defined its service population as those ages twelve through eighteen. This range includes someone who is not yet a teenager at the age of twelve but does not include those who are nineteen and are still teenagers.

Efforts to define "young adults," much less older teens, are not new; in 1975, Rosemary Young, then the Young Adult Services Coordinator at the Denver Public Library, stated: "But, adolescence may start as early as age ten and some individuals may continue in adolescence all of their lives, unwilling to accept a consistent role as an adult" (Young 1975, p. 84).

In 2003, the Supreme Court decision upholding the Children's Internet Protection Act (CIPA) put an interesting spin on the definition of "adult" because the ruling states that people aged seventeen are now adults, and that they can ask librarians to turn off Internet filters. Anyone younger, however, is considered to be a minor, and must search computers with filtered information. This

Supreme Court ruling will have an impact on older teens and librarians serving them because access to many types of information may be difficult. This situation is crucial for older teens who rely on unfiltered computer access for information related to school, life, and their future.

OLDER TEENAGERS TODAY

How would someone describe a typical older teenager in the United States? Many adults in the United States assume older teenagers are high school students who fit into one of a few different categories. They may be hard-working, college-bound, high school students. They may also be carefree, just biding their time until they are unchained from high school. Or they might have already dropped out of high school. Although many older teenagers can be labeled "typical high school students," this is a dangerous generalization, and librarians serving this age group should familiarize themselves with how much older teens may actually differ from one another.

> A Pizza Hut commercial that ran a few years ago advertising its "Big New Yorker" pizza features two teenagers sitting around and talking about the pizza. The narrator, who appears to be about fifteen or sixteen years old, talks in what sounds like a native New York City accent about the greatness of the "Big New Yorker" pizza. At the end of the commercial, the camera pulls back, showing that the teens are sitting on the back of a pickup truck in the middle of a field. The second teen, who has said nothing throughout the commercial, finally says something to his friend such as, "Come on, Bobby, you've never even been out of Iowa!" This commercial demonstrates how some aspects of the American teen are common to all, while others are not. Most teenagers throughout the United States love pizza and can relate to other teenagers who love pizza, no matter where they live. This depicts the assumption that some things in life, such as teens loving pizza, are typically standard despite other circumstances.

The United States is a very diverse country, and librarians serving older teens need to expand their thinking to grasp how different one teenager may be from someone else, even within a particular county or library service area. When planning your programs and services, take into account socioeconomic differences, religious beliefs, developmental differences, race, and cultural differences. Urban, suburban, and rural areas may differ greatly from one another, yet all three types of settings may be included in an area that your library serves. Also within one area, some people are living below the poverty line, whereas others are wealthy or middle class.

Family structures have also changed in the past twenty years. The average nuclear family no longer consists of a mother, a father, and children. Stepfathers and stepmothers, half-brothers and half-sisters, gay and lesbian parents, and adopted children are just some of the variations that have become widespread in our culture.

Demographics of Older Teens

Although stereotypes and generalizations can be harmful, understanding trends and general characteristics can be enlightening. Become familiar with national statistics and get a feel for the overall pulse of American teens who are about to enter adulthood.

There are approximately 16,209,000 people ages sixteen through nineteen in the United States. These older teens vary in ethnicity, educational attainment, geographical location, and possible participation in destructive behavior, such as using drugs, engaging in sexual intercourse, and riding with a driver who has been drinking.

As we head into the future, consider what life will be like with older teens on the planet. How many will there be, and will they be diverse, and of what gender? Fortunately, the U.S. Census Bureau has gathered a great deal of information and has published projections of the future population of teenagers.

The Horatio Alger Association of Distinguished Americans publishes *The State of Our Nation's Youth Report*. The report is a compilation of survey results based on the data collected from 1,013 students ages fourteen through eighteen across the country. Although the research does not specifically target older teens, the results may be valuable for librarians. Following are some of the results of the HAADA survey and Census Bureau data:

How High School Students Describe Their Last Report Card	
Mostly A's	20%
A's and B's	33%
Mostly B's	8%
Mix of B's and C's	26%
Mostly C's	7%
Mostly below C's	6%

Hours Per Week Most High School Students Spend on Homework	
0–5 Hours	58%
6–10 Hours	26%
11–15 Hours	9%
16–20 Hours	3%
More Than 20 Hours	3%

What Most Teens Plan to Do After High School

Continue my education	74%
Get a job	34%
Travel	18%
Join the armed forces	10%
Join a volunteer organization	8%
Get married	7%
Other	2%
Not sure	2%

Source: Horatio Alger Association of Distinguished Americans, *State of Our Nation's Youth Report*, as reported in *The Book of Lists for Teens* (Choron and Choron 2000, pp. 161–163).

Resident Population by Age and Sex: 2000 and 2001

	2000	2001
Females ages 15–19	9,829,000	9,844,000
Males ages 15–19	10,391,000	10,423,000

Source: U.S. Census Bureau, "Current Population Reports, P25-1095," in *Statistical Abstract of the United States* (2002, p. 14, Table No. 12).

Resident Population Projections by Sex and Age: 2005 and 2010

	2005	2010
Females Ages 15–19	10,202,000	10,536,000
Males Ages 15–19	10,788,000	11,132,000

Source: U.S. Census Bureau, "National Population Projections-Summary Tables" (published January 13, 2000), in *Statistical Abstract of the United States* (2002, p. 15, Table No. 13).

Resident Population by Race, Hispanic Origin, and Single Years of Age—2001

Age 16

Total	4,048,000
White	3,147,000
Black	611,000
American Indian, Alaska Native	52,000
Asian	149,000
Native Hawaiian and Other Pacific Islander	8,000
Two or more races	81,000
Hispanic origin	614,000
Non-Hispanic White	2,585,000

Age 17

Total	4,017,000
White	3,123,000
Black	605,000
American Indian, Alaska Native	51,000
Asian	151,000
Native Hawaiian and Other Pacific Islander	9,000
Two or more races	78,000
Hispanic origin	617,000
Non-Hispanic White	2,557,000

Age 18

Total	4,058,000
White	3,154,000
Black	606,000
American Indian, Alaska Native	51,000
Asian	161,000
Native Hawaiian and Other Pacific Islander	9,000
Two or more races	77,000
Hispanic origin	647,000
Non-Hispanic White	2,560,000

Age 19

Total	4,092,000
White	3,184,000
Black	607,000
American Indian, Alaska Native	50,000
Asian	167,000
Native Hawaiian and Other Pacific Islander	9,000
Two or more races	75,000
Hispanic origin	675,000
Non-Hispanic White	2,564,000

Source: U.S. Census Bureau, *Statistical Abstract of the United States* (2002, p. 16, Chart No. 14).

Marital Status of the Population by Sex and Age: 2000
Males 18 to 19 years old

Total	4,082,000
Never married	4,011,000
Married	70,000
Widowed	0
Divorced	1,000

Females 18 to 19 years old

Total	4,009,000
Never married	3,727,000
Married	270,000
Widowed	2,000
Divorced	10,000

Source: U.S. Census Bureau, "Current Population Reports, P20-537" and earlier reports, in *Statistical Abstract of the United States* (2002, p. 48, Chart No. 48).

Births to Unmarried Women by Age of Mother: 2000

15 to 19 years old	369,000

Source: U.S. National Center for Health Statistics, *Vital Statistics of the United States*, annual; and *National Vital Statistics Reports* (NVSR) (formerly *Monthly Vital Statistics Report*), in the *Statistical Abstract of the United States* (2002, p. 64, Chart No. 75).

School Enrollment by Race, Hispanic Origin, and Age: 2000

16 and 17 years old

White	5,845,000
Black	1,106,000
Hispanic origin	959,000

18 and 19 years old

White	3,924,000
Black	716,000
Hispanic origin	617,000

Source: U.S. Census Bureau, "Current Population Reports, PPL-148" and earlier PPL and P-20 reports, in *Statistical Abstract of the United States* (2002, p. 136, Chart No. 203).

Students Who Are Homeschooled by Selected Characteristics: 1999

Grades 9–12

Total	13,954,000
Homeschooled	235,000

Source: U.S. National Center for Education Statistics, "Homeschooling in the United States: 1999, NCES 2001-033, July 2001," in *Statistical Abstract of the United States* (2002, p. 147, Chart No. 223).

High School Dropouts by Age, Race, and Hispanic Origin: 2000

White

16 to 17 year olds	366,000
18 to 21 year olds	1,558,000

Black

16 to 17 year olds	84,00
18 to 21 year olds	383,000

Hispanic

16 to 17 year olds	121,000
18 to 21 year olds	733,000

Source: U.S. Census Bureau, "Current Population Reports, PPL-148," in *Statistical Abstract of the United States* (2002, p. 163, Chart No. 251).

General Educational Development (GED) Credentials Issued 2000

GED issued to those ages 19 and under   42,000

Source: U.S. National Center for Education Statistics, "Digest of Education Statistics," in *Statistical Abstract of the United States* (2002, p. 164, Chart No. 254).

College Enrollment of Recent High School Graduates 2000

Number of high school graduates	2,756,000
Percent enrolled in college	63.3

Source: U.S. National Center for Education Statistics, "Digest of Education Statistics," in *Statistical Abstract of the United States* (2002, p. 164, Chart No. 255).

Risk Behaviors in High School Students, 2001

	Grade 10	Grade 11	Grade 12
Rarely or never wear seatbelts	13.3%	13.6%	13.9%
Rarely or never wear bicycle helmets	83.5%	87.1%	86.3%
Who rode with a driver who had been drinking alcohol	30.6%	29.1%	32.8%

Source: Centers for Disease Control, "Youth Risk Behavior Surveillance—United States, 2001," in *The World Almanac and Book of Facts* (2003, p. 79).

Sexual Activity of High School Students, 2001: Ever had sexual intercourse

	Male	Female
Grade 10	42.2%	39.3%
Grade 11	54%	49.7%
Grade 12	61%	60.1%

Source: Centers for Disease Control, "Youth Risk Behavior Surveillance—United States, 2001," in the *World Almanac and Book of Facts* (2003, p. 80).

Deaths in the U.S. Involving Firearms, by Age, 1999
Ages 15–19

Total firearms deaths	2,896
Unintentional	126
Suicides	975
Homicides	1,708
Undetermined	68

Source: National Safety Council, in the *World Almanac and Book of Facts* (2003, p. 80).

Top Metropolitan Areas by Size of Teenage Population, in 2002

Los Angeles–Long Beach	836,393
New York	724,666
Chicago	723,487
Philadelphia	443,234
Washington metro area	411,989

Source: MapInfo Corporation, "Teens in the City," *USA Today*, February 3 2003, p. B9.

Older Teen Tidbits: Ten Statistics

1. In an average week during the 2001 school year, about 9% of youth ages 16 to 19 were neither enrolled in school nor working.

2. Older youth, ages 18 and 19, are three times as likely to be detached from the activities of school or work as youth ages 16 to 17. In 2001, 13% of youth ages 18 and 19 were neither enrolled in school nor working.

3. Long-term trends for high school seniors show that daily smoking declined from 21% in 1980 to 17% in 1992, increased to 25% in 1997, and declined to 19% in 2001.

4. Among 10th and 12th graders, males are more likely to drink heavily than are females. In 2001, 36% of 12th grade males reported heavy drinking, compared with 24% of 12th grade females. Among 10th graders, 29% of males reported heavy drinking, compared with 21% of females. As adolescents get older, the differences between males and females in this drinking behavior appear to become more pronounced.

5. Longer-term trend data for high school seniors indicate that past 30-day illicit drug use was reported by 37% in 1980, declined gradually to 14% in 1992, and then rose sharply, reaching 27% in 1997. Since that time illicit drug use has remained stable among high school seniors.

6. In 2000, the serious violent crime victimization rate for youth dropped more for younger teens (ages 12 to 14) than for older teens (ages 15 to 17). In 2000, the rate for older teens dropped to 19 per 1,000 and for younger teens dropped to 14 per 1,000.

7. In 2000, 87% of young adults ages 18 to 24 had completed high school with a diploma or an alternative credential such as a General Education Development (GED) certificate. The high school completion rate has increased slightly since 1980, when it was 84%.

8. Twenty percent of all 1998 high school graduates took the majority of their English courses at the honors level, an increase from 7% of 1982 high school graduates.

9. More high school students are taking foreign language courses. Thirteen percent of 1998 high school graduates had taken a 4th year or advanced placement course, compared with 6% of 1982 graduates.

10. Average reading scores have not improved among students ages 9, 13, or 17 since 1980. Girls had higher reading scores than boys at all three ages in 1999. (FIFCFS 2002, p. xx)

DEVELOPMENTAL STAGE OF LATE ADOLESCENCE

Most teenagers experience the same developmental stages, including psychological, physical, cognitive, emotional, and social transitions. Psychologists have designated three different stages of adolescence: early, middle, and late. In the late stage of adolescence, which is approximately ages sixteen through nineteen, teens prepare for adulthood and become more independent. Instead of spending time with family members, they are more likely to spend their time with peers and coworkers. They have a better sense of their identity. Unlike in earlier years, they are better able to think ideas through before making decisions. In addition, they have a more developed sense of humor and are better able to appreciate sarcasm. At this point in their lives they are more likely to have interests that remain the same over time, such as a liking for one type of sport or a particular hobby.

Older teens are more emotionally stable than younger adolescents. In most cases they are mature enough to make independent decisions and do not have to rely on the adults in their lives to help them with these decisions.

Career opportunities become a vital concern at this stage since older teens will soon have to make decisions that may have an impact on the rest of their lives. Teens in the late stage of adolescence also have more defined work habits, and by the age of eighteen or nineteen, many of them have already been working for several years.

Teens are also more likely to be sure of their sexual identity at this stage. Older teens may be involved in serious relationships, may have experienced love, and are more likely to have ongoing sexual relationships.

Psychologically, older teens seek more autonomy in their lives. They are more apt to challenge authority, not only because they have better cognitive abilities than younger teens, but also because they have more experience with the ways of the world. The cognitive abilities of teens increase as they grow older.

In terms of moral development, teens in high school are more likely to think about what is right and wrong.

There are physical changes as well. By age sixteen, females are close to their adult height, and they have developed physically. Male teens have also matured physically, although they will continue to have growth spurts until age twenty-one.

By the end of the late stage of adolescence, older teens often have mixed feelings about high school graduation and their future. They may feel a bit anxious about the future; they may be sad at the prospect of leaving friends and family behind. As older teens prepare to leave home, their relationship with their family changes. Whether they leave to attend college, enter the military, live independently, or join the workforce, they realize that life is going to change once they no longer live under the same roof with their parents.

In the late stage of adolescence, teenagers may look and act like adults, but it is important to remember that they are still teenagers. Some of them have not had much practice coping with the ups and downs of life, and although they are typically able to grow into adults, some would rather remain teenagers.

Milestones of Late Adolescence (17 to 18) (Adapted from Fenwick and Smith 1996)

1. Views world idealistically

2. Becomes involved in world outside of home and school

3. Sets goals

4. Relationships stabilize

5. Sees adults as "equals"

6. Seeks to establish independence firmly

Normal Adolescent Development (http://education.indiana.edu/cas/adol/
    development.html)

Late Adolescence (17–19 Years)

Movement Towards Independence
Firmer identity   Ability to delay gratification
Ability to think ideas through   Ability to express ideas in words
More developed sense of humor   Stable interests
Greater emotional stability   Ability to make independent decisions
Ability to compromise   Pride in one's work
Self-reliance   Great concern for others

Career Interests
More defined work habits   Higher level of concern for the future
                                         Thoughts about one's role in life

Sexuality
Concerned with serious   Clear sexual identity
    relationships   Capacities for tender and sensual love

Ethics and Self-Direction
Capable of useful insight   Stress on personal dignity and
                                             self-esteem
Ability to set goals and follow   Acceptance of social institutions and
    through   cultural traditions
Self-regulation of self esteem

(From the American Academy of Child & Adolescent Psychology)

LATE ADOLESCENCE VERSUS ADULTHOOD

So, why not consider older teens as adults?

> *I mean, it's like, today's teens, they just don't get it! Sure, for them,
> life is totally phine—er, phat. They are coming of age in an age
> that celebrates the coming of age. For every standard-issue ado-
> lescent yearning, there is a show that explores it on the WB. For
> each of life's clichéd ironies encountered for the first time, there is
> a chat room to lament it on TeenGripe.com. For every pimply
> punk buying a pop CD, another kid with a good complexion has
> just released a debut album. Being a teenager these days is as ef-
> fortless as being a Renaissance Man during the Renaissance.
> These kids have no idea how hard it is living in an era that has
> outgrown grownups.(Katz 1999, p. 126)*

Adults have stated that the lines between adulthood and adolescence are somewhat blurry. The drinking age, for example, is one issue that concerns many older teens because the law discriminates against people who are labeled "adult" at age eighteen, and sometimes younger, but who are prohibited from behaving as adults in many ways. Older teens often question why, at the ages of eighteen, nineteen, and twenty, they are allowed to vote, die for their country, and engage in other adult activities, but they are not yet allowed to drink alcoholic beverages.

"Can a nineteen year old really be treated as an adult?" is a question that can be asked in relation to the college-aged daughters of President George Bush and their difficulties refraining from drinking. It is sometimes said that society is asking adults, people who are age nineteen, to follow rules that are meant for children:

> *For all of her flaws—and Jenna Bush is hardly unique—the president's daughter is by every other definition an adult. She can vote; she can face down bullets in war; she can seek an abortion without her parents' consent; she can get married, have children and ruin 100 lives in a single hour in divorce court. In some states she can serve in public office, and everywhere else she can be prosecuted as an adult. Yet, we insist that when it comes to alcohol she conduct herself as a child. (Parker 2001, p. 15A)*

Legal issues raise another concern when determining whether an older teen is still a child or an adult—or somewhere in the middle. The age at which a juvenile is considered to be a legal adult varies from state to state. Older teens who have left home, or who are no longer under the control of their parents for whatever reason, may have difficulty with the age of maturity being defined as eighteen in most states.

Melaina Poore, who left home at age sixteen, comments, "How can the law act as an omniscient judge that stamps one age, 18, as the exact moment a person will become mature enough to fully participate in society and gain adult rights? It is impossible for all people to automatically and magically become independent mentally, spiritually, or financially on the date of their 18th birthday. It is just as impossible that anyone younger than 18 in not capable of meeting life's demands unless under the protective wing of a parent or guardian" (Poore 1994, p. 69).

In California, Proposition 21 gives prosecuting attorneys the power to decide when a teen criminal should be tried as an adult and not as a juvenile. More teens are tried as adults because the prosecutors represent the victims. Teens as young as fourteen can be tried as adults in California. In Connecticut, New York, and North Carolina, anyone aged sixteen or older can be tried as an adult. The age at which people are considered adults is seventeen in ten other states, and the rest of the states, including the District of Columbia, have determined that teens are adults once they turn eighteen (Ferdinand 2002, p. A03).

In 2002, Lee Boyd (John) Malvo, seventeen, was arrested for randomly shooting people outside stores, schools, and gas stations in Washington, D.C., Virginia, and Maryland. The fact that Malvo was only seventeen when the shootings occurred raised a lot of questions and controversy in the media and the public. People frequently asked whether Malvo should be tried as an adult or as a juvenile. Was Malvo developmentally mature enough to decide for himself to participate in the killings? At the age of seventeen, many people questioned, why would someone engage in such violent acts of random terrorism? These are tough questions that demonstrate some of the ambiguities and ironies facing older teens.

Do today's older teens differ from older teens of the past? There is evidence that some teenagers are growing up faster now, compared to previous times. Consider hazing rituals, which are common among college students, but typically not among high school students. In May 2003, several female high school students in Glenbrook, Illinois, were injured during a hazing ritual occurring during a powder puff football game that was not sponsored by the school. Senior high school students invited a group of juniors to participate, charging them $35 to $40, as an initiation into their senior year. Juniors were physically abused and showered with debris, including human excrement, pig intestines, and fish guts. School superintendent David Hales, who oversees the high school, was baffled why students participated in what appeared to be an unofficial tradition. "In 1977 the district ended its annual powder puff event during homecoming after students became too rough" (Black and Flynn, 2003, p. 1). Yet, twenty-six years later, the event became extremely rough, which leads to questions about the differences between teens today and those of the past.

Sometimes teenagers are almost in complete control of their own lives. Parents who realize that they have little control over their eighteen-year-old teenagers' plans were interviewed, and the results were published in "High School Seniors Are Going on the Kind of Unescorted Trips That Were Once Reserved for College Students" (Payne 2000). For example, female prom attendees, who used to wear long, flowing, dresses, are more likely to be dressed in short, tight, revealing dresses—similar to attire worn by stars attending award ceremonies. Older teens are also taking unescorted trips without their parents—the types of trips that used to be common among college students, not high school students. And consider how Craig Wilson describes his experiences at a "Sweet 16" party:

> *Their hair was sleek and sassy and looked as if it had been done by someone who might have spent some time down in the village, but not just any village. We're talking New York City's Village here. These girls had not missed an episode of Friends. And when did they start wearing dresses that could appear on that red carpet at the Oscars? I saw midriffs, a fair share of bare backs, and a gold lame skirt that was applied*

with a spray can. For some reason, this made me a tad sad.
Don't they realize they're going to be adults for a very long
time, but 16 only for a year?" (Wilson 2000, p. 01.D).

On the other hand, many adults are still trying to be teenagers. In "America
Loves Teens—But Wants Them to Act Like Adults," a marketing expert reports
on tastes and trends among people under age thirty. Not long ago there were specific behaviors and ways of dress that adults left behind as they entered their
twenties and thirties. In a more casual society, however, those rules are softened,
and there is not much distinction between how teenagers and adults dress
(Purdum 2000). Another article exploring the blurring of generations is "Visions
21/How We Will Live: Will Teenagers Disappear? As Kids Grow Up Even
Faster, That Carefree Age Known As Adolescence May Soon Be a Memory"
(Kirn 2000). Here modern teenagers are compared to teenagers of the past. Instead of pumping gas or working at the neighborhood soda fountain, today's
teens may be making serious money by helping adults trade stock on the Internet
or programming computers.

Coming of age is becoming a lifelong process, and the teenage years as a
preparation for life do not really make sense anymore since teen life resembles
adult life in many ways (Kirn 2000). One author even suggests the following:

> *Maybe we should abolish adolescence altogether. Not the bi-*
> *ological part, of course—the turbulent growth spurt and*
> *mental/physical/social adaptation. We are stuck with that.*
> *But it would be nice if we could get rid of the cultural mess*
> *we have made of the teenage years. Having deprived chil-*
> *dren of an innocent childhood, the least we could do is res-*
> *cue them from an adolescence corrupted by every sleazy,*
> *violent and commercially lucrative fantasy that untram-*
> *meled adult venality, high-horsing on the First Amendment,*
> *can conceive." (Morrow 1999, p. 110)*

Although many people believe that times have changed and that adults and
teens are more and more like each other than in the past, there is also a belief that
history repeats itself. Are today's teens really more like adults and vice versa? In
"Campus Cutie or Creep: What Were You Like in High School?" (Ragan 1994),
celebrities tell what their lives were like in high school. Sharon Stone says that at
age fifteen she was in eleventh grade, going to high school half a day and a nearby
college the other half. Tom Cruise explains how he left home for New York City,
and Dolly Parton tells why she left for Nashville as soon as she graduated from high
school. Cruise did not even bother to attend his high school graduation ceremonies.
Whitney Houston began cutting classes to take modeling assignments and to hang
out in Manhattan (Ragan 1994, pp. 270–274). These famous celebrities, who

were teenagers quite some time ago, were also as much like adults as today's older teens are.

"Adolescents behave like the adult society that raises them. They did not land on a meteorite. We raised them. They share our values. They act like us. When we criticize their behavior, we are really engaging in devastating self-criticism without a mirror" (Males 2001, p. 40). Indeed, many older teens share the same interests as adults, and many have the same values. They typically value their freedoms, including the freedom of speech and the freedom of expression, and the freedom to make decisions. Especially during late adolescence, like adults, older teens want a level of autonomy in their decision making. Unlike younger teens who may still be struggling with, for example, a parent who wants them to dress a certain way, older teens are far beyond that conflict. Like adults, older teens make decisions about how to spend, save, and make money; how to prepare for the future; and how to relate to other people. Adults who are disappointed with the overall behaviors and values of older teens should be reminded that in the past they may have had an influence on shaping the minds of those who will be our adults in the future.

ARE OLDER TEENAGERS USING THE PUBLIC LIBRARY?

When addressing the needs of older teens, it is helpful to know whether and how your library is already serving this group. If your library does not keep statistics on such factors, now is a good time to start.

In fact, libraries currently serve older teens, whether they realize it or not. Although very few libraries have separate sections just for older teens, this segment of the population does use the library—whether it involves a physical visit to the building, perhaps as part of a school field trip; a virtual tour of the library's Web site; or virtual reference service via live chat with a librarian. Using the library's Web site from home may also involve accessing electronic databases, another way in which older teens are using the library, albeit remotely.

Some libraries offer specialized programming just for older teens, usually in relation to pertinent topics such as research, career exploration, college and financial aid information, or at-risk teens. Often older teens are volunteers or employees in the public library, and they tend to be more likely to use the library.

To track library usage by older teens, some libraries can rely on statistics that are computer generated. For example, using Dynix, I can separate usage by age and determine how many library materials were checked out by males ages sixteen and seventeen in the past month or year at my library. I am also able to determine how many library cards were issued to people of different ages. Dynix also sorts information based on ethnicity; educational attainment; and residency in a specific city, county, or state.

Relying on computer-generated statistics is not always the best way to determine usage, though. Take a look around. Some older teens may use the library on a regular basis, but they may never check anything out. The reasons vary; they may have overdue fines, they may not want to carry around a bunch of books, or they may be too embarrassed about the topic they're interested in to approach the circulation desk.

SPECIAL CONSIDERATIONS IN SERVING OLDER TEENAGERS

Consider some of the circumstances, including some ethical issues, that you are more likely to encounter when serving older teens than when serving other age groups.

What types of policies does your library have for Internet usage by older teens? Are specific types of material under- or overrepresented in your collection because of self-imposed censorship? Work with library administrators to set or reform policies that have an impact on library services for older teens. Realize, however, that this may take time. Library directors and administrators, despite the concrete beliefs of some library staff, do not always have a lot of power in changing policies and procedures. They also have bosses to report to, and in many cases that boss is a group of many library board members, all with different opinions about how public libraries should operate. Often there are other outside forces that have an impact on library policies and procedures, and in some cases library administrators (even if they want to) cannot discuss many of these matters with library staff. Whereas library staff may feel left out of the loop and as though library administrators are not communicating well, in some instances the situations that arise are of a confidential nature.

Train your staff to work with teens and be sensitive to these ethical issues. If finding qualified trainers is a challenge, consider YALSA's Serving the Underserved (SUS) program and share your suggestions with library administrators. You can also advocate for youth by being involved in state library associations and having a voice in the training of librarians in teen services at conferences. Also, become aware of how involved your state library and state library association are in services to young adults and young adult librarians, and whether standards exist for serving young adults.

In 1999, as a representative of the Young Adult Section of the North Carolina Library Association, I was awarded the Frances Henne/YALSA/VOYA Research Grant along with John P. Bradford, who at the time represented the Arizona Library Association. We studied state-level commitment to young adult library services, and via survey results we gathered information about statewide standards, current services to teens and young adult librarians by state libraries and state library associations, and young adult book awards. We also gathered information about continuing education opportunities in each state

(Anderson and Bradford 2001, p. 25). Let your library administrators know that through your attendance at state and national library conferences, the information you gather will benefit the end user, teenagers needing library services.

Following are a few ethical situations that may be encountered by librarians serving older teens:

- Confidentiality and privacy are typically important concerns for older teens, especially in smaller communities where the library staff may know the family members of older teens. Become familiar with the USA Patriot Act and other laws about the privacy of library records. When using the Internet, patrons leave a search history, a record of where they have been. Remember that older teens may be searching for materials that they would like to keep private.

- Internal censorship within libraries can be detrimental to older teens. Work to build a diverse collection, without allowing your personal feelings (or someone else's) to invade the informational needs of teens. Do you or your colleagues refrain from purchasing materials that contain sexual descriptions? Are staff members hiding copies of materials, or processing them and instantly marking them "lost" on the computer catalog before the items ever make it to the shelf? If so, it may be necessary for librarians to work with library administrators to curb these practices. Librarians or administrators may have to physically check to make sure that certain items make it to the shelves, or even place the items on hold and check them out the first time to begin the circulation process. In libraries where certain materials have historically not been purchased, new librarians and administrators may find it difficult to change the traditional attitudes of staff.

- If older teens are able to access certain materials at home, in bookstores, at the movies, in music stores, and in video stores, shouldn't they be allowed to access them at the library? Do teens have to be eighteen to check out videos, DVDs, and certain musical selections? These policies may hamper your service to older teens and need to be reconsidered.

- Librarians and library administrators need to consider the Children's Internet Protection Act (CIPA) decision by the Supreme Court in 2003. According to the ruling, people age seventeen and older are allowed to have unfiltered Internet access in public libraries, whereas those under the age of seventeen must use computers with filters. With the age set at seventeen, libraries are faced with difficult choices, especially since the legal age—whether it be sixteen, seventeen, or eighteen—differs throughout the United States. Some librarians believe that teenagers should be allowed to have unfiltered access in libraries. Karen G. Schneider, director of the Librarian's Index to the Internet, comments: "I predict also that when it comes to small children, we'll find that many of us very strongly believe in loco parentis, and we would no more let a 4-year-old have unsupervised open access to the Internet than we would sit on our hands and watch a toddler walk into rush-hour traffic. And finally, I believe many of us would agree that—however complex and amorphous this issue can be—communities can and should emancipate Internet access for teens, who are now held hostage by CIPA's guidelines, which deny adolescents any unfiltered access in libraries that receive the e-rate" (Schneider 2003, p. 16).

- Older teens may ask about sensitive topics. Older teens are more likely to ask for help about sensitive topics because they are usually more at ease with problems. If a teenager asks for information about abortion, or Wicca, or trees, or any other topic, it is important that you do not question why, nor should you give your opinion about the subject. This is true of all subjects. Comments, and even body language, can send a negative message to teens. Ask library administrators to require all library staff to read and sign a copy of the American Library Association's *Library Bill of Rights*.

- Older teens may be emancipated from their parents. If a parental signature is required for those under eighteen to obtain a library card or use the Internet, it may be necessary to work with library administrators to ensure that emancipated teens are not excluded from library privileges. If a teenager has become emancipated and is legally responsible for his or her actions, public libraries should take into account special considerations for this segment of the teen population. In some instances, emancipated teens may be caring for younger siblings, as the situation in *Chicago Blues*. In the novel, Marnie, eleven, protests having to live with her sister, and one of her many reasons is, "I left my library card at home" (Deaver 1995, p. 9). Lissa, seventeen, tells Marnie that she will get her a new library card. How difficult would this be in your library? Would the staff allow someone age seventeen to be responsible for the library account of a sibling who is eleven?

- Truancy raises more ethical questions for librarians serving older teens. If you are familiar with older teens, you probably do not assume that all people ages sixteen through eighteen are supposed to be in a classroom during the day. If you suspect that a student is skipping school, do you think it is your responsibility to contact the school? Consider this scenario, which occurred while I was managing the Young Adults' Services Department at the Allen County Public Library in Fort Wayne, Indiana: I was helping a high school senior with a research project, and the student admitted that his mother had called him in sick so that he could go to the library to finish his term paper so that he would graduate. The student asked to use the library's telephone, saying that he really needed to get in touch with his teacher about how to cite something. When calling the teacher, it was obvious that the teacher inquired about his whereabouts, and the student admitted to being at the public library.

Should librarians use their own professional judgment regarding truancy in a situation such as this one? The student may be better off in the public library, finishing a term paper that will lead to graduation, but it is also arguable that the library may be contributing to the delinquency of a minor by knowing that a student should be in school instead of at the public library. The answer to this scenario depends on community standards, rules governing the use of the library, and local laws in your area—and, in some cases, a bit of empathy and common sense on the part of the librarian and the library administration.

NONTRADITIONAL OLDER TEENAGERS

Just as stereotypes and generalizations may be detrimental, it is important to consider the needs of teens who don't fit the usual mold. When determining your library audience, remember that some older teens may not be involved in educational and living situations that are considered to be mainstream. As in any situation, the term "mainstream" will mean different things to different people. In some parts of the country, for example, the number of older teens learning English as a second language may be few, and these teens may be considered "nontraditional." In areas with many people who have moved to the United States from other countries, teens learning English as a second language may be considered to be more mainstream.

Although librarians may assume that older teens are still attending high school, this is not always true. Some teens may be enrolled in college, some may have opted to drop out of high school, and others may be homeschooled. Older teens may be illiterate or severely below the educational levels of their peers. In contrast, others may be extremely gifted. Some older teens have already earned advanced degrees. Others are juggling high school and college simultaneously and have special needs from public, school, and college libraries. Homeschooled teens typically rely heavily on the public library for curricular needs. High school dropouts may need information about GED classes and other opportunities.

Not all older teens are living in family environments that include a parent. Older teens may be homeless, runaways, incarcerated, living alone, or residing in a group home. Some older teens have been labeled by youth advocates and social workers as "throwaways," meaning that they are asked to leave home or they are forced to do so. Homeless teens and runaways may find that the public library is a safe haven, or they may consider it a place that they would rather avoid. Whereas some public libraries specifically cater to homeless and runaway teens, others shun them. Some older teens are already married and living with their spouses. Besides the typical stresses that burden teens, some teens may also have the responsibility of parenting their own child or children. Others are raising their siblings.

Incarcerated teens and those who reside in group homes may not be library users because it is physically impossible, or illegal, for them to even visit the library. It is not uncommon for libraries to provide outreach services to incarcerated teens and group home residents. Some libraries have created deposit collections at juvenile detention centers and other youth service agencies. For example, the Young Adults' Services Department of the Allen County Public Library in Fort Wayne, Indiana, administers the Teen Agency Program (TAP), in which staff are provided with a generous budget to supply books, magazines, comic books, and graphic novels to incarcerated teens. Library staff also involve teens in the summer reading program and in book discussion groups.

Some older teens have decided to become emancipated, meaning that they have gained legal independence from their parents or legal guardians. The age at which teenagers can become emancipated varies in different states. The laws about emancipation may tie in to special circumstances, such as whether a teen is expecting a child or if he or she has joined the military. Older teens may decide that it is necessary to become emancipated if they are getting little assistance from their parents, if their parents are dangerous, or if they are already living on their own. Some find it necessary to become emancipated due to health issues, for instance, older teens who have refused certain medical treatments for religious or cultural reasons. Some older teens with a chronic illness become emancipated from their parents due to arguments about their treatment or their right to die. In some states, emancipated teenagers have rights such as being allowed to live in their own place, get medical care without the permission of their parents, enroll in a school or college without parental permission, buy and sell property, sign contracts, obtain a marriage license, get a driver's license, or join the military without parental permission.

CONCLUSION

In summary, it is important to remember that older teens are not all alike. They may have similarities, but for the most part, every teen is a unique individual, and it is imperative that they be treated as individuals. All teenagers go through the same developmental stages, and they all have that in common. Even within the context of the older teen category, between sixteen and nineteen, teenagers may differ due to their ages and stages. On a local level, teens may differ from one area to the next.

Becoming familiar with the older teens in your particular service area is the best way to prepare for serving older teens. You may face ethical issues when serving older teens that would not be a concern with younger teens or adults. You may face other challenges in serving older teens as well. Older teens are on the last rung of the ladder to adulthood, but often they have not yet finished climbing the ladder. As librarians, we are in a prime position to help older teens over the last hurdles of the teenage years.

REFERENCES AND SUGGESTED READINGS

Adler, Jerry, and John McCormick. 1999. "The Truth About High School." *Newsweek* 133, no. 19 (May 10): 56–58.

Anderson, Sheila B. 2000. "Best of the Best Revisited: Bo Jo Jones and Beyond." *Journal of Youth Services in Libraries* 14, no. 1 (Fall): 18–20.

Anderson, Sheila B., and John P. Bradford. 2001. "State-Level Commitment to Public Library Services to Young Adults: Frances Henne/YALSA/VOYA Research Grant Results." *Journal of Youth Services in Libraries* 14, no. 3 Spring: 23–27.

Black, Lisa, and Courtney Flynn. 2003. "Glenbrook North, Cops Investigate Brawl at Hazing; 5 Girls Are Hurt During 'Initiation'." *Chicago Tribune*, May 7: 1.

Choron, Sandra, and Harry Choron. 2000. *The Book of Lists for Teens*. Boston: Houghton Mifflin.

Deaver, Julie Reece. 1995. *Chicago Blues*. New York: HarperCollins.

Federal Interagency Forum on Child and Family Statistics (FIFCFS). 2002. *America's Children: Key National Indicators of Well Being*. Washington, DC: U.S. Government Printing Office.

Fenwick, Elizabeth, and Dr. Tony Smith. 1996. *Adolescence: The Survival Guide for Parents and Teenagers*. New York: DK Publishing.

Ferdinand, Pamela. 2002. "Seventeen an Awkward Age, N.H. Juvenile Justice Finds; in Reversal, State Moves to Raise Criminal Adulthood to 18." *Washington Post*, March 27: A03.

Fisher, Marc. 2001. "Adolescent Woes Are a Big Joke to These Students." *Washington Post*, March 27: B1.

Hersch, Patricia. 1998. *A Tribe Apart: A Journey into the Heart of the American Adolescent*. New York: Fawcett.

Hine, Thomas. 1999. *The Rise & Fall of the American Teenager*. New York: Avon.

Holmes, George R. 1995. *Helping Teenagers Into Adulthood: A Guide for the Next Generation*. Westport, CT: Praeger.

Howe, Neil, and William Strauss. 2000. *Millenials Rising: The Next Great Generation*. New York: Vintage.

Katz, Mark. 1999. "Power Children." *Time* 154, no. 20 (November 15): 126.

Kessler, Rachael. 1999/2000. "Initiation—Saying Goodbye to Child-hood." *Educational Leadership* 57, no. 4 (December/January): 30–34.

Kirn, Walter. 2000. "Will Teenagers Disappear? As Kids Grow up Even Faster, That Carefree Age Known As Adolescence May Soon Be a Memory." *Time* 155, no. 7 (February 21): 60–61.

Males, Mike A. 2001. "Debunking the 10 Worst Myths About America's Teens." *Teacher Librarian* 28, no. 4 (April): 40–42.

Morrow, Lance. 1999. "The Boys and the Bees: The Shootings Are One More Argument for Abolishing Adolescence." *Time* 153, no. 21 (May 31): 110.

Parker, Kathleen. "2001. Can a 19-Year-Old Really Be Treated As an Adult?" *USA Today*, June 5: 15A.

Payne, Melanie. 2000. "High School Seniors Are Going on the Kind of Un-escorted Trips That Were Once Reserved for College Students." *Akron Beacon Journal*, March 21: F1.

Poore, Malaina. 1994. "Let Us Claim Our Place in Society." *Social Work in Education* 16, no. 1 (January): 69.

Pruitt, David B., ed. 1999. *Your Adolescent: What Every Parent Needs to Know: What's Normal, What's Not, and When to Seek Help*. New York: HarperCollins.

Purdum, Todd S. 2000. "America Loves Teens—But Wants Them to Act Like Adults." *Minneapolis Star Tribune,* October 1: 01E.

Ragan, David. 1994. "Campus Cutie or Creep: What Were You Like in High School?" *Cosmopolitan* 216 (May 1): 270–274.

Rapp, Melanie. 1998. "Adolescent Development: An Emotional Roller Coaster." In *Young Adults and Public Libraries: A Handbook of Materials and Services.* Edited by C. Allen Nichols and Mary Anne Nichols. Westport, CT: Greenwood Press: 1–10.

Rutherford, Deanna. 2002. "My Life As a Rodenite." *Young Adult Library Services* 1, no. 1 (Fall): 8–10.

Schneider, Barbara, and David Stevenson. 1999. *The Ambitious Generation: America's Teenagers, Ambitious But Directionless*. New Haven, CT: Yale University Press.

Schneider, Karen G. 2003. "Let's Begin the Discussion: What Now?" *American Libraries* 34, no. 7: 14–16.

Stepp, Laura Sessions. 2000. "We Should Celebrate Our Teenage Children." *Washington Post*, June 23: C06.

Sweeting, Helen, and Patrick West. 1994. "The Patterning of Life Events in Mid- to Late Adolescence: Markers for the Future?" *Journal of Adolescence* 17: 283–304.

U.S. Census Bureau. 2002. *Statistical Abstract of the United States.* Washington, DC: Government Printing Office.

Wilson, Craig. 2000. "The Glow of Sweet 16 Seems a Bit Too Bright." *USA Today* (October 25): 01.D.

World Almanac and Book of Facts. 2003. New York: World Almanac Books.

Young, Rosemary. 1975. "Toward Defining 'Young Adults'." *School Library Journal* 22, no. 2 (October): 84.

2

Need to Know, Chance to Grow: Nonfiction Resources and Programming Ideas for Older Teens

Sheila B. Anderson

Providing a combination of related nonfiction materials and specialized programming strengthens your services to older teenagers. The teens receive the materials they need to become knowledgeable about different subjects along with a chance to assimilate and process that information by exploring these topics in a structured setting run by caring librarians. Older teens have unique needs in the library, just as toddlers have different library needs than infants and school-aged children. Youth service librarians usually go to great lengths to match age-appropriate library materials and programs with the population served. Marketing efforts extend these services in public libraries, where displays are created to promote library materials, booklists and bookmarks are produced and distributed, and suggested reading lists are included on library Web pages—all based on reading levels and ages. This is the most effective strategy for promoting suitable materials and programs for teens of different ages and in different stages as well.

Keep in mind that people ages sixteen through nineteen are not exactly full-fledged adults yet, but they are not children either. Most public libraries concentrate their efforts on providing materials for teens that relate to homework assignments, but older teens usually have needs and interests that go beyond homework. In fact, during the late teen years, adolescents are almost like adults. In many ways, older teens may behave more like and identify more closely with adults than with teens who are their own age but less mature.

NEED TO KNOW: IMPORTANCE OF NONFICTION

Older teens are often goal-oriented, and the reaching of these goals may be enhanced through nonfiction materials available at the public library. Being aware of the goals that teens in your community are seeking to achieve is one of the first steps in developing a useful library collection. Some of the goals relate to hobbies, whereas others may be a result of schoolwork and career aspirations.

Consider Randy Gardner, seventeen, who set a record of staying awake for 264 hours and 12 minutes for the purpose of completing his school science fair project on the effects of sleep deprivation. Jeffrey J. Dunkel was also inspired by his school studies. After attending political meetings because of a school requirement, he became interested in politics after determining that nothing was getting done. He ran for mayor of Mount Carbon, Pennsylvania, when he turned eighteen—and won.

Sarah Hughes, seventeen, reached a goal relating to her hobby when she became an Olympic gold medalist in women's figure skating. Sean Frawley and Dan Getz, high school students in Warwick, New York, shared a passion for flying machines and wanted to create a toy ornithopter. Since they only found a few build-it-yourself kits, they launched an online company called Ornithopter Technologies and invented their own kit based on a design by a nineteenth-century French inventor. All of these teens, who reached amazing goals, may have used the public library. By targeting your efforts to older teens in the public library, through collection development of nonfiction materials and programming, you can help teens reach their goals.

Teens in the late stage of adolescence are often involved in activities that are different from activities enjoyed by younger teens. Planning for careers and vocations, higher education and training, and even marriage and family, older teens seek out activities that complement their changing interests.

Yet there is also great diversity within the group. Older teens who are still in high school may be striving to excel so that they can attend college. Many older teens are extremely busy with schoolwork and extracurricular activities. Other older students may be biding their time in high school, knowing that they are going to inherit a family business or begin a job; others may be anxious to enter the military, perhaps after having served as a Junior ROTC member. Some students are barely getting by academically, and they might not even graduate from high school. Other students are involved in co-op programs with their high schools that allow them to work part-time during the day. Some attend regular high school as well as a vocational school. Other teens may be students in boarding schools, where they both live and attend classes, and heavily use the library on campus instead of the public library. Despite these differences, many older teens have similar information needs as they strive to reach adulthood.

Teens on the brink of adulthood need information about education and recreation. They need information about furthering their education, college life, scholarships, entering the workforce, or entering the military. Older teens are also about to begin driving or have already begun driving, so they need information about that topic as well. Since they soon may be living on their own, in a dorm, or with a roommate, they may require information about independent life skills—caring for clothes, cooking, nutrition, and financial management. In preparation for turning eighteen, teens may require information about politics, voting, and the selective service. Like teens in the middle stage of adolescence, older teens still need information about careers, colleges, dating, sex, friendships, and getting along with others. Unlike younger teens, they also need information about becoming independent and about senior trips, proms, and more. They also may be more interested in the popular culture usually enjoyed by adults. For example, as teens become mobile, they may more frequently attend popular movies.

In the late stage of adolescence, teens see adults more as equals; and they perceive themselves as adults. They make efforts to become a part of the adult world. They may actually enter the adult world through the doorway of the college world. What better way to feel like an adult than to be matched with college students on an intellectual level? Some older teens who live near colleges and are in high school may find that they prefer to crash college keg parties or to attend college cultural events.

Some teens may be debating whether they should take a year off before attending college after graduating from high school. You can be prepared and waiting with materials to help them research possible opportunities. Some teens are burned out by the time they finish high school and need an alternative to higher education (Wilgoren 2001). Some colleges, such as Harvard University, suggest that students take a break before coming to campus, because it gives them an opportunity to get a perspective on their lives. A recent trend among high-achieving students (those who can afford it) is to spend a year doing something else before attending college. These activities include working with sled dogs in Alaska, building guitars in England, becoming fluent in Swahili, teaching disabled people to ski, hiking the Appalachian Trail with a dog, working on a forty-eight-foot sailboat, and taking a cross-country trip in a covered wagon (Wilgoren 2001).

Some older teens are busy and do not use the public library. Many are computer savvy and would rather conduct research using their own computers, without giving much thought to the reliability of the information found. Others may have some basic knowledge about research skills, but they also may need assistance in finding appropriate and relevant information. Older teens may not be familiar with the Dewey Decimal Classification System, and they may question why the library is not set up exactly like a bookstore. Also, they may need help writing term papers and reports. Older teens may not be as visible in your library as younger teens. Many still use the library for social purposes and recreational needs, but probably not as often as younger teens, due to time constraints and the demands of other activities. On the other hand, some older teens may find that a quiet study room in a public library is the only place where they can find silence after being in noisy schools during the day and hectic households in the evenings and on weekends. Older teens may visit the library for nonfiction relating to a hobby, an interest, or just plain old curiosity.

How can you prepare yourself and your library to serve all of these diverse needs and interests? First, build your library collection in such a way that it represents diverse topics that might be useful for older teens who are striving to reach adulthood. Don't assume that all teens are the same. Keep in mind that the living situations, educational levels, and reading levels of older teens can and do differ. Whereas many older teens are still attending high school, some are already in college, some have dropped out of high school, and others are being home-schooled. Many older teens still live with their parents, but some are already married, some are emancipated and living on their own, and others are living on the streets or in shelters.

The reading levels of teenagers will also differ. Some teens may be reading Toni Morrison, some may be reading Danielle Steele, some may be struggling with The Boxcar Children series, and others may be reading in languages other than English.

Once you have established a diverse library collection, create bookmarks and booklists, either in print or virtual, to promote your collection. Make sure that the lists are available to youth service workers who may come into contact with older teens. For example, if there is a group of high school dropouts studying to take the GED, reach out to the leader of the group and promote your library as the place where high school dropouts can seek information.

Consider offering customized programs for special populations within the older teen population. After determining the information needs of these groups, connect with youth service workers to provide services that will enhance the role of the library in the lives of these teenagers. Offer to provide your outreach services to groups who may not be able to physically travel to the library, such as incarcerated teens.

As when serving any group, librarians who work with older teens should shape their collection and design their programming in response to the needs and interests of the group. With older teens, nonfiction and informational material and programming can be a powerful combination. In addition, there has been an increase in the publishing of nonfiction specifically for teens, so, if you're looking for a title that addresses a certain need, chances are you'll find it. Many of these nonfiction topics are also popular with adults, but authors have found a market writing specifically for teens.

There are nonfiction books about virtually any topic for older teens. For example, adults have read horoscopes for years, as have teens. Astrology provides teenagers with the opportunity to think about their lives in a different context, from the viewpoint of a complete stranger. Many teens enjoy comparing their daily horoscopes with their daily lives. *Teen Astrology: The Ultimate Guide to Making Your Life Your Own* (Abadie 2001) explains the signs of the Zodiac, horoscopes, and the cycles of becoming an adult.

Another example is the Complete Idiot's Guide series by Alpha Books. Not only are there hundreds of books published for adults, there is a new series specifically focusing on topics that are popular with teens, such as friendship, dating, volunteering, and spirituality. There have been other spin-offs of adult books into additional titles for teens. Stephen Covey's popular *The Seven Habits of Highly Effective People* resulted in a book just for teens about the same topic. *Who Moved My Cheese? for Teens*: *An A-Mazing Way to Change to Win,* by Spencer Johnson is also a spin-off of a very popular book for adults about dealing with change.

Other topics are typically exclusive to older teen readers. For instance, many high school juniors and seniors are concerned with preparing for the prom. They can find answers to their questions in *Prom! The Complete Guide to a Truly Spectacular Night* (Krulik 2002). The book, designed for young female readers, covers all aspects of prom attendance, including clothes, hair, and makeup.

Organizing and time management has been a popular topic for adults in recent years, and professional organizer Julie Morgenstern and her daughter, Jessi Morgenstern-Colon, seventeen, decided that a book about the subject needed to be written for teens. Together they wrote *Organizing from the Inside Out for Teens* (Morgenstern 2002). The book shows teens how to organize their rooms, their desks, and their time. (This book also demonstrates how one teenager can influence the types of materials being published and made available to youth.)

CHANCE TO GROW: SIGNIFICANCE OF PROGRAMMING

Public library programming at its best offers participants an opportunity to grow. For older teens, programs can expand their horizons and even change their lives, and in the best programming, the experience promotes library services and collections.

If older teens have not had access to a public library that offers a great deal of programming for younger teens or children, they may not accept the concept of programming at first. In some cases, it takes time. Also, some older teens stopped using the library years ago, and it may be necessary for you to rebuild a connection with older teens to draw them into the library for programs. Since many older teens are extremely busy, some public librarians have discovered that a good focus for teen programming is nonfiction topics that relate to teen lives and interests.

Some public libraries offer programs for older teens in conjunction with adult programming. Older teens will quite likely attend a program that is geared for adults, or especially for college students, since older teens and younger college students are both striving toward independence. When designing programs for older teens, consider networking with other adult and youth service organizations, as well as schools and colleges, to maximize resources and to acquire new ideas. For in-depth suggestions about teen programming, the three editions of *Excellence in Library Services to Young Adults: The Nation's Top Programs* (Chelton 1994, 1997, 2000) are extremely valuable resources because each entry includes an intended age range or grade level. A fourth edition of the publication will be available in 2004. The libraries featured in the books were selected as having administered the best programs in the United States, as determined by the YALSA Executive Committee. The following are samples of public library programs especially for older teens featured in the second and third edition of the books:

1. (High School) Senior Sunday: Jackson County Library Services, Medford Library, Medford, Oregeon: The public library offered special Sunday library hours, when the library is typically closed, to high school seniors working on senior research projects. The high school seniors benefited from individualized assistance from librarians (Chelton 1997).

2. Teen Parenting Course: Chicago Public Library, Woodside Regional Library, Chicago, Illinois: Senior high students were offered parenting classes, covering topics including nutrition, budgeting, child development, and discipline. The library collaborated with the Department of Public Aid and Sinai Parenting Institute (Chelton 1997).

3. Teen Study Center: Chicago Public Library, Northtown Branch, Chicago, Illinois: Senior high school students were welcomed into the Teen Study Center, a section of the library for high school students. The center houses reference materials, computers, and videos. High school students assisted in planning for the space (Chelton 1997).

4. Teen Job Fair: Shaker Heights Public Library, Shaker Heights, Ohio: Targeting teens ages sixteen and older, library staff collaborated with the Shaker Heights Recreation Department to match seasonal and summer employers with teens seeking employment. Library staff provided a handout with suggested reading related to resume writing, job searching, and successful job interviews (Chelton 2000).

5. Page Fellows Program: Queens Borough Public Library, Jamaica, New York: Library employees ages seventeen through twenty-one who are high school or college students, called Page Fellows, are matched with a librarian who serves as a mentor for a fifteen-week period. During these weeks, the librarian and the Page Fellow take field trips to libraries and learn about the career of librarianship (Chelton 2000).

SUGGESTED NONFICTION RESOURCES AND PROGRAMMING IDEAS

Following are suggested programming topics for use with older teens and lists of related nonfiction resources. This is just a sampling. Many nonfiction books for older teens have been published, but in most cases the most recent ones published or extremely valuable older titles have been chosen for these selective lists. The books listed can be used in conjunction with programs for the purpose of promoting the library collection.

Beauty: "Mirror, Mirror, on the Wall . . ."

Many older teens would be interested in attending a library program about beauty. Would those attending the prom be interested in free makeovers? How about teens who are getting married or who are interested in cosmetology as a career or even just as a hobby? Consider inviting beauty and health professionals into your library to give a presentation on topics such as skin care, fashion, or makeup. Body piercing, body art and painting, and tattooing are also popular with teens, and the purpose of these practices is to enhance beauty. If these topics are popular in your community, it may be useful to offer programs on safe practices or finding samples of artwork for tattoos. Encourage library staff who are uncomfortable with these topics, or who discriminate against those with a body piercing or tattoos, to visit the Modified Librarian Web site at http://www.bmeworld.com/gailcat/, a forum for librarians to show off their own tattoos and body piercing.

Aveline, Erick. **Temporary Tattoos.** Buffalo, NY: Firefly Books, 2001.
    Everything you always wanted to know about using temporary tattoos.

Brown, Bobbi. **Bobbi Brown Teenage Beauty: Everything You Need to Look Pretty, Natural, Sexy & Awesome.** New York: Cliff Street Books, 2000.

Makeup, beauty rules, prom beauty, modeling, hair, athletic looks, and more are discussed in this in-depth book that is chock-full of color photographs. There is also specific beauty information for African Americans, Asian Americans, and Latin Americans. Especially appealing to those about to turn sixteen is the section on "sweet 16 beauty bashes."

Cooke, Kaz. **Real Gorgeous: The Truth About Body & Beauty.** New York: Norton, 1996.

Gives practical information to teens about shapes, weight, whether body parts are normal, fashion victims, makeup, perfume, hair, self-image, and more.

Dickey, Anthony. **Hair Rules!** Villard, 2003.

A celebrity hairstylist advises women on how to have beautiful and healthy hair.

Forney, Alfred. **Born Beautiful: The African American Teenager's Complete Beauty Guide.** New York: John Wiley, 2002.

Provides practical information for African American teens about skin, complexion, makeup, nail care, hairstyles, fashion, and more.

Lutz, Ericka. **The Complete Idiot's Guide to Looking Great for Teens.** Indianapolis, IN: Alpha Books, 2001.

Includes in-depth information about a multitude of topics including the history of beauty standards for women, how to change looks, healthy eating, safe and effective weight loss, exercise, team sports, martial arts, dance, skin, hair, grooming, hormones, stress, and more.

Marron, Maggie. **Stylin': Great Looks for Teens.** New York: Michael Friedman Publishing Group, 2001.

Glossy color photographs enhance this thorough book that includes information about makeup, hairstyles, dressing, accessorizing, body art, nails, navel rings, and more.

Miller, Jean-Chris. **The Body Art Book: A Complete Illustrated Guide to Tattoos, Piercings, and Other Body Modifications.** New York: Berkley Books, 1997.

Provides useful illustrations and advice for those who want to be pierced and tattooed.

Careers: Still Asking, "What Do I Want to Be When I Grow Up?"

While digging through files in my garage, I came across a "Kuder Occupational Interest Survey (KIOS) Report Form" dated December 22, 1987. I was reminded how my high school tried to help me chart the course for my future when I was sixteen. My KIOS form indicated that I was most likely to become a film/TV producer or a librarian. I was least likely to become a farmer or a plumber. I do not believe that the report had much influence on my future as a librarian; by that age, I already loved to read and had no interest in unclogging toilets or doing anything else that required mechanical abilities. But I do remember how interested I was in the results. The fact is, most teens are avidly interested in their career options.

Consider attending or hosting career workshops or job fairs for older teens. Invite guest speakers to talk about different types of careers each month. Maintain a broad collection of materials about possible careers. Many publishers create series that focus on careers. Why not put some of the series on standing order? Don't limit the career information to materials only suitable for college-bound students. Older teens also need information about careers that do not require any further education and about careers that are available after attending a trade or vocational school.

Career programs give you an excellent opportunity for promoting librarianship. You may even wish to participate in the Job Shadow Day, in which teens shadow someone for a day to learn about different career choices. Also, the American Library Association (ALA) Office for Human Resources Development and Recruitment (HDRD) can assist with recruiting efforts, information about library careers and educational requirements, and scholarship opportunities. The HDRD has created a brochure entitled *Become a Youth Services Librarian*. It is available through ALA and you can make it available to teens in your library.

Clinton, Susan. **Cosmetology.** Mankato, MN: Capstone Press, 2000.

> Provides in-depth information about job responsibilities, educational or on-the-job training requirements, and long-term career development opportunities for a cosmetologist. Other titles in this series, called Careers Without College, discuss careers such as dental hygienist, fire fighter, paralegal, surgical technician, and corrections officer.

Csikszentmihalyi, Mihaly, and Barbara Schneider. **Becoming Adult: How Teenagers Prepare for the World of Work.** New York: Basic Books, 2000.

> The authors, a psychologist and a sociologist, answer the following questions: How do young people envision their future careers? What can families, schools, and communities do to help teenagers develop habits and values that will be useful in their occupational lives? What do teenagers think about their schooling and after-school work, and how do these experiences affect their passage to adult work?

Eberts, Marjorie. **Careers for Bookworms & Other Literary Types.** Lincolnwood, IL: VGM Career Books, 2003.

Discusses careers in the book industry, publishing fields, and library science. This is one book in the VGM Careers for You series. Some of the others are *Careers for Night Owls and Other Insomniacs, Careers for Fashion Plates & Other Trendsetters*, and *Careers for Shutterbugs & Other Candid Types*, all published in 2003.

Gershenfeld, Alan, et al. **Game Plan.** New York: St. Martin's Press, 2003.

An insider's guide to producing video games for successful game companies.

Kamen, Gloria, ed. **Heading Out: The Start of Some Splendid Careers.** New York: Bloomsbury, 2003.

A collection of twenty-four autobiographical essays describing how notables have chosen their career paths. Features those who are writers, artists, scientists, doctors, politicians, and athletes.

Kwatinetz-Wood, Danielle. **The UnCollege Alternative: Your Guide to Incredible Careers and Amazing Adventures Outside College.** New York: Regan Books, 2000.

Gives advice to those who are interested in starting a business, interning, and working in careers that do not require college degrees.

Pasternak, Ceel. **Cool Careers for Girls as Environmentalists.** Manasas Park, VA: Impact Publications, 2002.

Explores career information related to the environment and provides useful Web sites, books, and places to contact for mentoring and educational programs. This is part of a series; other books by the same publisher focus on careers for girls in air and space, animals, computers, construction, criminology, engineering, food, health, law, the performing arts, and sports.

Phifer, Paul. **Quick Prep Careers: Good Jobs in 1 Year or Less.** Chicago: Ferguson Publishing, 2003.

Introduces fifty jobs that require a year or less of preparation, either in school or on the job, and twenty-five additional jobs for which certification is required, including personal requirements, salary, work environment, job future, and sources for more information.

Schwager, Tina, and Michele Schuerger. **Cool Women, Hot Jobs ... And How You Can Go For It, Too!** Minneapolis, MN: Free Spirit, 2002.

Describes out-of-the-ordinary jobs that have been held by women, including dolphin trainer, stuntwoman, fighter pilot, and Disney imagineer.

Weissman, Dick. **The Music Business.** 3rd ed. New York: Three Rivers Press, 2003.

Provides essential career information for those seeking to enter the music industry.

Young Person's Occupational Outlook Handbook. 4th ed. Based on information from the U.S. Department of Labor. Indianapolis, IN: JIST, 2003.

This thorough guide is based on the Department of Labor's *Occupational Outlook Handbook* for adults. It has been written especially for teens and it includes icons, boxed information, and extensive information about a variety of careers.

College: Four More Years of WHAT?

Some public libraries offer programs specifically for college-bound students. The San Leandro (California) Public Library administers the College Bound Club, in which high school students receive assistance with research and improving their SAT scores so they'll have a better chance of being accepted by the college of their choice. Meeting monthly, members are given information by guest speakers, provided with workshops on writing college application essays and financial aid, and taken on field trips to local colleges and universities (Peck 1999, p. 40).

At the Olean (New York) Public Library, Young Adult/Reference Librarian Rosemarie Grainer conducts a Colleges on the Web program for high school students and parents. Teens are given a presentation on how to find information about colleges on the Internet. Grainer suggests that public libraries work with school guidance counselors in promoting this type of program.

In the novel *Catalyst* (Anderson 2002), high school senior Kate has only applied to one college, MIT. When she gets her rejection letter, she decides to take a year off from school. She had her heart set on MIT, but most students know that applying to only one college is risky. Consider asking local college admissions officers to speak about the college admissions process, especially since the process is becoming more competitive. Those who have worked in the field are familiar with the ins and outs of how applicants are selected and may be a valuable resource to high school students. If admissions officers are not available, you can promote such books as *Admissions Confidential: An Insider's Guide of the Elite College Selection Process* (Toor 2001). If you want to learn what today's older teens are thinking, read the sample college essays included in the book. I found two especially intriguing—one about a teenager who was suspended for admitting that she used drugs, and another from a teenager who explains why she decided to join the American Civil Liberties Union (ACLU).

The novel *This Lullaby* (Dessen 2002) tells the story of Remy and her friends during the summer after high school graduation. Librarians often neglect to provide services for recent high school graduates. This summer of limbo, or just before it, when students suffer from senioritis, may be the perfect time to target older teens. Teens often have more free time during that last summer, as they let go of high school and prepare for college, the military, the working world, or some adventure. Perhaps you can attract teens who are suffering from senioritis with programs that will prepare them for college. Bibliographic instruction, research, and writing skills are obvious choices, as well as workshops about what to expect in college, how to get along with roommates, how to stay safe on a college campus, what to bring, and how to cope with homesickness.

In the early 1990s, two librarians held a workshop for high school, public, and college librarians that resulted in a list of information-seeking strategies that high school graduates should be familiar with. The strategies included perspective, familiarity, search strategies, basic library skills, awareness of the variety of information available, ability to analyze materials, and respect for librarians' expertise. Although the resulting article was published in 1992 and some of the research methods may be outdated, the basic concepts presented are still valid (Knudsen and Orpinela 1992). Perhaps during summer months before teens leave for college, when boredom kicks in, you could offer bibliographic instruction to help teens hone research skills that will be needed in college. A more casual approach might be a book discussion group or journaling class, where teens can share mutual concerns or write about the transitions they're going through.

Do not shy away from serving average students, or less-than-average students, who may not be planning to attend Ivy League colleges or other elite universities. Many students decide to attend state schools or community colleges. Teens choose these colleges for a variety of reasons: the degrees offered; lower costs; proximity to their friends, families, and jobs; and because they did not excel in high school. Often community colleges and state systems of higher education offer the course work and degree programs needed for a variety of careers. Although community colleges are sometimes called "thirteenth grade," they can be valuable starting places for students who are not necessarily ready, either academically or financially, to attend a four-year school.

"I was one of those underachieving high school graduates who was not supposed to go to college," Bob Templin told faculty and staff members. Today, Templin is the president of Northern Virginia Community College. He was once a student at Harford (Maryland) County Community College. After earning a bachelor's degree at Towson University, he went on to earn a master's from Georgetown University and a doctorate in adult and community college education from North Carolina State University (Samuels 2002). Templin is just one example of many underachieving high school students who have become top administrators and leaders in their fields of study.

Asher, Donald. **Cool Colleges for the Hyper-Intelligent, Self-Directed, Late Blooming, and Just Plain Different: Including Addresses, Phone Numbers, and Web Sites for Every Accredited Four-Year Institution in the United States and Canada. Berkeley**, CA: Ten Speed Press, 2000.

Describes unique colleges, such as those that are totally free, where students can design there own degree programs, where grades are not given, where students can attend before they graduate from high school, and more.

Black, Isaac. **African American Student's College Guide: Your One-Stop Resource for Choosing the Right College, Getting in, and Paying the Bill.** New York: John Wiley, 2000.

Gives advice about choosing a college, test scores, college essays, financial aid, scholarships, and top colleges for African American students. Appendix information includes sample essays, a list of organizations that sponsor tours of historically black colleges, and other educational organizations.

Cohen, Harlan. **Campus Life Exposed: Advice from the Inside.** Princeton, NJ: Peterson's, 2000.

Discusses topics relating to college life such as homesickness, depression, roommates, relationships, dating and sex, drugs and alcohol, and campus safety.

Fudzie, Vince, and Andre N. Hayes. **Your Brain Is a Muscle Too: How Student Athletes Succeed in College and in Life.** New York: Amistad, 2001.

Provides a balance between athletics and academics by giving student athletes information about deciding on a school, preparing for college, fitting in, study skills, money issues, substance abuse, and more.

Gottesman, Greg. **College Survival: A Crash Course for Students by Students.** Laurenceville, NJ: Arco, 1999.

Clothing, packing, roommates, choosing classes, time management, computers, the Internet, Greeks, dorm life, laundry, athletics, dating, partying, and commuting are discussed in this practical book for college students and for those who are preparing to attend college.

Greene, Howard R., and Matthew R. Greene. **Presenting Yourself Successfully to Colleges: How to Market Your Strengths and Make Your Application Stand Out.** New York: Cliff Street Books/HarperCollins, 2001.

Provides step-by-step advice for writing a college essay, getting recommendations from mentors, and packaging the college application.

Hernandez, Michele A. **Acing the College Application: How to Maximize Your Chances for Admission to the College of Your Choice.** New York: Ballantine, 2002.

Provides detailed information about completing college applications and also gives examples of excellent college application essays.

Light, Richard. **Making the Most of College: Students Speak Their Minds.** Cambridge, MA: Harvard University Press, 2001.

After interviewing Harvard seniors for ten years, Light tells why some students make the most of college while others struggle, how decisions made by students can improve their college experiences, and how diversity affects education.

Nist, Sherrie, and Jodi Patrick Holschuh. **College Rules! How to Study, Survive, and Succeed in College.** Berkeley, CA: Ten Speed Press, 2002.

The authors, who are college professors, provide advice on maximizing the college experience, studying, handling stress, maintaining motivation, how college is different from high school, taking exams, professors, selecting courses, understanding a course syllabus, and using textbooks.

Toor, Rachel. **Admissions Confidential: An Insider's Guide of the Elite College Selection Process.** New York: St. Martin's Press, 2001.

Written by a former admissions officer at Duke University, this insightful book explains the process of how students are chosen to attend the university. Toor reveals why some valedictorians are rejected while others are admitted and why independent college counselors can sometimes hurt an applicant's chance at being admitted. Some essays written by applicants are also included in one chapter. Although the book was not specifically published for teens, anyone applying to competitive colleges should read it, especially if rejection letters arrive instead of acceptance packets.

Valverde, Leonard A., ed. **The Latino Student's Guide to College Success.** Westport, CT: Greenwood Press, 2002.

Written by Latino education experts, this book provides information specifically to Latinos who are contemplating, preparing for, or already in a college setting.

Help with Growing into Adulthood: Almost an Adult, But Not Quite

In *The Sound of Music,* naíve Liesel succumbs to the charms of her handsome suitor, Rolf. During the song "Sixteen, Going On Seventeen," Rolf serenades Liesel, saying that at the age of sixteen she needs to be careful because young lads will offer her food and wine. She is told that she is unprepared to face a world of men and that she needs someone older and wiser to protect her. Rolf is that older man, of course—for he is seventeen, going on eighteen. Times have changed since the world of Rolf and Liesel. Although turning sweet sixteen is still a rite of passage for teen girls, teens at this age are not as sweet and innocent as in years past. They are more mature and knowledgeable about the world around them. But female teens still crave information about the process of growing up, especially now with so many opportunities and pressures to succeed in college, advance in careers, and make a difference in the world.

In the song "The Circle Game," Joni Mitchell sings about growing up, using metaphors to compare the life of a child-turned-man to the seasons and carousels. She suggests that humans are captive on a carousel of time. We can only look behind, but it is impossible to return to where we once were. After sixteen springs and summers have passed, the boy is turning car wheels through the town instead of cartwheels. He is cautioned to take his time, because before he knows it, he will be dragging his feet and walking slowly as an old man. It is intriguing that Mitchell uses an example of driving a car as a coming-of-age theme. What could be more apt? Being able to drive is undoubtedly still important to teen males, as are many other rites of passage, including independence from parents, sexual experiences, and preparation for the future. In a country where male teens have gotten a bad reputation in recent years, partly due to highly publicized school shootings, it is imperative that librarians supply them with materials to make the transition to adulthood a bit less difficult.

Older teens may be interested in attending library programs that focus on helping them succeed. Many older teens may lack life skills that are necessary as an adult. For example, some older teens still do not know how to do laundry, eat a balanced diet, or balance a checkbook. Guest speakers at the library could focus on one or more of these topics, especially for teens who are planning to leave home after high school graduation.

The books listed below are essential for older teens who need written guidance about growing up. Some of the titles are specifically for males or females, while others are appropriate for either gender. You can offer programs that are exclusively for males or females, although by late adolescence both males and females are usually concerned about many of the same issues: growing up, moving on to bigger and better things after high school, and learning to become independent.

Brain, Marshall. **The Teenager's Guide to the Real World.** Raleigh, NC: BYG Publishing, 1997.

> Provides information to teens about how to become a successful adult. Topics include jobs, relationships, attitudes, success, finances, and more.

Carlson, Richard. **The Don't Sweat Guide for Graduates: Facing New Challenges with Confidence.** New York: Hyperion, 2002.

> Shows readers who have recently graduated from high school, college, or any other institution of higher learning how to survive in the real world without experiencing too much stress.

Carter-Scott, Cherie. **If High School Is a Game, Here's How to Break the Rules: A Cutting Edge Guide to Becoming Yourself.** New York: Delacorte, 2001.

> Presents ten truths about the teen years and dealing with these circumstances, including "Your Body Will Change," "You Will Be Presented with Choices," "Support Is Out There," "You Will Question Authority," "Your Identity Will Emerge," "Your Inner World Is Your Safety Zone," "Deal with the Things You Cannot Change," "Mistakes Can Be Valuable Lessons," "What You Make of School Is Up To You," and "Adolescence Is the Tunnel to Your Future."

Chiawei O'Hearn, Claudine, ed. **Half and Half: Writers on Growing Up Biracial and Bicultural.** New York: Pantheon, 1998.

Eighteen essays address the difficulties of not fitting in and the benefits of being part of two worlds while growing up.

Colman, Penny. **Girls: A History of Growing Up Female in America.** New York: Scholastic, 2000.

Reveals everyday experiences of girls through diaries, letters, photographs, memoirs, popular magazines, and household manuals.

DeVillers, Julia. **Teen Girlfriends: Celebrating the Good Times, Getting Through the Hard Times.** Berkeley, CA: Wildcat Canyon Press, 2001.

Interviews with more than 100 teenage girls provide a look at various aspects of friendship between young women.

Fox, Annie. **Can You Relate? Real-World Advice for Teens on Guys, Girls, Growing Up, and Getting Along.** Minneapolis, MN: Free Spirit, 2000.

The creator of a Web site for online advice targeted toward teens, Fox presents answers to frequently asked questions about issues related to growing up.

Goldstein, Mark A., and Myrna Chandler Goldstein. **Boys Into Men: Staying Healthy Through the Teen Years.** Westport, CT: Greenwood Press, 2000.

Focuses on the enhancement of the physical and mental health of teen males.

Graham, Stedman. **Teens Can Make It Happen: Nine Steps to Success.** New York: Fireside, 2000.

Presents nine steps that teens should take to prepare for the future, make life-changing decisions, create a vision, and more.

Gray, Kenneth. **Getting Real: Helping Teens Find Their Future.** Thousand Oaks, CA: Corwin Press, 2000.

Advice about careers, college, and military service for teens.

Gurian, Michael. **From Boys to Men: All About Adolescence and You.** New York: Price Stern Sloan, 1999.

Answers questions about the physical, emotional, sexual, and social changes that teenage boys undergo during adolescence.

Jacob, Iris. **My Sisters' Voices: Teenage Girls of Color Speak Out.** New York: Henry Holt, 2002.

Collection of writings by teenage girls about topics including family, friendships, sex, love, racism, loss, and oppression. The author, Jacob, was age eighteen when the book was published.

Johnson, Kevin. **Where Ya Gonna Go?: Now That You're a Graduate.** Minneapolics, MN: Bethany House, 2001.

From a religious perspective, provides advice to older teens about life after high school.

Jukes, Mavis. **Guy Book: An Owner's Manual for Teens.** New York: Crown Publishers, 2002.

Using a theme of automobiles, this book provides practical information to boys about sexual topics, drugs, girls, nutrition, and more.

Kahaner, Ellen. **Everything You Need to Know About Growing Up Female (Need to Know Library).** New York: Rosen, 2001.

Gives advice to teen girls about growing up female.

Martin, Sam. **How to Mow the Lawn: The Lost Art of Being a Man.** New York: Dutton, 2003.

Provides helpful advice to men about many things that are considered to be manly.

Nikkah, John. **Our Boys Speak: Adolescent Boys Write About Their Inner Lives.** New York: St. Martin's Press, 2000.

Older male teens from across the country write about their lives, including topics such as friendship, love, high school, drug abuse, and depression.

Paul, Anthea. **Girlosophy: A Soul Survival Kit.** St. Leonard's, NSW: Allen & Unwin, 2001.

Provides a variety of information about being female, including debates about whether to have children, live together, or become married; how to focus on goals; falling in love; beauty; nutrition; meditation; death; emotions; and more. The color photographs throughout the book are exceptionally appealing. Teens may also enjoy *Girlosophy: The Love Survival Kit* (St. Leonard's, NSW: Allen & Unwin, 2000).

Viorst, Judith. **You're Officially a Grown-Up: The Graduate's Guide to Freedom, Responsibility, Happiness, and Personal Hygiene.** New York: Simon & Schuster, 1999.

With lots of humor and drawings, high school and college graduates are reminded that now they will have to sew, vote, balance a checkbook, write thank-you notes, pay bills, and do more tasks that are required of independent adults.

Wells, Donna K., and Bruce C. Morris. **Reality Quest: Teens Making the Facts.** Deerfield Beach, FL: Health Communications, 2002.

Teens talk about issues that have an impact on their lives in this book, which is somewhat in the format of an Internet instant messaging session. The book also includes quizzes for teens to take so that they can ponder their lives and their futures.

Woods, Len. **I'm Outta Here: Facing Tough Choices After High School.** Grand Rapids, NJ: Baker Books, 1999.

> A practical guide for recent high school graduates, this book presents fifty ethical situations for teens to ponder relating to finance, education, work, sexuality, relationships, and spirituality.

Death, Grief, and Depression: Hard to Keep Your Chin Up?

Many teenagers have an obsession with death and depression, and this may not be entirely strange, considering that at the late stage of adolescence, the critical thinking skills of teens shift into high gear. As teens mature, it is natural for them to think about their own mortality. Many teens also experience the death of a loved one or a friend. Some teens watch videos portraying ways in which death happens, such as *Faces of Death*, over and over again. This series is now available on DVD, proof that it has stood the test of time.

The early death of cultural icons, such as rock stars Kurt Cobain and Jim Morrison, is often a topic of conversation among older teens. The song "The End" by the Doors is played repeatedly in the bedrooms of teens across the country.

Coping with death, grief, and depression is not easy for anyone, adult or teen. Although it is not practical for librarians to act as grief counselors or psychologists unless they are also trained in this field, you might consider working with schools when tragedy occurs in your community. Library displays with books about death and grief may catch the eye of teens who need these materials but who might not seek them otherwise. When high school students commit suicide, are killed in automobile accidents, or are the victims of violence, you can partner with school counselors to promote library resources that help ease the pain. Inform school personnel, including library media specialists, about the resources your library has concerning depression. Disseminating information about community resources, such as suicide hotlines or professionally guided support groups, is another way to meet the information needs of teens.

Bolton, Martha. **Saying Goodbye When You Don't Want To: Teens Dealing with Loss.** Ann Arbor, MI: Vine Books, 2002.

> Uses personal experiences, poetry, and scripture verses to provide advice on how to cope with all kinds of loss in one's life.

Cobain, Bev. **When Nothing Matters Anymore: A Survival Guide for Depressed Teens.** Minneapolis, MN: Free Spirit, 1998.

> A guide to understanding and coping with depression, discussing the different types, how and why the condition begins, how it may be linked to substance abuse or suicide, and how to get help. Written by the aunt of Kurt Cobain.

Fitzgerald, Helen. **The Grieving Teen: A Guide for Teenagers and Their Friends.** New York: Simon & Schuster, 2000.
 Provides in-depth information about support groups; hospital visits; when death is sudden; funerals; understanding grief; and suggested books, organizations, and Web sites. Focuses on sensitive topics such as discovering the body, what a dead body looks or feels like, cremation, witnessing death, suicide, and AIDS.

Klebanoff, Susan. **Ups & Downs: How to Beat the Blues and Teen Depression.** New York: Price Stern Sloan, 1999.
 Assists with problems relating to difficulties in school and at home, mood swings, and suicidal thoughts.

Murphy, James M. **Coping with Teen Suicide.** New York: Rosen, 1999.
 Suitable for teens considering suicide, helping someone who is suicidal, or anyone who is just writing a paper about suicide, this book concentrates on stress, depression, and getting help.

Fitness, Dieting, and Eating Disorders: Every Body Has Body Issues

Don't dunk that donut. Stop chomping on chocolate. Learn to love lima beans. Broccoli is easy to befriend. Strawberries are not slimy, grapes are grand, and mushrooms are marvelous. Obesity has been a problem with adults in the past, but more recently it has become a growing problem for children and teens. Children who are overweight are 20 to 30 percent heavier than they were ten years ago (Brownlee 2002). Overweight youth suffer from high blood pressure, heart disease, and diabetes—as well as low self-esteem. Television, video game playing, Internet surfing, and other sedentary activities can be blamed, along with a poor diet. My late maternal grandmother, who cooked healthy meals for generations of students in the school cafeterias of Wellsville, New York, would not be too happy to hear that fast-food franchises have invaded schools. Youth are eating Whoppers and Chalupas in school cafeterias.

 Librarians serving older teens should be especially aware of issues relating to eating disorders. High school wrestlers have been forced to gain and lose weight at unhealthy rates. Some athletes are prone to using steroids, while many teen girls are suffering from bulimia and anorexia. Others are just plain skinny, though—not necessarily because they are eating vegetables and drinking lots of water, but because it is in their genes to be naturally thin.

 Although it may be impractical to offer library programs for teens suffering from eating disorders, it is realistic to offer general programs relating to nutrition and fitness. Employees from local health clubs are usually willing to demonstrate different types of exercise, such as weight training and aerobics. Health workers and nutritionists can be contacted to speak about overall nutrition or nutrition relating to student athletes.

Barrett, CeCe. **The Dangers of Diet Drugs and Other Weight-Loss Products.** New York: Rosen, 1999.

Discusses the use of over-the-counter, prescription, and herbal diet drugs as well as liquid and prepackaged diet foods and explains their relation to eating disorders and proper nutrition.

Bellenir, Karen, ed. **Diet Information for Teens: Health Tips About Diet and Nutrition, Including Facts About Nutrients, Dietary Guidelines, Breakfasts, School Lunches, Snacks, Party Food, Weight Control, Eating Disorders, and More.** Detroit: Omnigraphics, 2001.

Thorough coverage of issues relating to food, meal planning, weight control, and eating disorders.

Gaede, Katrina, Alan Lachica, and Doug Werner. **Fitness Training for Girls: A Teen Girl's Guide to Resistance Training, Cardiovascular Conditioning and Nutrition.** San Diego: Tracks Publishing, 2001.

Thorough fitness guide for girls covering stretching, resistance training, sport-specific strength training, medicine balls, eating, and more.

Kaehler, Kathy. **Teenage Fitness: Get Fit, Look Good, and Feel Good.** New York: Cliff Street Books, 2001.

Discusses body types, nutrition basics, creative fitness, workouts, and more.

Kolb, Joseph J., Stewart Smith, and Joe Kolb. **Get Fit Now for High School Basketball: Strength Conditioning for Ultimate Performance on the Court.** New York: Hatherleigh Press, 2003.

Provides advice specifically for high school basketball players.

Luby, Thia. **Yoga for Teens: How to Improve Your Fitness, Confidence, Appearance, and Health—and Have Fun Doing It.** Santa Fe, NM: Clear Light Publishers, 2000.

Explains the philosophy and benefits of yoga to teenagers, and provides photographs and step-by-step instructions for a variety of poses.

Monroe, Judy. **Understanding Weight Loss Programs.** New York: Rosen, 1999.

Discusses the weight-loss industry, including why this business is thriving, the many products and services offered, and the pros and cons of various weight-loss methods.

Schwager, Tina, and Michele Schverger. **The Right Moves: A Girl's Guide to Getting Fit and Feeling Good.** Minneapolis, MN: Free Spirit, 1998.

Interspersed with quizzes is information about building self-esteem, nutrition, eating disorders, fitness plans, cross-training, warming up, flexibility, sports injuries, and more.

Smith, Stewart, and Chris Johnson. **Get Fit Now for High School Football.** New York: Hatherleigh Press, 2001.

Interspersed with useful black-and-white photographs is information on stretching, calisthenics, strength and weight training, and workouts for high school football players.

Steinfeld, Jake. **Get Strong! Body by Jake's Guide to Building Confidence, Muscles, and a Great Future for Teenage Guys.** New York: Fireside, 2002.

Provides teenage boys with principles and fitness techniques to assist with developing a positive self-image and becoming both mentally and physically stronger.

Vedral, Joyce L. **Toning for Teens: The 20-Minute Workout That Makes You Look Good and Feel Great!** New York: Warner Books, 2002.

Provides practical advice to teen girls on weight training and building strong bodies.

Wilson, Leslie. **The Ultimate Guide to Cheerleading.** New York: Three Rivers Press, 2003.

This development guide provides practical instructions for cheerleading squad members and coaches.

Driving: Freedom at Last!

April 21, 2085: My sixteenth birthday. Sad, sad day. What I mind most—what I've been dreading most—is losing my license . . . At least Anny Beth can still drive, since she's only eighteen. I don't know what I'd do without Anny Beth. I don't know what we'll do when she hits sixteen. (Haddix 2000, p. 1)

So begins the intriguing story *Turnabout*. In this futuristic novel, Anny Beth and Melly grow younger after engaging in an age-reversing experiment. They have both enjoyed driving for years, and as they become younger, they dread losing this privilege and their freedom. They realize that not being able to drive will have an incredible impact on their lives, and that the ability to drive marks the division between childhood and adulthood.

Ask teens in middle adolescence what they anticipate most, and chances are that they will mention the right to drive. Driving ages differ in various states. In rural areas, the age may be lower. Some states set progressive stages for teen drivers, such as with an adult at a certain age and alone after a certain amount of time. In New Jersey, a very populated state with extremely high automobile insurance, teens cannot drive until age seventeen, which is later than many states. As a teen growing up in New Jersey, I learned that some parents with multiple residences allowed their teens to obtain a driver's license from another state where the age requirement was younger. Parents often want teenagers to have the freedom to drive as much as teens do. Driving is a convenience for some teens, a necessity for others, a freedom for still others, and for some it may be a hobby. One of my friends in high school and his buddies would pitch in to buy cheap cars and intentionally drive them recklessly and smash them into trees and other objects.

Not many books have been written for teens on driving, although there are plenty of magazine and newspaper articles about the topic, mostly concerning accidents and safety. Automobile accidents are the leading cause of death for people ages fifteen through nineteen. So driving is not just an area of interest for teens—it is a subject of vital concern.

Stock your library with multiple copies of driving manuals in both English and Spanish. Allow some to be available for check out, and keep at least one copy in the reference section. Some insurance companies, such as State Farm, publish free brochures specifically for drivers. For example, *Preparing Your Teen to Drive* by State Farm advises parents and teens on purchasing a vehicle that is safe. Perhaps you could invite representatives from insurance companies or employees from the Department of Motor Vehicles to present information to older teens about driving and safety. Representatives from automobile dealerships could also present programs on selecting a new or used automobile. Some organizations, businesses, or even a high school teacher from an auto shop class may be willing to demonstrate some of the basics of car maintenance such as changing a tire and checking fluid levels.

Library displays about driving, safety, laws related to driving, and road trips are another way to promote books to older teens who are about to drive or who are already driving. Tangible objects are useful for displays. Dangle keys from a display board, use photographs of automobiles, and place a spare tire in the middle of the display, surrounded by books.

Berardelli, Phil. **Driving Challenge: Dare to Be Safer and Happier on the Road.** Vienna, VA: Nautilus Communications, 2001.

> Explains different types of accidents that occur and gives advice for staying safe on the road.

Berardelli, Phil. **Safe Young Drivers: A Guide for Parents and Teens.** Vienna, VA: Nautilus Communications, 2000.

> Includes information about driving in different types of conditions, choosing a car, coping during accidents, using maps, parking in garages, using parking lots and spaces, getting insurance, using cell phones, coping with pot holes in the road, and more.

Duval, Jacques, and Denis Duquet. **The Auto Guide 2002.** Willowdale, ONT: Firefly, 2002.

> Useful for teens buying their first car, this guide is filled with information about evaluating the strengths and weaknesses of different types of new cars, cost of new cars, and a used car section covering models back to 1995.

Winters, Adam. **Everything You Need to Know About Being a Teen Driver.**
Need to Know Library. New York: Rosen, 2000.
Presents basic information to new teen drivers and is especially appro-
priate for reluctant readers.

Wong, Janet S. **Behind the Wheel: Poems About Driving.** New York: Margaret K. McElderry Books, 1999.
Thirty-five poems look at various aspects of driving, including passing the written driver's test, being pulled over by a cop, and having an accident, and treat them as a metaphor for life.

Money and Finance: Don't Let It Burn a Hole in Your Pocket

As teens begin to earn money at a job or get allowances from parents, they
need to learn how to handle finances, banking, budgeting, investing, and money.
Consider asking local experts to speak about these topics to older teens. Some
teens may still not know basic information about banking, such as maintaining a
checking account and the importance of a savings account. As older teens become more independent from their parents, being able to manage money will
become even more important.

Like adults, teens have been known to abuse credit cards. Then again, some
parents acquire credit cards in the names of their teenagers. An Ohio college student applied for her first credit card and was sent a rejection letter. There were already four credit cards in her name and her father had put her $50,000 in debt.
Another teen, who is now twenty-nine, tells how he got into financial trouble
when his mother used his Social Security number. This teen said that maybe seventeen year olds are not worried about their mothers taking stuff from them, but
perhaps they should be (Irvine 2002). Teens can run credit reports on themselves
if they discover that their parents have money problems to determine whether
identity theft and credit card fraud have occurred.

Burkett, Larry. **Money Matters for Teens.** Adapted from materials by Larry
Burkett with Marnie Wooding; illustrated by Chris Kielesinski. Chicago:
Moody Press, 2001.
Teaches teens how to manage their money wisely.

Gardner, David, and Tom Gardner. **The Motley Fool Investment Guide for
Teens: 8 Steps to Having More Money Than Your Parents Ever
Dreamed Of.** New York: Simon & Schuster, 2002.
Interspersed with numerous quotations from teens who have managed
money well are explanations of mutual funds, banking practices, IRAs, in-
vesting, and more.

Liebowitz, Jay. **Wall Street Wizard: Sound Ideas from a Savvy Teen Inves-
tor.** New York: Simon & Schuster, 2000.
Teen finance guru Liebowitz explains investing, managing and selling
stocks, taxes, starting a company, and more.

Modu, Emmanuel, and Andrea Walker. **TeenVestor: The Practical Investment Guide for Teens and Their Parents.** New York: Berkley Publishing, 2001.

> Practical information about helping teen investors manage money, understanding the stock market, mutual funds, taxes, online brokers, and more.

Silver, Dan. **The Generation Y Money Book: 99 Smart Ways to Handle Money.** Los Angeles: Adams-Hall, 2000.

> Targeting high school students and older teens, this book includes practical advice on saving receipts, tipping, avoiding credit cards, when not to shop, managing checking accounts, and planning for college.

Jobs: Workin' for a Livin'

Since the age of fourteen, I have worked, not necessarily because I needed the money, but because I love to work. At age thirteen, I began babysitting, which is not unusual for young teens. I began delivering newspapers when I was fourteen, and lifeguarding during the summer at fifteen.

During my senior year of high school, I was involved in the Distributive Education Clubs of America (DECA). I happily left school at 11:43 A.M. every day. I worked as a photographer for half of the year and at a movie theater the other half. Looking back, I do not regret my decision to be involved in DECA instead of taking a lot of college preparation courses. While biding my time in high school, waiting to be released so that I could begin college, I put my energies into the working world. Despite my academic apathy, lazy was not a word that described me, and I knew that I would work hard as a college student.

Whatever the motivation—social, financial, career preparation, a vocational interest—many teens have jobs. The world of work can teach teens, as it did me, a lot about people, customer service, and management. I did not always find it easy to work with adults. I had a boss who yelled at me in front of a customer. The customer asked me if it was typical for her to talk to her staff in that manner. When I responded yes, she told me that she would never shop there again due to the behavior of my boss and she left. To this day, I do not give negative feedback to staff in front of library patrons, and I try to instill the same practice in my library managers. Being a lifeguard for seven years was my first management training. I learned the importance of being observant, being consistent with rules, and taking preventive measures to avoid accidents. It is not easy being sixteen, wearing a bikini, and telling an intoxicated adult not to dive into three feet of water.

My work experiences as a teen have shaped my adult life. To this day, I still swim, I am an avid photographer, I read the newspaper, and I love spending time with my niece and my nephews. DECA is still a function at my former high school, and other students are also benefiting from being able to learn via the working world. Nationwide, there are 170,000 marketing students, according to DECA, Incorporated, so there are probably students in your library service area who are also involved in this co-op program.

Older teens need information about jobs that they may currently be working in or that they would like to be working in. Many teens work in the retail trade and service industries, such as at the mall, amusement parks, and restaurants. In the late 1990s, teenagers in the Silicon Valley made as much as $20 per hour writing computer codes.

There has been a great deal of debate about whether students should be encouraged to work while they are still in school. Teens do not work just for spending money but also to gain independence. By working, teens can acquire basic life skills, such as learning to dress properly, time management, how to write resumes, and what to expect during job interviews. Future employers may be impressed to see that students were able to juggle school life and work. Others argue that working cuts into learning and that teens working too much are too tired for school. Laurence Steinberg, a professor of psychology at Temple University in Philadelphia, believes that the number of hours a teen should work depends on age. High school juniors should be able to handle fifteen hours per week, and that number increases to twenty for seniors.

Programs for teens who are about to begin a part-time job or who are already working might cover such topics as sexual harassment and other legal issues, health and safety concerns, resume writing, interview skills, people skills, and time management. Intergenerational issues are also pertinent for older teens, and they may need guidance regarding relationships with people of different ages who have various ethical beliefs and work habits. Also, consider holding a job fair, where teens can meet face to face with recruiters from a variety of businesses. There are also overseas opportunities for older teens in the summer months, and you could invite employers and former teen participants to speak about that topic.

Coon, Nora E. **Teen Dream Jobs.** Hillsboro, OR: Beyond Words Publishing, 2003.
> Presents advice to teen job seekers, features teens who have been successful in starting businesses, and gives suggestions for writing cover letters and resumes.

Fry, Ron. **101 Smart Questions to Ask on Your Interview.** Franklin Lakes, NJ: Career Press, 2003.
> Gives practical information to job seekers, even first-time job seekers, about appropriate questions to ask at job interviews.

Ireland, Susan. **The Complete Idiot's Guide to Cool Jobs for Teens.** Indianapolis, IN: Alpha Books, 2001.
> Discusses how to get a job, determine what job type suits certain skills and interests, learn about different types of jobs, write resumes, ace interviews, intern, and more.

Lancaster, Lynne C., and David Stillman. **When Generations Collide: Who They Are. Why They Clash. How to Solve the Generational Puzzle at Work.** New York: Harper Business, 2002.

Gives detailed information about people from four different generations, including the Traditionalists, the Baby Boomers, the Generation Xers, and the Millennials. Provides advice about recruiting, retaining, and managing people from different generations. For the sophisticated older teen, this thorough book will provide assistance with interpersonal relationships at work, either at current jobs or in future work situations.

Morem, Sue. **How to Get a Job and Keep It: Career and Life Skills You Need to Succeed.** Chicago: Ferguson Publishing, 2002.

Discusses different types of jobs, writing resumes, job searching, and more.

Nadler, Burton Jay. **The Everything Resume Book: Great Resumes for Every Situation.** 2nd ed. Avon, MA: Adams Media Corporation, 2003.

Includes practical advice about creating a resume and also covers how to post a resume online. Part of the Everything series.

Summer Jobs for Students: Explore More Than 45,000 Paid Positions! Princeton, NJ: Peterson's, 2003.

State-by-state listing of jobs available for students.

Law: Miranda and More

The subject of law appeals to teens on many different levels, and the motivations for learning about law vary from the fear of being arrested, to the dream of practicing law, to an avocational interest engendered by television shows such as *Cops* and those featuring hard-nosed judges. Older teens are sometimes faced with making difficult choices, and having books that outline laws relating to youth is crucial. Remember that not only teens who have legal problems are interested in this topic. Many teens simply want to know their legal rights. Older teens, especially, may need library materials about compulsory attendance laws, school searches, confidentiality of school records, how to seek emancipation, and obligations of employers. Information about legal matters should be as up-to-date and as thorough as possible. Since laws are different in every state, and generic law books for teens will not cover everything, librarians serving older teens should ensure that the library's reference section includes information about state laws.

Programs relating to the rights of teenagers may also be popular, especially those concerning laws about driving, search warrants, and emancipation. Local law firms or law enforcement agencies may be willing to speak at library programs about law. Ask these individuals to speak about careers in law and law enforcement as well.

Some high schools have mock trial clubs, and libraries may benefit by linking with these groups to offer programs relating to law. The club typically has mock trials in real courtrooms, and perhaps the public library could promote library resources relating to these topics. A book such as *Teens on Trial: Young People Who Challenged the Law—And Changed Your Life,* edited by Thomas A. Jacobs, J.D., could be used as debate material for library programs.

Cary, Eve, editor. **The Rights of Students (ACLU Handbook for Young Americans).** New York: Puffin, 1997.
> Provides legal information pertinent to the lives of students.

Hempelman, Kathleen A. **Teen Legal Rights.** Westport, CT: Greenwood Press, 2000.
> Provides practical information about legal rights concerning a variety of topics such as driving, school newspapers, dress codes, student records, minimum wage, income taxes, voting, marrying, drug abuse, crime, discrimination, entering into contracts, and court.

Jacobs, Thomas A., J.D., ed. **Teens on Trial: Young People Who Challenged the Law—And Changed Your Life.** Minneapolis, MN: Free Spirit, 2000.
> Presents information about court decisions that relate to the life of teenagers.

Jacobs, Thomas A., J.D., ed. **What Are My Rights?: 95 Questions and Answers About Teens and the Law.** Minneapolis, MN: Free Spirit, 1997.
> In a question-and-answer format, this thorough book gives law information to teens about topics such as sexual harassment, dress codes, drug testing, school prayer, the death penalty, and freedom of expression. Although slightly out of date, much of the information is still pertinent.

Truly, Traci. **Teen Rights: A Legal Guide For Teens and the Adults in Their Lives.** Naperville, IL: Sphinx, 2002.
> The author, who is an attorney, explains the laws with regard to situations that teens encounter today, with summaries of court cases, information about different types of laws, and a fifty-state legal guide to laws about abortion, age of majority, driver's licenses, curfews, emancipation, and more.

The Military: Just One More Push-Up!

In 2003, when the United States went to war with Iraq, the media turned their attention to the military. As CNN and other television stations provided extensive coverage of the war, this exposure inevitably sparked interest in the military, especially in older teens who may have been contemplating service to their country as a soldier. The story of nineteen-year-old POW Jessica Lynch being rescued by other soldiers may have touched the lives of many people, especially older teens, since Lynch is also an older teenager.

All branches of the military spend time and money recruiting high school students. Recruiters visit shopping mall arcades and post literature at the library, attempting to attract potential soldiers. Visit a theater and you may see an advertisement for joining the military before the flick begins. At Dover Downs International Speedway in Dover, Delaware, a stock car called "Rover" (Recruiting Outreach Vehicle) represents the Air Force and is used to recruit young adults to the military. As part of the pageantry before the NASCAR race, a pair of B1 bombers and F-16 fighters from Dover Air Force Base fly over the grandstands. Similarly, the Marines have a car in the NASCAR Busch Grand National series, and the Army's dragster is used as a recruitment tool on the National Hot Rod Association circuit.

In the past, schools were off-limits to military recruiters. In fact, 2,000 out of 217,000 schools nationwide barred military recruiters (Hutcheson 2002, p. 2). As part of the No Child Left Behind Act, Congress ordered that schools turn over the names, addresses, and telephone numbers of students to military recruiters. Only parents can block the release of the information. The law also requires school administrators to allow military recruiters onto their campuses. There has been controversy about whether the act is an invasion of privacy. In the meantime, the Defense Department predicts that recruitment costs will decrease now that recruiters have direct access to high schools.

Older male teens with no intention of joining the military may also need military information, since males turning eighteen must register for the Selective Service. Familiarize yourself with the Selective Service, so you can provide this information to older teens. If Congress and the president approve a reinstatement of the draft, the Selective Service would begin a lottery program based on birthdays to determine who is called. Unlike in past years, full-time college students cannot claim an exemption from the draft unless they are ministerial students.

With increased promotion of military service opportunities to older teens by the government and by military recruitment campaigns entering the mainstream via sporting events, you may discover that a greater number of older teens are requesting information about the military. They will need ASVAB study guides and information about military life, homesickness, different branches of the service, applying to military academies, becoming physically fit in preparation for basic training, and available vocations and educational opportunities associated with the military. Familiarize yourself with Junior ROTC and Civil Air Patrol programs in preparation for any questions from teens. Those contemplating joining one of the services may also need information from the library about college tuition reimbursement, which is offered to military personnel. Also, the military's delayed entry program allows older teens to join the military but to delay entry for a specific amount of time. Whereas in the past many high school seniors began basic training the Monday after high school graduation, many now spend a leisurely summer with family and friends before leaving. Consider hosting programs for teens who are contemplating military service. Most recruiters would be very willing to be a part of such a program. Current military personnel from the area who are home on leave, preferably those who are ages eighteen or nineteen, could also be part of a panel to talk about joining the military.

Flach, Andrew. **The Official United States Navy SEAL Workout.** New York: Five Star, 2003.

Presents information about physical training for sailors at BUD/S, the Navy SEAL basic training program.

Flach, Andrew. **The United States Marine Corps Workout.** New York: Five Star, 1999

Designed for Marines and future Marines, this manual provides practical fitness advice, information about Marine fitness requirements, and guidance on becoming a Marine.

Green, Michael. **U.S. Army Special Operations Forces.** Mankato, MN: Capstone Press, 2000.

Focuses on the major missions, training, and weapons of the Airborne Rangers. This is one in a series about special operations of the Army, Navy, and Air Force.

Korman, Lewis J., and Matthew Naythons. Foreword by Walter Cronkite. **A Day in the Life of the United States Armed Force: Photographed by 125 of the World's Leading Photojournalists on a Single Day, October 22, 2002.** New York: HarperCollins, 2003.

Through photographs, this book gives readers a glimpse of life in the armed forces at 125 locations throughout the world.

Ostrow, Scott A. **Arco Guide to Joining the Military.** Laurenceville, NJ: Arco, 2001.

Designed to help potential military personnel make decisions about military service and careers.

Thiebes, Raquel D. **Army Basic Training: Be Smart, Be Ready.** Philadelphia: Xlibris Corporation, 2000.

Prepares new Army recruits for the physical training requirements in basic training.

United States Department of Defense. **America's Top Military Careers.** Indianapolis, IN: JIST, 2001.

Describes twenty military careers in great depth.

Philosophy and Psychology: Deep Thinkers

Teens of any age are grappling with the truths of the universe and trying to learn how their brains work. By late adolescence, they may be even more interested in the fields of psychology and philosophy, since they are more mature and better able to think about more complicated issues and grasp more difficult concepts. Programs relating to psychology could revolve around personality types. Consider introducing teens to the Enneagram, which is a system for determining nine different personality types—reformer, helper, motivator, artist, thinker, loyalist, generalist, leader, and peacemaker—and how they interact with one another. I have used this method during booktalk programs. I have linked Enneagram types with different characters in books to exemplify to teens the various personality types that people may have, and how people relate to one other based on their Enneagram type (Anderson and Mahood 2001, pp. 108–109). Taking this concept a step further, perhaps librarians, after studying the basics of the Enneagram, could offer library programs in which teens discuss personality types in relation to fictional characters.

Teens may also be interested in the Myers Briggs Type Indicator test as they strive to learn more about themselves. This test involves an acronym of four letters that stand for traits relating to personality and work habits, such as ESTP, which refers to Extrovert, Sensitive, Thinker, Perceiver. Invite guest speakers to discuss the Myers Briggs Type Indicator and how it relates to the world of work and management. Many psychologists, career counselors, and business consultants have expertise in this area, and they may be willing to share their knowledge with a group of teens.

Dream analysis workshops may also be popular with teens. Books about dream interpretation are typically popular items in many libraries, and psychologists could visit libraries and speak about how to analyze dreams.

Regarding philosophy, you may want to work with speech teachers and debate coaches to assist with academics and plan programs. Many older teens will be thrilled by the thought of being able to sharpen their tongues at the library by participating in dialogues using the Socratic method. There have been several books published relating popular culture to philosophical ideas, and these may be used as a basis for library programs.

Baron, Renee. **What Type Am I? Discover Who You Really Are.** New York: Penguin, 1998.
>Features the Myers-Briggs Type Indicator personality theory and assists readers with discovering their personality type.

Callahan, William J. **The Enneagram for Youth.** Chicago: Loyola University Press, 1992.
>Introduces youth to the Enneagram personality theory.

Carlson, Dale, and Hannah Carlson. **Where's Your Head? Psychology for Teens.** Madison, CT: Bick Publishing House, 1998.
>Explains the psychological differences between early childhood, early adolescence, adolescence, and adulthood; explains theories of human behaviors; explains mental illness; and discusses therapy.

Covey, Sean. **The 7 Habits of Highly Effective Teens: The Ultimate Teenage Success Guide.** New York: Simon & Schuister, 1998.
Discusses seven habits for highly effective teens, including "Be Proactive," "Begin with the End in Mind," "Put First Things First," "Think Win-Win," "Seek to Understand, Then to Be Understood," and "Synergize."

Irwin, William. *The Simpsons* **and Philosophy: The D'oh! of Homer.** Chicago: Open Court, 2001.
Links the television show *The Simpsons* with the core elements of philosophy.

Johnson, Julie Tallard. **I Ching for Teens: Take Charge of Your Destiny with the Ancient Chinese Oracle.** Rochester, VT: Bindu Books, 2001.
This translation of the Chinese oracle that has been guiding people for more than 2,000 years helps teens cope with decisions about truth, opportunities, disappointment, happiness, coming-of-age rituals, and more.

Johnson, Spencer. **Who Moved My Cheese? for Teens: An A-Mazing Way to Change to Win.** New York: Putnam, 2002.
Presents the author's parable about change framed in a story about a group of high school friends trying to handle change in their lives.

Law, Stephen. **Philosophy Rocks! Find Out What It All Means.** New York: Hyperion, 2000.
Each chapter tackles a truth-seeking question, such as "Who Am I?" "Where Do Right and Wrong Come From?" and "What Is Real?"

Pickels, Dwayne. **Am I Okay? Psychological Testing and What Those Tests Mean.** Philadelphia: Chelsea House, 2001.
Explains different types of psychological tests, ways tests are given, and the history of testing.

Riso, Don Richard, and Russ Hudson. 2003. **Discovering Your Personality Type: The Essential Introduction to the Enneagram.** Boston: Houghton Mifflin.
This manual provides thorough information, including charts, boxed information, and quotations, about the Enneagram and the nine personality types associated with the personality theory.

Shaw, Tucker. **Who Do You Think You Are? 12 Methods for Analyzing the True You.** New York: Alloy Books, 2001.
Provides teens with information about different ways to analyze themselves, such as using numerology, the seven types of intelligence, psychological profiles, chakras, the Enneagram, and more.

music and learning about musicians. I became familiar with many musicians when I was an older teenager. For both teens and adults, music may be just the thing to get them crying, laughing, motivated, or interested in library resources.

Music is somewhat of an obsession for many teens. Consider Rad, a character in *Tomorrow Wendy: A Love Story* (Stoehr 1998). Rad only talks in song lyrics. The book is a treasure for music lovers. Older teens may be listening to new musicians as well as those who performed at Woodstock, or to those musicians who are too senile to even remember Woodstock. You do not need to blare Eminem's "White America" in your living room (although this always wakes me up), but you should be aware that Eminem is a musician, not a small, multicolored chocolate candy, and that his music is very popular with many teens. When serving older teens and building library collections for them, knowing the culture of music is essential.

To successfully work with any segment of the public on an adult reference desk, librarians must be familiar with world events, current events, and culture. Older teens have interests similar to adults', and library collections should reflect these cultural interests. Howard Stern may not be popular in the location where you are serving older teens, but Jerry Springer might, or televangelists, or stars from the reality TV show *American Idol*, or Kelly Osbourne, or country musicians, or . . . well, the possibilities are endless. The point is, you must accommodate the needs and interests of your public, whether you share those needs and interests or not. To do that you must remain open-minded.

Before you build a library collection and reach an older teen audience, familiarize yourself with teen heroes, fads, and trends. You can read teen magazines, watch television, and browse Web sites for teens. To test your teen cultural knowledge, take the culture quizzes in each April, August, and December issues of *Voice of Youth Advocates*, created by Erin V. Helmrich and Wendy Woltjer. Also, read "Up To Date Or Out of Date: Test Your Teen Knowledge" by Kimberlee Ried and Kaite Mediatore (2003, p. 22). You might be surprised to discover that you are out of date in your knowledge of pop culture.

Popular culture can even be used in library programs relating to bibliographic instruction. As a young adult librarian in North Carolina, I offered a program called "Rockin' Research" in which participants dissected the lyrics of the song "One Week" by the group Barenaked Ladies. The song includes references to historical and recent cultural figures including Aquaman, Leanne Rimes, and Harrison Ford. Another song that is useful for this purpose is "We Didn't Start the Fire," by singer and songwriter Billy Joel. It references tons of topics, such as hula hoops, the movie *Psycho*, Chubby Checker, and James Dean. Some Web sites list the song lyrics, with links to information about each topic. In this case, the research has already been completed for the participants. Nevertheless, the song contents can be used as a framework for seeking information about each topic.

Barson, Michael, and Steven Heller. **Teenage Confidential: An Illustrated History of the American Teen.** San Francisco: Chronicle Books, 1998.
> A history of popular culture in relation to teens, this illustrated book shows how teenagers have been portrayed in books, comics, movies, TV, advertising, and music throughout the years.

Chase, David, et al. **The Tao of Bada Bing! Words of Wisdom from the Sopranos.** n.p.: Carhil Ventures, 2003.
> Features memorable quotations from all four seasons of the television show *The Sopranos.*

Epstein, Dan. **20th Century Pop Culture.** Philadelphia: Chelsea House, 2000.
> With many colorful photographs, this thorough book chronicles pop culture, including movies, music, television, and news, beginning with Coca Cola and ending with the Y2K bug. "On December 20, *Life* magazine ran a cover story on teenagers, underscoring the fact that, for the first time in American history, teenagers were viewed as a demographic unto themselves. Thanks, in part, to the many extra jobs that were created by World War Two, teenager had plenty of spending money, and it became Madison Avenue's avowed mission to get them to spend it on various clothing, dance and music fads" is a quotation from page 29.

George-Warren, Holly, Patricia Romanowski, and Jon Pareles, eds. **The Rolling Stone Encyclopedia of Rock & Roll.** New York: Fireside, 2001.
> This thorough encyclopedia presents essays on critical and historical perspectives about musicians and includes discographies.

Humphries, Reynold. **The American Horror Film.** New York: Columbia University Press, 2003.
> Features movies such as *Dracula,* which was produced in 1931, as well as present-day movies, including *Scream* and *The Sixth Sense.* Includes an extensive filmography of horror films.

LeKich, John. **Reel Adventures: The Savvy Teens' Guide to Great Movies.** Willowdale, ONT: Annick, 2002.
> Highlights memorable lines and scenes from movies; includes modern-day blockbusters, classics, cult films, and Oscar-winning films.

Osgood, Charles, ed. **Funny Letters From Famous People.** New York: Broadway Books, 2003.
> Collection of humorous letters written by politicians, writers, and show business figures including Fred Allen, Groucho Marx, and Oscar Wilde, and others.

Rollin, Lucy. **Twentieth-Century Teen Culture By the Decades: A Reference Guide.** Westport, CT: Greenwood Press, 1999.

    Decade by decade, discusses the music, fashion, language, reading interests, educational, medical, economic, political, and technological elements of American teen life.

Schlosser, Eric. **Reefer Madness: And Other Tales from the American Underground.** Boston: Houghton Mifflin, 2003.

    The author of *Fast Food Nation* considers the hypocrisy of economy and American culture, especially relating to the issues of marijuana, pornography, and illegal migrant workers.

Walley, David. **Teenage Nervous Breakdown: Music and Politics in the Post-Elvis Age.** New York: Insight Books, 1998.

    Explores how popular teen culture, especially music, has been important in the shaping of society during the past several years.

Older Teen Tidbits: Ten Songs About Late Adolescence

1. "Be True to Your School," by the Beach Boys
2. "Edge of Seventeen," by Stevie Nicks
3. "I'm Eighteen," by Alice Cooper
4. "I Love Rock 'n' Roll," by Joan Jett and the Blackhearts
5. "Jack and Diane," by John Cougar Mellencamp
6. "Seventeen," by Janis Ian
7. "Summer of ''69," by Brian Adams
8. "Sweet Little Sixteen," by the Beatles
9. "Sixteen Going on Seventeen," from *The Sound of Music*
10. "Young Turks," by Rod Stewart

Older Teen Tidbits: Ten Movies About Late Adolescence

1. *American Pie*
2. *American Graffiti*
3. *Bill and Ted's Excellent Adventure*
4. *Breakfast Club*
5. *Disturbing Behavior*
6. *Fast Times at Ridgemont High*
7. *Ferris Bueller's Day Off*
8. *Grease*
9. *Risky Business*
10. *Sixteen Candles*

Older Teen Tidbits: Ten TV Shows About Late Adolescence

1. *Beverly Hills 90210*
2. *Boston Public*
3. *Buffy the Vampire Slayer*
4. *Dawson's Creek*
5. *Heartbreak High*
6. *My So-Called Life*
7. *Party of Five*
8. *Sabrina the Teenage Witch*
9. *Saved By the Bell*
10. *Welcome Back Kotter*

Reading and Book Groups: Now, That's Entertainment!

Book discussions that concentrate on nonfiction are highly popular with older teens, as are writing workshops for those who wish to fine-tune their skills in writing nonfiction. Since most expository writing involves research, in a nonfiction writing workshop you can naturally progress to information literacy and teach older teens how to find magazine articles, reference materials, radio transcripts, and more. Explore nonfiction topics in a variety of formats: magazine articles, lists, poetry, autobiographies, and graphic novels. Older teens may be especially interested in reading nonfiction that has been written by other teens.

Also, teens in late adolescence are better able to understand humor, including parodies and sarcasm, so be sure your collection includes a variety of materials on humor.

Since older teens typically have well-developed cognitive abilities compared to younger teens, they may be more likely to be more critical about topics such as politics and current events. Following are just a few of the resources that can help you select titles for teen reading and writing groups.

Cart, Michael, editor. **The Best American Nonrequired Reading.** Boston: Houghton Mifflin, 2002.

> Selection for readers under twenty-five of the best literature from mainstream and alternative American periodicals including *The New Yorker*, *Jane*, *Spin*, *Esquire*, *Time*, and others.

Choron, Sandra, and Harry Choron. **The Book of Lists for Teens.** Boston: Houghton Mifflin, 2002.

> Provides over 250 lists for teens on a variety of topics in categories including "Me, Myself, and I," "The World Out There," "Relationships," "School," "That's Entertainment," and "Facts on File." Lists include "100 Things to Do When There's Nothing to Do," "37 Ways to Fight Censorship," "6 Helpful Hints for Teens Buying Cars," "9 Nobel Prizewinners

Who Hated School," "5 Common Scholarship Scam Come-ons," and "10 Teen Inventors."

Espeland, Pamela. **Life Lists for Teens: Tips, Steps, Hints, and How-tos for Growing Up, Getting Along, Learning, and Having Fun.** Minneapolis, MN: Free Spirit, 2003.

Similar to *The Book of Lists for Teens* by Sandra Choron and Harry Choron, this book also includes lists for teens in the categories of "Health and Wellness," "Getting Along," "Staying Safe," "School and Learning," "Going Online," "Planning Ahead," "Saving the World," and "Focus on You."

Fisher, David. **Chicken Poop for the Soul: Stories to Harden Your Heart and Dampen Your Spirit: A Parody.** New York: Pocket Books, 1997.

This parody of the popular series includes twisted tales about similar topics. For more chicken poop, try *Chicken Poop for the Soul II: More Droppings,* published in 2000.

Franzen, Jonathan. **How to Be Alone: Essays.** New York: Farrar, Straus & Giroux, 2002.

This collection of fourteen essays by noted social critic Jonathan Franzen presents answers to questions about how to be alone in a noisy and distracting mass culture.

Fulghum, Hunter S. **Don't Try This at Home: How to Win a Sumo Match, Catch a Great White Shark, and Start an Independent Nation, and Other Extraordinary Feats (for Ordinary People).** New York: Broadway Books, 2002.

Chock-full of humor, this unique book describes how readers can perform silly stunts.

Janeczko, Paul B., ed. **Seeing the Blue Between: Advice and Inspiration for Young Poets.** Cambridge, MA: Candlewick Press, 2002.

Collection of poems and advice to young poets from well-known poets including Nikki Grimes, Liz Rosenberg, Janet S. Wong, and others.

Meyer, Stephanie H., and John Meyer. **Teen Ink 2: More Voices, More Visions.** Deerfield Beach, FL: Health Communications, 2001.

Teens write about family, friends, challenges, love, imagination, school days, fitting in, milestones, and memories.

Mezrich, Ben. **Bringing Down the House: The Inside Story of Six MIT Students Who Took Vegas for Millions.** New York: Free Press, 2002.

Tells the story of how six MIT students visited the casinos in Las Vegas, Nevada, and took advantage of the statistical nature of blackjack.

Paint Me Like I Am: Teen Poems from WritersCorps. Foreword by Nikki Giovanni. New York: HarperCollins, 2003.

A collection of poetry written by teenagers involved in the nonprofit organization WritersCorps.

Remnick, David, and Henry Finder, eds. **Fierce Pajamas: Selections From an Anthology of Humor Writing from** *The New Yorker.* New York: Random House, 2001.

Collection of humorous writings by Groucho Marx, Woody Allen, Steve Martin, E. B. White, Ogden Nash, and more. An especially interesting selection for teens from this anthology is "Teen Times" by Paul Rudnick, published in *The New Yorker* on November 6, 2000. The author comments that there have been several versions of adult magazines created for teens, such as *Teen People*, and presents hilarious make-believe cover lines for magazines targeted at teens in the United States.

Vizzini, Ned. **Teen Angst? Naah: A Quasi-Autobiography.** Minneapolis, MN: Free Sprit, 2000.

The author, nineteen at the time the book was written, reflects on his earlier teen years.

Vowell, Sarah. **The Partly Cloudy Patriot.** New York: Simon & Schuster, 2002.

A collection of humorous personal essays that explore the relationship of American history to citizenship. Most of the commentaries derive from Vowell's radio appearances on NPR's *This American Life*.

Weston, Carol. **For Teens Only: Quotes, Notes, & Advice You Can Use.** New York: HarperCollins, 2002.

With tons of quotations from celebrities, this book provides advice to teens about being true to oneself.

Winnick, Judd. **Pedro and Me: Friendship, Loss, and What I Learned.** New York: Henry Holt, 2000.

Cartoonist Judd Winnick, portrayed on MTV's *Real World,* describes his friendship with Pedro, who was diagnosed with AIDS at age seventeen.

Relationships and Sexuality:
"And I Met This Great Guy But My Parents Hate Him . . ."

Older teens often find that their relationships with family members and peers change over the course of their teen years. A best friend from middle school may now be someone to avoid. While someone aged twenty-five may have seemed old to a thirteen year old, teens in late adolescence are more likely to socialize with people who are in their twenties. In the late stage of adolescence, teens generally view adults as their peers. Parents are usually not considered aliens to older teens, and many older teens are building more positive relations with their parents and other relatives. Teens who work may have a lot of contact with adults in job situations. Older teens already attending college may be surrounded by older peers and may have platonic or romantic relationships with these peers.

The Internet has opened an entire new world for some teens, especially shy teens who have difficulty communicating in person. Many teens spend hours in chat rooms and have virtual friends from all over the world. Parents and others who care about the well-being of youth have faced some challenges in the past few years with teens forming online relationships with strangers and deciding to meet these strangers in public. There can be many dangers involved in meeting people online, as discussed in *Katie.com: My Story* by Katherine Tarbox. This autobiography tells about Katie's negative experience with an online relationship.

In some cases, however, online relationships may be safer compared to face-to-face relationships. One exceptional work of fiction that explores this topic is *Romiette and Julio,* by Sharon M. Draper. In this modern-day Romeo and Juliette story, Romiette, sixteen, who is African American, meets Julio, also sixteen, who is Hispanic American, in a chat room. After much discussion they discover that they attend the same high school. They become friends and begin dating. It is soon apparent that other people, gang members they meet face-to-face, have a problem with the fact that they are involved in a biracial relationship. This book, and others that explore the topic of online relationships, could be used for book discussions with teens.

Romantic and sexual relationships, of course, are always a major focus at this time of life. Teens may be looking for Mr. or Ms. Right, trying to figure out if they should "get serious," or looking for support in ending a relationship. As described in *Heartbreak and Roses: Real Life Stories of Troubled Love*, edited by Janet Bode and Stan Mack, some teens may be struggling with abusive relationships. Although it is doubtful that a group of abused teens will show up at the library for a program about the topic, librarians can at least have the materials available and provide information referral services as well. Some older teenagers may already be married or engaged. Librarians may want to become familiar with laws relating to marriage and cohabitation. Married teens may need legal advice and referrals to free legal aid.

> *"Sybil Davison has a genius I.Q. and has been laid by at least six different guys,"* begins *Forever* (Blume 1975, p. 1).

By late adolescence, many teenagers are already in relationships where regular sexual activity is not uncommon. Some teens, like Sybil Davison, have had multiple sexual partners.

In Thailand, teenagers download a "Sperm Screensaver" and a game called "Sperm Invader" from the Durex Web site. Teens are also given advice on safe sex and have the opportunity to talk to Durex-selected doctors about sex, sharing information on message boards. Durex is not just targeting Thai teens. There are thirty-six Durex Web sites targeting specific cultures, and Durex condoms are promoted in many languages.

Durex, Trojan, French ticklers, and other condoms are not exactly unknown to many of these older teens. Teens have undoubtedly already been lectured about pregnancy, diseases, contraception, and rape. By late adolescence, most males have already released enough sperm to repopulate the entire world. These males usually understand sexual desire. For females, however, there is a different story. "Adolescent Girls and Sexual Desire" in the *New Moon Network* explains that teen females are not given enough information about sexual pleasure and that they should be provided with this information along with other sexuality information. Deborah L. Tolman's *Dilemmas of Desire: Teenage Girls Talk About Sexuality* thoroughly explores the topic of teen females and sexuality.

Although many adults believe that all teenagers think about is sex, teens are not always as sexually active as adults may believe. Some teens have taken virginity pledges and have decided to abstain from sex until they are married. Although these types of pledges are successful among those who are fifteen and sixteen, they are not as successful for eighteen year olds, according to the National Institute of Child Health and Human Development. Many adults assume that all teenagers are engaging in sexual activity. Not all teens are having sex, and many of those who are have given a lot of thought to the decision to become sexually active (McClelland 2001).

Keep in mind that sex sometimes occurs between teenagers and adults. In most cases, especially if the sex is consensual, teenagers will not be likely to divulge this information to adults unless it is absolutely necessary. Teens who are the victim of rape by an older person may not be likely to let adults know about the situation. As older teens enter the working world and have more contact with adults, they are more apt to find themselves in romantic and sexual situations involving adults. Also, in many college and military towns, a lot of older teen females are more likely to be involved with soldiers and college students instead of high school males, who are typically more immature.

Older teens may be pregnant, may have had an abortion or two, and may already have a child or many children. Pregnant and parenting teens may be an audience that your library is not currently targeting. Consider working with children's librarians to provide story times for children of teenagers. Invite pregnant and parenting teens to the library for a tour of library facilities and to promote library materials. Morning Glory Press sells board games designed specifically to teach parenting skills to pregnant and parenting teens, as well as fictional books about teen pregnancy with discussion guides. Consider holding book discussion groups for teen parents. Pregnant and parenting teens may need library materials about parenting, custody, child support, adoption, abortion, abortion alternatives, fatherhood, financial issues, breast-feeding, and prenatal care. Since pregnant and parenting teens may be too embarrassed to visit the library, or it may be physically impossible for them to visit the library, consider providing outreach services to groups serving them.

Like teens in middle and early adolescence, older teens may also still be seeking information about sexuality from the public library. This information should be readily available. The alternatives—the Internet or word of mouth from peers—may propagate misinformation. Besides buying materials that are geared specifically for teens, consider also buying books that are for adults, since older teens are more likely to use these for information and research purposes. *The Sex Lives of Teenagers: Revealing the Secret World of Adolescent Boys and Girls* (Ponton 2000), for example, was seemingly intended for adults; namely, the parents of sexually active teenagers. Older teens, however, who are usually able to evaluate information much as adults do, would also benefit from reading about the research that Ponton has conducted on the topic.

By the stage of late adolescence, many older teens are comfortable with their sexual identity. Many have decided whether they are straight, bisexual, gay, or lesbian by the time they reach age sixteen. Despite their own acceptance, there is still a lot of hatred and misunderstanding of older teens who are not straight. A 1999 national survey by the Gay, Lesbian, and Straight Education Network (GLSEN) found that 69 percent of gay, lesbian, bisexual, and transgendered students reported having been verbally, physically, or sexually harassed or physically assaulted at school (Tuttle 2000, p. 7). Although many efforts have been made to improve relations between gay and straight students, there is still name-calling and violence in schools. Older teens need information about all types of sexuality, not just heterosexuality. Your library collection should reflect the community, and since it is estimated that approximately 10 percent of the U.S. population is gay, lesbian, or bisexual, it is imperative that information on this segment of the population be available.

Ayer, Eleanor H. **Everything You Need to Know About Teen Fatherhood.** New York: Rosen, 1998.

> Especially appropriate for reluctant readers, this book in the Need to Know series provides teen fathers with information about their new role in life. The book includes many glossy photos and easy-to-read text.

Ayer, Eleanor. **Everything You Need to Know About Teen Marriage.** New York: Rosen, 1997.

> Provides advice to teens who are thinking about getting married and to those who are already married

Bode, Janet, and Stan Mack. **Heartbreak and Roses: Real Life Stories of Troubled Love.** New York: Franklin Watts, 2000.

> Teens from around the United States reflect on love and relationships with their parents and friends.

Canfield, Jack, ed. **Chicken Soup for the Teenage Soul on Love and Friendship.** Deerfield Beach, FL: Health Communications, 2002.

Stories about falling in love, breaking up, friends, and family.

Carle, Dr. Gilda. **Teen Talk with Dr. Gilda: A Girls' Guide to Dating.** New York: Quill Books, 2003.

Dr. Gilda Carle, a therapist, advises girls about being confident and independent without allowing boys to rule their lives.

Cherniss, Hilary, and Sara Jane Sluke. **The Complete Idiot's Guide to Surviving Peer Pressure for Teens.** Indianapolis, IN: Alpha Books, 2002.

In a world full of cliques and conformists, teens are provided with practical advice about telling people what they are and are not willing to do, avoiding pressure, and maintaining friendships in difficult situations.

Endersbe, Julie K. **Teen Fathers: Getting Involved.** Mankato, MN: Lifematters Press, 2000.

Provides practical advice to new teen fathers about becoming involved in the life of their child.

Flaming, Allen, and Kate Scowen. **My Crazy Life: How I Survived My Family.** Toronto: Annick Press, 2002.

Ten teens write about growing up in families where they dealt with loneliness, divorce, abandonment, alcoholism, abuse, or mental illness.

Garber, Marjorie. **Vice Versa: Bisexuality and the Eroticism of Everyday Life.** New York: Simon & Schuster, 1995.

Provides a thorough, historical account of bisexuality in society and explores how bisexuals are faced with challenges by people who do not understand bisexuality and its differences from homosexuality.

Hershor, Michael. **Cool It: Teen Tips to Keep Hot Tempers from Boiling Over.** Far Hills, NJ: New Horizon Press, 2003.

An essential guide specifically for teenagers who need assistance in dealing with anger management, especially regarding relationships with other people that may include bullying, teasing, assaults, and rebellion.

Huegel, Kelly. **GLBTQ: The Survival Guide for Queer and Questioning Teens.** Minneapolis, MN: Free Spirit, 2003.

Gives practical advice and reassurance to gay, lesbian, bisexual, transgendered, and questioning teens about relationships, facing prejudice, getting support, and surviving high school.

Jennings, Kevin. **Telling Tales Out of School: Gays, Lesbians, and Bisexuals Revisit Their School Days.** Los Angeles: Alyson Publications, 1998.

Thirty essays by gay, lesbian, and bisexual adults who reminisce about their experiences in school.

Lindsay, Jeanne Warren. **Teenage Couples: Expectations and Reality: Teen Views on Living Together, Roles, Work, Jealousy, and Partner Abuse.** Buena Park, CA: Morning Glory Press, 1996.

Provides practical advice to teen couples who have decided to live together. Lindsay has also written other books that are appropriate for teen couples, all published by Morning Glory Press, including *Teenage Couples: Caring, Control, and Change: How to Build a Relationship That Lasts* (1995) and *Teenage Couples Coping with Reality: Dealing with Money, In-Laws, Babies, and Other Details of Daily Life* (1995).

Locker, Sari. **Sari Says: The Real Dirt on Everything from Sex to School.** New York: HarperCollins, 2001.

The columnist for *Teen People* presents advice about all types of relationships, including those with family members, friends, boyfriends, and girlfriends.

Montpetit, Charles, ed. **The First Time: True Stories, Volume 2.** Custer, WA: Orca, 1995.

Short stories about true accounts of the emotions and desires associated with sexual relations.

Musgrave, Susan, ed. **You Be Me: Friendship in the Lives of Teen Girls.** Toronto: Annick Press, 2002.

Collection of autobiographical essays about older teen girls as they struggle with cliques, death, identity, and beginning adult life.

Ponton, Lynn. **The Sex Lives of Teenagers: Revealing the Secret World of Adolescent Boys and Girls.** New York: Plume, 2001.

The author, a psychiatrist, shows parents and teens how to cope with sexuality via dialogue in therapy sessions. Explores topics including pregnancy, abortion, masturbation, sexual orientation, Internet dating, gender roles, drugs, and AIDS.

Rashid, Norrina, ed., and Jane Hoy. **Girl2Girl: The Lives and Loves of Young Lesbian and Bisexual Women.** London: Diva Books, 2000.

A collection of poems, advice, autobiographical information, and jokes by young women ages fourteen through twenty-one who are trying to cope in a homophobic world.

Rich, Jason. **Growing Up Gay in America: Advice for Teen Guys Questioning Their Sexuality and Growing Up Gay.** New York: Franklin Street Books, 2002.

Specifically for older gay teen males, this book explores the gay social scene; provides advice about relationships and sex, gives words of advice about cyberspace; and supplies a detailed list of gay-friendly organizations, help lines, colleges, churches, and more.

Roberts, Tara, ed. **Am I the Last Virgin? Ten African American Reflections on Sex & Love.** New York: Aladdin, 1997.
A collection of essays about the sexual experiences of African American women.

Roy, Jennifer Rozines. **Romantic Breakup: It's Not the End of the World.** Berkeley Heights, NJ: Enslow, 2000.
Includes information about dating today, healthy relationships, date abuse, and breaking up.

Shaw, Tucker, and Fiona Gibb. **Any Advice?** New York: Alloy Books, 2000.
Alloy.com's advice experts, Tucker and Fiona, answer questions that teens have about relationships with friends, crushes, dates, family members, and more. The bright cover is sure to attract a lot of attention among teens. It includes bright boxes of color, including red, yellow, blue, and orange, along with the words, "MY MOM READS MY E-MAIL, A LOSER'S TRYING TO HOOK UP WITH ME, I JUST KISSED MY BEST FRIEND'S BOYFRIEND, AND MY LIFE BASICALLY SUCKS."

Shaw, Tucker, and Fiona Gibb. **This Book Is About Sex.** New York: Alloy Books, 2000.
Provides information about sex, contraceptives, sexually transmitted diseases, masturbation, pregnancy, and more.

Sonnie, Amy. **Revolutionary Voices.** Los Angeles: Alyson Books, 2000.
Celebrates queer youth culture through a collection of prose, poetry, artwork, letters, and diaries written by people of various races, classes, and religion.

Soong, Jennifer, ed. **Love Stories: Stories of True Romance.** New York: Avon Books, 2001.
Teen People presents information about real-life teen couples and advice from famous people.

Tanenbaum, Leora. **Slut! Growing Up Female with a Bad Reputation.** New York: Perennial, 2000.
Presents stories of girls and women who have finally overcome their sexual labels.

Tarbox, Katherine. **Katie.com: My Story.** New York: Dutton, 2000.
Katherine Tarbox wrote this story at age eighteen, reflecting on her life at the age of thirteen, when she met "Mark," twenty-three, in an online chat room.

Tolman, Deborah L. **Dilemmas of Desire: Teenage Girls Talk About Sexuality.** Cambridge, MA: Harvard University Press, 2002.
Portrays how teenage girls understand their sexual feelings and experiences and how society has a role in shaping these experiences.

Vitkus, Jessica, and Marjorie Ingall. **Smart Sex: Honest, Expert Information To Answer All Your Questions.** New York: Pocket Books, 1998.

    This frank and honest book about sex covers topics including virginity, masturbation, same-sex information, birth control, safer sex, pregnancy, sexual harassment, date rape, and more.

White, Emily. **Fast Girls: Teenage Tribes and the Myth of the Slut.** New York: Scribner, 2002.

    Explores the legacy of the high school slut, including interviews with several women who were given this label as teens and are now adults.

Religion and Spirituality:
"Are You There, God? It's Me, Margaret."

From the ages of 16 to 18, John Walker had transformed himself from a quiet, smooth-cheeked American teenager to a devout, bearded Muslim studying in Yemen. That he could grow the requisite beard was something of a miracle. Were his parents really onboard with all this? With the new name? The move to Yemen? Frank Lindh said yes. "He was always intellectually coherent, and he had a wonderful sense of humor," Lindh told reporters. (Tyrangiel 2001)

Older teens may wish to take matters of religion into their own hands, as John Lindh Walker demonstrated to Americans soon after the terrorist attacks in September 2001. Older teens may have been educated in a certain faith at a younger age, but now that they are more mature, they are more likely to question the religious beliefs of their parents. For others, religion may not have been an aspect of their lives growing up, and they now wish to explore the topic. Some teens have rejected religion altogether and have preferred to say that they are spiritual but not religious. Books about spirituality are also useful for teens who are thinking about the whys and hows of the world. It is important to provide materials about all types of religions and represent the beliefs of everyone in your community, regardless of your own religious beliefs or disbelief.

Albom, Mitch. **Tuesdays with Morrie: An Old Man, a Young Man, and Life's Greatest Lesson.** New York: Doubleday, 1997.

    Years after his college days, Mitch Albom reconnects with his college professor, Morrie Schwartz, who is dying. For several weeks, Mitch would visit with Morrie every Tuesday, and they would discuss the meaning of life. Mitch, who was a young college student and a nontraditional older teen, states: "It is my freshman year. Morrie is older than most of the teachers, and I am younger than most of the students, having left high school a year early. To compensate for my youth on campus, I wear old gray sweatshirts and box in a local gym and walk around with an unlit cigarette in my mouth, even though I do not smoke" (p. 30). The recorded book version of this work includes actual conversations between Mitch and Morrie.

Barrett, Jon, and Megan Howard, eds. **Faith: Stories of Belief and Spirituality.** New York: Avon, 2001.
> Presented by *Teen People*, this is a description of how spirituality has shaped the personal experiences of teens and celebrities.

Cotner, June. **Teen Sunshine Reflections: Words for the Heart and Soul.** New York: Harper Trophy, 2002.
> An interfaith collection of poems, prayers, and reflections that address challenges faced by teens, including words from Mother Teresa, Mahatma Gandhi, the Dalai Lama, and teenaged authors.

Gordhamer, Soren. **Just Say Om! A Teenager's Guide**. Avon, MA: Adams Media Corporation, 2001.
> Presents Buddhist and Zen meditations for teens who are struggling to cope with life.

Healy, Mark. **Spiritualized: A Look Inside the Teenage Soul.** New York: Alloy Books, 2000.
> This collection of personal essays by teenagers and interviews with teenagers about their beliefs includes all types of religions including Mormon, Quaker, Hindu, Muslim, Evangelical Christian, Wiccan, Greek Orthodox, Unaffiliated, and more.

Lunde, Paul. **Islam: Faith, Culture, History.** New York: DK Publishing, 2002.
> Explains the Islam faith and corrects misconceptions about the faith.

Mauck, Scott. **Daily Groove: A Big Fat Scary Devotional.** Nashville, TN: Thomas Nelson, 2002.
> Geared to males, this provides prayers and devotions for Christian teens.

Moorey, Teresa. **Spellbound: The Teenage Witch's Wiccan Handbook.** Berkeley, CA: Ulysses Press, 2002.
> Presents information about who witches are and what they believe, ways to celebrate pagan festivals, ways of explaining witchcraft to parents, and more.

Walsch, Neale Donald. **Conversations with God for Teens.** New York: Scholastic, 2001.
> With a foreword by singer Alanis Morissette, this books helps teens answer questions about religion and God.

Watkins, James N. **Are There Really Ghosts?: Questions and Answers About Angels, the Supernatural, and the Psychic Friends Network.** St. Louis, MO: Concordia Publishing House, 2001.

> One book in the series of the Why Files, this focuses on the supernatural, including UFOs, witches, and psychics, God and angels, and cults, from a Christian viewpoint.

Wilkinson, Bruce. **The Prayer of Jabez for Teens.** Sisters, OR: Multnomah Publishers, 2001.

> Provides prayers for teens relating to the situations in their lives.

Secondary Education: High School, Home School, and More

In the song "Kodachrome," Paul Simon sings about his high school education. He is not very positive about his experiences, but he admits that he can read the writing on the wall. Attending high school is the major activity of many older teens. Be sure to have an ample supply of materials about this subject. Success in high school is often viewed as a requirement for getting into the college or job of choice. And like Paul Simon, some teenagers are not too thrilled about having to set foot in a high school. Others are making the most of high school.

Secondary education has changed greatly in recent years. There are magnet schools that focus on certain topics. Charter schools are a relatively new type of school. Some high school students are attending classes via the Internet, especially in some rural parts of the United States where the nearest physical school building is many miles away. To better serve older teens, it is necessary to educate yourself about all types of high schools and the different types of curriculum offered. Are there specific courses on different types of trades, and if so, what are they? Do the high schools in your area focus on specific topics due to demand? On the other hand, is there a lack of focus on certain subjects, resulting in the need for the public library to buy more materials in these areas? For example, high schools may not offer certain foreign languages, and students wishing to learn these languages may have to take correspondence courses. Your public library can enhance the education of the student learning the foreign language by ensuring that materials are available.

Not all older teens attend high school, and some of those who don't may be homeschooled. The public library is a natural spot for homeschoolers of all ages. Consider reaching out to homeschool groups in the area to promote library resources, give tours, and provide specific bibliographic instruction based on curricular needs. Librarians may also want to survey the older homeschooling population to determine how to build collections. Buy materials specifically for older homeschoolers relating to college, curriculum, and study skills.

Many public schools sponsor foreign exchange students from other countries. Students in these programs are usually high school juniors and seniors. There are many ways for you to reach out to these students. For example, offer orientations to the public library, introducing them to your facility, collection, and services. You can have students apply for their library cards at that time. If the students are under eighteen, it may be necessary to make sure that the host family is considered the legal guardian if a signature is required for a library card. And remember, many foreign exchange students are connected with their friends and families back home through the Internet, so explain to them that Internet access is typically free in most public libraries.

Likewise, consider specialized services for American teenagers who have opted to become foreign exchange students in other countries. You may be able to conduct programs geared to high school students who are contemplating an exchange in another country. By working with guidance counselors and agencies responsible for foreign exchange programs, you can help to educate teens about the benefits and possible conflicts with exchange programs. Besides asking someone from the foreign exchange program agency to speak about going to school in another country, you could invite former exchange students, even college students, to speak with potential exchange students and their parents about what to expect while living and going to school in another country.

In the library, make available any free publications offered by student exchange programs. For example, AFS (American Field Service) sends more than 1,600 students to forty-two countries each year and annually awards more than $1 million in financial aid and scholarships. They also place students from abroad with more than 2,600 U.S. families per year. AFS produces a thorough brochure with information about each country where American students can live for an extended period of time.

Adams-Gordon, Beverly. **Home School, High School and Beyond: A Time Management, Career Exploration, Organization, and Study Skills Course.** Lynwood, WA: Castlemoyle Books, 2000.
> Provides in-depth information that is valuable in administering a homeschool program.

Cohen, Cafi. **And What About College? How Homeschooling Leads to Admission to the Best Colleges and Universities.** Cambridge, MA: Holt Associates, 2000.
> Details how homeschooled students can prepare for college.

Cohen, Cafi. **Homeschooling: The Teen Years: Your Complete Guide to Successfully Homeschooling the 13 to 18 Year Old.** Roseville, CA: Prima Publishing, 2000.
> Both parents and teens will benefit from the multitude of information in this book about homeschooling and being a homeschooled teenager.

Ekeler, William J., ed. **The Black Student's Guide to High School Success.** Westport, CT: Greenwood Press, 1997.
> Designed for African American high school students, this book gives information about planning for the future, high school politics, study habits,

athletics, extracurricular activities, leadership, black pride, self-esteem, integrating with others, working part-time, and choosing a career.

Farrell, Juliana, and Colleen Rush. **High School, the Real Deal: From GPAs to Graduation.** New York: Alloy, 2001.
Includes information about academics, extracurricular activities, working, handling stress, social scenes, and life after high school.

Fisher, Douglas, Caren Sax, and Ian Pumpian. **Inclusive High Schools: Learning from Contemporary Classrooms.** Baltimore: Paul H. Brookes Publishing, 1999.
Covers inclusive education, exceptional children, curriculum, and model high schools.

Greene, Rebeca. **The Teenagers' Guide to School Outside the Box.** Minneapolis, MN: Free Spirit, 2001.
Teens are given practical information about alternative types of education, including volunteering, dual enrollment, mentoring, job shadowing, interning, camping, traveling overseas, and studying abroad.

Hawks, John. **Youth Exchanges: The Complete Guide to the Homestay Experience Abroad.** Facts on File, 1995.
This is a guide to foreign exchange programs, with an index by country. Although it was published in 1995, much of the information is still relevant, and there are few books that have been published on this topic.

Jones, Steve. **The Internet for Educators and Homeschoolers.** Palm Springs, CA: ETC Publications, 2000.
Assists educators and homeschoolers with the use of the Internet for research and other purposes.

Lieberman, Susan Abel. **The Real High School Handbook: How to Survive, Thrive, and Prepare for What's Next.** Boston: Houghton Mifflin, 1997.
Provides practical advice for those attending high school. Page 3 states that "High school is not simply an idea adults cooked up to keep teenagers off the streets and out of the house. You are laying the foundation for your adult life."

Pride, Mary. **Mary Pride's Complete Guide to Homeschool Grades 7–12.** Eugene, OR: Harvest House, 2003.
Addresses getting ready for the ACT and SAT, financial aid options, and resources to help parents homeschool teens.

Ransom, Marsha. **The Complete Idiot's Guide to Homeschooling.** Indianapolis, IN: Alpha Books, 2001.
Assists home schooling parents with curricular materials, resources, and various academic subjects.

Riera, Mike. **Surviving High School.** Berkeley, CA: Celestial Arts, 1997.

Gives advice to high school students about relationships, driving, alcohol and drug abuse, economics, parents, safety, grief, making decisions about college, and more. The first chapter includes a chart of how teens can expect things to change in ninth, tenth, eleventh, and twelfth grades in the following categories: physical growth and thinking changes, friendship and social development, family changes, and issues of spirituality.

Stress: I Scream, You Scream, Edvard Munch Screams!

Older teens may suffer from stress for several reasons, such as trying to make decisions about their future and trying to juggle jobs, schoolwork, and social lives. Many are worried about the future, especially with the threats of terrorism and war so prevalent in the news. Collaborate with local health care workers to disseminate information and provide workshops on stress management.

Carlson, Richard. **Don't Sweat the Small Stuff for Teens.** New York: Hyperion, 2000.

Offers 100 insightful suggestions for a variety of difficulties, such as managing stress, recognizing meaningful contributions, trusting inner signals, and more.

Hipp, Earl. **Fighting Invisible Tigers: A Stress Management Guide for Teens.** Minneapolis, MN: Free Spirit, 1995.

Provides practical advice to teenagers about life management skills and how to handle stressful situations.

Powell, Mark. **Stress Relief: The Ultimate Teen Guide.** Lanham. MD: Scarecrow Press, 2002.

As part of the It Happened to Me series, this book provides up-to-date information about stress relief with facts, suggested reading, Web sites, and more.

Seaward, Brian Luke. **Hot Stones & Funny Bones: Teens Helping Teens Cope With Stress & Anger.** Deerfield Beach, FL: Health Communications, 2002.

Provides candid conversation with teens from all over the country about topics including stress, anger, sexuality, depressing, faith, humor, and compassion.

Shores, Steve. **Stressbusters: For Teens Under Pressure.** Ann Arbor, MI: Servant Publications, 2000.

Advises teens about ways to reduce the stress in their lives and to manage various demands.

Sluke, Sara Jane, and Vanessa Torres. **The Complete Idiot's Guide to Dealing With Stress for Teens.** Indianapolis, IN: Alpha Books, 2002.

Explains stress, burnout, and depression; gives reasons why growing up is hard to do; and focuses on peer pressure, family problems, decision-making skills, and more.

Volunteerism: Need a Hand?

> We work at the library. But we're clerks. Not librarians. If we were librarians, we might actually have to lift a finger every now and then. Locate arcane shit. They, the public they, are always calling in to find the most random info: the original copyright date on The Old Man and the Sea, the name of the third witch in Macbeth. When we get a call like that, Andrew and I just hand the phone off to one of the librarians. They're making the big money. We're volunteers. Slave labor, really. We're here because Lee High requires two hundred hours of community service for graduation." (Thomas 1997, pp. 17–18)

Each short story in *Doing Time: Notes from the Undergrad* involves a different community service project completed by a variety of high school students. Although the book is fictional, many high school students throughout the United States are required to do service learning and to work as volunteers before they can graduate. Other teens volunteer out of interest or goodwill. Teens are a core group of volunteers for libraries. Besides purchasing materials about volunteerism, you might also invite representatives from organizations who need volunteers to speak to teens about volunteer opportunities available at their locations.

Ausenda, Fabio, ed. **World Volunteers.** Oxford, England: Vacation Work Publications, 2003.

Provides information on hundreds of humanitarian volunteer opportunities, with details about costs and the application process.

Blaustein, Arthur I. **Make a Difference: Your Guide to Volunteering and Community Service.** Berkeley, CA: Heyday Books, 2002.

A thorough guide presenting many aspects of volunteering and performing community service.

Canfield, Jack, ed. **Chicken Soup for the Volunteer's Soul: Stories to Celebrate the Spirit of Courage, Caring and Community.** Deerfield Beach, FL: Health Communications, 2002.

Volunteers describe their experiences with helping others.

Gralla, Preston. **The Complete Idiot's Guide to Volunteering for Teens.** Indianapolis, IN: Alpha Books, 2001.

    Discusses how to find volunteer opportunities, why volunteering is beneficial, and creating a solo volunteer opportunity; provides a list of resources and more.

Mintzer, Richard. **Helping Hands: How Families Can Reach out to Their Communities.** New York: Chelsea House, 2003.

    Provides real-life examples of ways that young people and families can reach out as volunteers.

Murdico, Suzanne. **Volunteering to Help the Environment.** New York: Children's Press, 2000.

    Presents information about volunteer opportunities that benefit the environment.

Perry, Susan K. **Catch the Spirit: Teen Volunteers Tell How They Made a Difference: Stories of Inspiration from 20 Remarkable Recipients of the Prudential Community Spirit Award.** New York: Franklin Watts, 2000.

    Twenty teens describe how volunteerism has enriched their lives and their communities.

War, Peace, and Terrorism: The World Around Us

Information about current events is crucial for older teens, who are better able to think critically about world events than younger teens, whose cognitive abilities are less developed. Those who are eighteen, or who are about to turn eighteen, may be especially interested in world affairs as they make decisions about voting and political party affiliation. The war with Iraq in 2003, terrorism, and the aftermath of the 9/11 attack will probably be popular topics for generations. Although librarians know that the most current information is usually gained from weekly publications such as *Time* and *U.S. News and World Report,* as well as Web sites featuring news, books are also useful in learning about these timely topics. Publishers have produced books about terrorism specifically for teenagers. On the first anniversary of the terrorist attacks, many libraries throughout the country had some type of remembrance event. These books might also be used for future remembrances.

Work with your community high schools to offer relevant courses in civics and current events. Some students may be interested in joining discussions at the library about current events, war, peace, or terrorism. Any of the following books could be used as discussion books. *With Their Eyes,* by Annie Thoms, a collection of monologues and photographs about September 11, 2001, could be used for readers' theater programs with older teens.

Berman, Paul. **Terror and Liberalism.** New York: Norton, 2003.
> Considers how liberals can respond to the threat of terrorism.

Butler, Smedley D. **War Is a Racket.** Reprint ed. Los Angeles: Feral House, 2003.
> This antiwar classic by America's most decorated general presents an argument against war.

Frank, Mitch. **Understanding September 11th: Answering Questions About the Attacks on America.** New York: Viking, 2002.
> Overview of the economic, political, cultural, and religious conflict between the United States and the Middle East.

Fridell, Ron. **Terrorism: Political Violence at Home and Abroad.** Berkeley Heights, NJ: Enslow, 2001.
> Explores the motivation of terrorists and explains how terrorist actions affect politics throughout the world.

Gitlin, Todd. **Letters to a Young Activist.** New York: Basic Books, 2003.
> Gitlin recalls his experience as president of the Students for a Democratic Society in the sixties and gives advice to those who wish to explore the spirit of activism.

Hess, Stephen, and Marvin Kalb, eds. **Media and the War on Terrorism.** Washington, DC: Brookings Institution Press, 2003.
> A series of conversations among journalists and politicians, including Ted Koppel, Joe Lockhart, and Michael Murray, about media coverage of terrorism.

Lewis, Bernard. **The Crisis of Islam: Holy War and Unholy Terror.** New York: Modern Library, 2003.
> Examines the historical roots of the resentments that dominate the Islamic world today and that are increasingly being expressed in acts of terrorism.

Moussaoui, Abd Samad, with Florence Bouquillat. **Zacarias, My Brother: The Making of a Terrorist.** New York: Seven Stories, 2003.
> This book reveals information about the extremist Wahabi sect, to which hijacker Zacarias Moussaoui belonged.

Shaw, Tucker. **Peace.** New York: Alloy Books, 2002.
> Filled with ideas and anecdotes from teens and quotations from celebrities and leaders about peace, this book asks teens to consider if it is possible to live a peaceful life in a nonpeaceful world and how their lives have changed since September 11, 2001. Focuses on the students of Stuyvesant High School in New York City and the use of the school as a staging area for rescue workers.

Thoms, Annie. **With Their Eyes.** New York: HarperCollins, 2002.
  Collection of monologues and photographs from Stuyvesant High School's theatrical event relating to global fears and tragedy.

Wells, Donna K., and Bruce C. Morris. **Live Aware, Not in Fear: The 411 after 9-11: A Book for Teens.** Deerfield Beach, FL: Health Communications, 2002.
  Topics include terrorism, bioterrorism, economic impacts of terrorism, and more.

Writing, Research, and Study Skills: Life Essentials

Most seniors in high school, and some juniors, have to write a research paper in English class before graduating. Some students even begin learning how to conduct research at a much younger age. My earliest memory of doing research goes back to the third grade. My skills were fine-tuned in eleventh grade due to a research project that required extensive library use, and I remember spending a great deal of time using the *Readers' Guide to Periodical Literature*. I recall using the high school library and the public library for this project, as well as two nearby college libraries. When assisting teens in the library with research now, and showing them how to use electronic databases, I usually let them know how lucky they are that they do not have to use microfilm. Accompanying parents typically smile and agree.

Stock your shelves with research how-to materials to make this process as easy as possible. Although some researchers still use printed note cards, more technologically savvy teens may compile all of their research in an electronic format. Either way, you should have a collection representing both methods of organizing data. Teens may also need books about grammar and writing skills for general homework assignments. Information literacy is a topic that can be used as a basis for programming. If older teens are not familiar with using electronic library resources, the staff can offer classes or individualized instruction. The components of the program could address evaluating information, using preselected Web sites, search engines, plagiarism and intellectual property, and citations.

The next Walter Dean Myers, David Almond, An Na, or Aidan Chambers may be lurking in the stacks of your library. Writing is a hobby for many teenagers. Resources about writing fiction, nonfiction, screenplays, poetry, diaries, and more may be sought by eager writers. Some high school students take creative writing classes at the high school or college level. I remember one day when my entire high school expressive writing class took a field trip to the football stadium bleachers, where we were instructed to stare at the clouds and write about whatever came to our minds. Not all high school creative writing teachers will be as innovative as my teacher was, and looking back, I realize that she wanted to get us out of the classroom environment in hopes that the change of scenery would send a spark through our brains. Since not all high schools still offer creative writing classes, and not all high school libraries include materials about the topic, it is imperative that the public library house these materials—so that we will have books or other written materials to buy for the library in the future. Without books for teens to learn about creative writing, it is less likely the publishing field will flourish in the future with excellent fiction, poetry, and essays. Perhaps a future winner of the Michael L. Printz Award will look back on his or her teen years and give credit to your library for access to creative writing materials.

Bankhead, Betty, Janet Nicols, and Dawn Vaughn. **Write It! A Guide for Research.** Englewood, CO: Libraries Unlimited, 1999.
    Provides information on researching specific topics, using search engines, and citing resources.

Edgerton, Leslie. **Finding Your Voice: How to Put Personality in Your Writing.** Cincinnati, OH: Writer's Digest Books, 2003.
    Practical advice for beginning writers on developing a unique voice.

Hambleton, Vicki, and Cathleen Greenwood. **So, You Want to Be a Writer? How to Write, Get Published, and Maybe Even Make It Big.** Hillsboro, OR: Beyond Words Publishing, 2001.
    Exploring different genres, time management, writing tools, how to get unstuck, how to get published, writing as a career, and resources for writers are discussed in this book specifically for young writers.

Hamlett, Christina. **Screen Teen Writers: How Young Screenwriters Can Find Success.** Colorado Springs, CO: Meriwether Publishing, 2002.
    Advises teens about writing screenplays, including how to write good dialogue, how to pace scenes, keeping people from stealing movie ideas, rewriting, and more.

Harmon, Charles, ed. **Using the Internet, Online Services, and CD-ROMs for Writing Research and Term Papers.** New York: Neal-Schuman, 2000.
    Particularly useful for high school and college students, this handbook explains how to use online library catalogs, electronic databases, and the Internet for research purposes.

Kiester, Jane Bell. **The Chortling Bard: Caught 'ya! Grammar with a Giggle for High Schools.** Gainesville, FL: Maupin House Publishing, 1998.
    Discusses a method for teaching grammar, mechanics, usage, vocabulary, and literary devices with plots and vocabulary borrowed from Shakespeare.

Koch, Stephen. **Modern Library Writer's Workshop: A Guide to the Craft of Fiction.** New York: Modern Library, 2003.
    Great modern writers provide commentary about the art of writing fiction.

Mirriam-Goldberg, Caryn. **Write Where You Are: How to Use Writing to Make Sense of Your Life: A Guide for Teens.** Minneapolis, MN: Free Spirit, 1999.

Provides advice and exercises for individuals to become more confident and more competent writers.

Rosenberg, Mandie L. **Get Wise! Mastering Grammar Skills: Don't Use No Double Negatives.** Laurenceville, NJ: Peterson's, 2002.

This entertaining instruction book provides cool activities for high school students seeking to improve grammar skills. Other books in the series are *Get Wise! Mastering Vocabulary Skills,* by Nathan Barber and *Get Wise! Mastering Writing Skills,* by Laurie Bennett..

Rowland, Robin. **The Creative Guide to Research: How to Find What You Need—Online or Offline.** Franklin Lakes, NJ: Career Press, 2000.

Provides practical advice about using online resources for research purposes. An especially useful section focuses on interviewing people using e-mail.

Schumm, Jeanne Shay. **School Power: Study Skill Strategies for Succeeding in School.** Minneapolis, MN: Free Spirit, 2001.

In-depth information about homework, taking notes, listening, class discussions, becoming a better reader, improving writing skills, and studying.

CONCLUSION

Humans, especially those who are about to make major life changes, crave information. Consider the person who is about to be divorced and needs legal information as well as information about being single again. Think about future brides, and how they tend to check out all the materials available on wedding planning. Future parents tend to horde baby name books and baby care materials. Those who are about to retire typically seek information about being happy in their retirement—whether that involves moving to a state with a better climate, traveling in an RV, or just spending time with grandchildren. Whatever the milestone, the age, or the stage, there is typically information about these topics in the public library for specialized populations. Older teens are also about to make major life changes, like expectant parents, future brides, future divorcees, and those who have reached retirement. Teens in the late stage of adolescence also need information about a multitude of topics relating to the large leap into the future. Librarians who take the time to promote these resources through programming may find that teens have an easier time as they transition to adulthood.

REFERENCES AND SUGGESTED READINGS

Abadie, M. J. 2001. *Teen Astrology: The Ultimate Guide to Making Your Life Your Own.* Rochester, VT: Bindu Books.

Anderson, Laurie Halse. 2002. *Catalyst.* New York: Viking.

Anderson, Sheila B. 2000. "I Stink and My Feet Are Too Big!: Training Librarians to Work with Teens" *Voice of Youth Advocates* 22, no. 6 (February): 388.

Anderson, Sheila B., and Kristine Mahood. 2001. "The Inner Game of Booktalking." *Voice of Youth Advocates* 24, no. 2 (June): 107.

Blume, Judy. 1975. *Forever.* New York: Pocket Books.

Brownlee, Shannon Brownlee. 2002. "Too Heavy, Too Young." *Time* January 21: 3.

Chelton, Mary K, ed. 1994. *Excellence in Library Services to Young Adults: The Nation's Top Programs.* 1st ed. Chicago: American Library Association.

———. 1997. *Excellence in Library Services to Young Adults: The Nation's Top Programs.* 2nd ed. Chicago: American Library Association.

———. 2000. *Excellence in Library Services to Young Adults: The Nation's Top Programs.* 3rd ed. Chicago: American Library Association.

Dessen, Sarah. 2002. *This Lullaby.* New York: Viking.

Haddix, Margaret Peterson. 2000. *Turnabout.* New York: Simon & Schuster.

Hutcheson, Ron. 2002. "U.S. Military Recruiters Get New Hand From Law." *Delaware State News,* November 29: 2.

Irvine, Martha. 2002. "Strapped Parents Taking Kids' Credit." *Los Angeles Times,* December 13: C19.

Knudsen, Carmeile, and Johnette Orpinela. 1992. "Preparation High School or What Students Should Know About Libraries When They Leave High School." *Emergency Librarian* 19, no. 5 (May/June): 12.

Krulik, Nancy E. 2002. *Prom! The Complete Guide to a Truly Spectacular Night.* New York: Grosset & Dunlap.

McClelland, Susan. 2001. "Not So Hot to Trot: Despite Popular Opinion to the Contrary, Only About Half of Teens are Currently Engaged in Sex." *Maclean's* (April 9): 50–51.

Morgenstern, Julie, and Jessi Morgenstern-Colon. 2002. *Organizing from the Inside Out for Teens.* New York: Henry Holt.

Peck, Penny. 1999. "Bound for Glory." *School Library Journal* 124, no. 12 (July): 40.

Ponton, Lynn. 2000. *The Sex Lives of Teenagers: Revealing the Secret World of Adolescent Boys and Girls.* New York: Dutton.

Ried, Kimberlee, and Kaite Mediatore. 2003. "Up To Date Or Out of Date: Test Your Teen Knowledge." *Young Adult Library Services* 1, no. 2 (Winter): 22.

Samuels, Christina A. 2002. "Former 'Underachiever' Has Big Aspirations at NVCC; New President Seeks to Publicize School's Successes, Importance." *Washington Post*, September 22: T10.

Sheffer, Susannah. "Adolescent Girls and Sexual Desire." 1997. *New Moon Network* (Fall): 78–80.

Stoehr, Shelley. 1998. *Tomorrow Wendy: A Love Story.* New York: Bantam.

Thomas, Rob. 1997. *Doing Time: Notes From the Undergrad.* New York: Simon & Schuster.

Toor, Rachel. 2001. *Admissions Confidential: An Insider's Guide of the Elite College Selection Process.* New York: St. Martin's Press.

Tuttle, Chris. 2000. "High School Confidential." *The Advocate* (February 1): 7.

Tyrangiel, Josh. 2001. "The Taliban Next Door: At 16, John Walker Was a Quiet California Kid. At 20, Was a Taliban Warrior. How Did He Get from Marin County to Mazar-I-Sharif?" *Time* (December 17): 36–38.

Wilgoren, Jodi. 2001. "Before College, Year Off Beckons to Well Off." *New York Times,* April 17: sec. A, col. 1: 4.

3

Respect for the Future: Making Space for Older Teens

Amy Alessio

The importance of creating an inviting space for teens in the library cannot be overestimated. A comfortable area with seating and attractive, age-appropriate displays will tell older teens that they are welcome in the library and even encouraged to stay, whereas a space situated poorly, uncomfortable, or with a disappointing collection clearly sends a negative message to teens. High school teens balance school, jobs, applications for college or other training for the future, social life, hormones, and more. Why should they come to the library? An efficient, successful space for them in the library lets them know immediately that there are worthwhile reasons for them to be there, and it sells itself even when staff are not immediately present to reinforce this message.

The National Center for Education Statistics reported in 1995 that 23 percent of patrons coming to the public library are young adults. They are coming in the door, but are they staying? High school media centers devote 100 percent of their space to older teens. How many public libraries devote even 23 percent of their space to this group?

If teens are not visibly present in your library, reexamine the space devoted to their materials:

- Is it distinctive from the younger children, or mixed in with the youth department?

- Is it near a place where they can ask for help?

- Conversely, are painfully self-conscious teenagers allowed some privacy to choose reading materials?

- Is the collection organized in a way that teens can easily find the materials they need?

- Does it have new materials to attract attention, and are they creatively displayed?

- Does it acknowledge that older teens may have different, future-thinking interests than younger adolescents?

When you can answer "yes" to all of these basic questions, you will see teens in the library, happily using the materials. If you answer "no" to any of the questions, well, you have adjustments to make.

Planning an entirely new space is daunting and unreasonable for many facilities, but it can be broken down into steps: planning, designing the dream space, a reality check, and keeping it fresh. Even if an entirely new space is not needed or possible, reviewing these steps can help you best utilize what you already have for older teenage patrons. These steps will help you find out how to accommodate new services while maintaining existing services.

PLANNING

Your first step in creating a successful space for teens is to understand older teens and their distinct needs and interests. High school teens have some universal interests, such as dating, defining their selves, their future, and family life. However, many could be dealing with adult problems. Why would high school teens need to come to the library? Why would they want to? High school teens may first come to the library because of necessity. Homework projects require the reading of literature; other subjects require reading articles and doing research. People with limited resources at home often need to use the library to complete papers or use the Internet.

Teens may also want to explore options for the future, including careers, college, financial aid, and catalogs. Some may be taking college classes already. Many need a comfortable and safe place to go after school. Others are searching between the covers of novels for ways to understand themselves and their world. For teens, the library is not simply a luxury. Certainly some of these needs may be addressed in school libraries, but school resources may not be available during all of the hours teens have free to work on these things. Your collection must support all these needs—and it must support them at appropriate levels.

In *Exploding the Myths: The Truth About Teenagers and Reading*, Marc Aronson writes:

> *The fate of YA today just as the demographics tilt again and YAs are on the rise: we have library sections that are used by readers from about eleven to fifteen or sixteen; we have bookstore sections aimed at readers up to about age fourteen; we have a genre of literature defined by what it was about twenty years ago; and we have an expanding set of authors and subjects." (Aronson 2001, p. 35)*

At the most basic level, then, an effective teen space for older teens in a public or school library will address these needs: research materials for schoolwork, information about colleges and careers, computers, and a place for socialization. To retain its target audience, a teen space will also offer leisure materials and attractions.

What's in Demand?

You can begin updating your space for older teens by assessing how easy it is for teens to find information they need at your library. What are teens repeatedly asking for? College guides, articles on abortion for a debate, classics for school reading assignments? Sure, the staff probably know just where to find the answers when these questions are asked, but the fact that they are being asked repeatedly indicates that there may be a problem with signage or handouts. Keep track of the questions high school teens are asking at the service desks for a period of three to four months during the school year, and you'll discover some of the most popular subjects and areas of need. You can make it easier for staff by providing them with a list of popular subjects, so hash marks can be placed next to the subjects. Be sure to allow enough space for marking down specific titles when they are asked for repeatedly. This will generate a list of library items that are used heavily by teens, along with information on where they are used. You will begin to see the traffic patterns of this age group in the facility.

Of course, your circulation statistics also indicate what items are being used heavily. Your catalog can probably generate demographic reports, such as how many fourteen versus eighteen year olds have active library cards. Circulation statistics on young adult books will immediately reveal hot topics for this age group.

In *Teen Spaces: The Step-by-Step Library Makeover*, Kimberly Bolan Taney offers a "Comparison Worksheet" that separates out library statistics by patron groups such as children, young adults, and adults, cross-tabled by items and budget, staff, program attendance, and square footage (Taney 2002, p. 114). This resource clearly illustrates that teens do not get their statistical share of library resources. Teens may be congregating in areas away from the books designated for their age group. More comfortable chairs or more privacy may be available in the adult reading room, or teens may have to work on group projects near the adult reference section.

Documenting locations where older teens congregate may also indicate that certain features in your teen space should be duplicated to attract more teen users. *Output Measures and More: Planning and Evaluating Public Library Services for Young Adults*, outlines several ways to measure the areas of the library most used by young adults. For example, as reported in "Building Use by Young Adults Data Collection Form," staff counted how many young adults are in the YA area, the children's room, the reference areas, the circulation area, and the AV area at different times of the day (Walter 1995, p. 47).

By performing some of these simple assessments and tracking your observations of teens, you may find that a daunting number of subjects are used by teens. In fact, it may seem that they use the entire library. Often moving materials already owned by the library, or placing duplicate copies in teen space, or even providing a space where teens can talk, will help attract users to the teen space. Pathfinders and marketing tips are explored later in this chapter, as well as some ways to catch teens' attention in different areas of the facility. Before purchasing anything new for a teen space, take a good look at what your library already has.

What Materials Are Already Available?

Knowing what the library owns already for teens will further define the direction your new teen space will take. In addition to the list of subjects being asked for by teens at the service desks, compile a list of the teen homework and reading assignments that you know occur during the school year. High school teachers are a good source, and school librarians probably already have a list available. Compile a list of the local colleges, and make certain you have handouts on each one, and possibly catalogs and applications for the upcoming semester. Do your financial aid books need updating? Is there an online or CD-ROM product that can best update this information? Match each one with titles in your collection and look for titles to help fill any gaps. Conversely, this list can also be used to weed subjects or redundant items not used by teens.

Don't forget to take into account that self-conscious teens may not be asking for what they want at service desks. Walter (1995) outlines a way to find out which materials are used most in the library. She describes how to identify hot items with an "In-Library Use of Young Adult Materials Log." With this system, materials found on tables and on carts that are ready to be reshelved (e.g., Cliffs Notes, reference books, fiction books, and magazines) are systematically counted at different hours of the day (p. 58). This is just one more method you might consider using to find out what's being used in your library.

Do Teens Know What the Library Offers?

The best reference section for teens, complete with CD-ROMs of literature criticism, is useless if no one knows about it. One group of teens who should know what your library has to offer is your teen employees. Teen employees are usually at the oldest end of the teenage years, and because they are familiar with the library, their awareness will be a strong indicator of how accurately the library is serving teen needs. Provide teen employees with a survey. Since they may feel uncomfortable criticizing their employer on paper, you can make it anonymous. Allow teen employees to complete the survey during work hours. If there are not many teens employed by your library, give the survey to staff members who have or know teens that could fill it out. Keep it simple. Open-ended questions can be useful for data collectors, but since older teens have to write many papers for school, your questionnaire should not be so complex that it is regarded as a sort of assignment. Make as many answers as possible multiple-choice. Some sample questions follow:

- Which areas do you enjoy reading in? (Genres such as science fiction, graphic novels, and popular nonfiction subjects may be listed for check off, with an "other" category followed by a blank for respondents to fill in.)

- How do you find out about the types of materials that you like to read? (Possible answers include genre signs, bookmarks, *What Do I Read Next* online, *Novelist* database, print readers' advisory guides, or staff suggestions. If none of these answers is given, marketing of these products and services, or more prominent browsing copies in the teen area, are clearly needed.)

- Do you use magazine articles for homework? How easily can you find them in the library or online?

- How often per month do you use the library to work on group projects for school?

- Where is the literature criticism or Cliffs Notes section located in the library?

- On a scale of 1 to 5, with 5 being the easiest, how easily can you find the books you are looking for in the library? (You may wish to separate finding materials in the online catalog from finding them on the shelves.)

- Which of these items have you checked out in the last two months?: recorded books, DVDs, pamphlets, computer software, college guides.

- Approximately how many times has an item you wanted been checked out or not owned by the library in the past two months?

- Did you know there is a teen summer reading program? A teen advisory board? Have you every participated in these activities? (Programming questions help design a teen space, as they will indicate whether you need to put a bulletin board advertising teen programs in a more prominent place.)

- What features does your school media center have that this library may not? (Have choices for teens to check off here, such as more convenient hours, more computers, and certain types of library materials.)

- (As a checklist, ask the following question): Have you ever used the library Web page to put items on hold, search the catalog, use databases, or link to Internet sites?

- What can the library do to make your life easier or improve its services to you? (Give choices, but leave space for comments as well. Choices should include things you think you may be capable of doing, such as providing more magazines and graphic novels, having seating available away from the children's area, and having more computers available.)

After compiling the results from your "insider" teens, survey some of the teens visiting the library. Offer some incentive for patrons and staff teens alike, asking for addresses, e-mail addresses, and phone numbers for a raffle for those who fill out the survey. This is also a good way to compile a mailing list to notify teens about upcoming events and new library materials of interest to them. Many libraries have teen advisory boards (TAB) that meet regularly. Surveying the TAB can be done more informally, at a meeting, making it clear that teens' continued input is necessary for the success of the area.

Is there something about the library that is currently discouraging older teens from using it, or from staying when they have to visit? Discouraged teens should be surveyed as well. Erin Pierce, teen librarian at the Carnegie Library in Pittsburgh, Pennsylvania, handed out teen space surveys at local concerts and during Teen Read Week. She also implemented focus groups of library users and nonusers, and selected a group from these teens to work directly with the architect.

Although it may be painful to read the results of these surveys, they are important for getting library administration and library boards to realize why a teen area is important. Negative comments by teens or data showing that even teen staff members do not know about the availability of library materials are powerful incentives to offer change.

In 1998, the Schaumburg Township District Library in Illinois moved into a new 166,000-square-foot building. At that time, there was no young adult specialist to help with the planning, and the TAB had only existed for six months. The Teen Corridor was between the youth area and adult fiction sections and contained a few stylized chairs, magazine spinner racks, a table for handouts, and the book collection on plain shelving against the walls. This area was on the first floor, and tables and reference books for high school teens were located on the second floor, a designated quiet study area.

It quickly became apparent that the teens were working in noisy groups on homework assignments upstairs, constantly clashing with staff and other patrons. They had no other space, as adults filled the discussion rooms and meeting rooms. Because of the disturbances, the teens were often kicked out of the library. Trying to keep teens from working in groups (as they were assigned to do by their teachers) and to be quiet was futile and frustrating to everyone involved. The solution was to provide a space where they could work or talk in groups without disturbing others.

The library board listened to input from the TAB and its leader, a youth services librarian. They showed that more teens were coming to programs and using the collection, but they outlined what they felt was wrong with the Teen Corridor. The library board approved a teen coordinator librarian and began discussing the redesign of the space. The board would not fund the redesign of the teen space without knowledge of each facet of the TAB's input. The TAB voted on a sports theme and chose several features of the section, including lockers and astro turf carpeting. Semiprivate dividers were put at each end of the corridor, replicas of the entrance to the Chicago Cubs' Wrigley Field. Tables with embedded board games could double as homework and leisure areas. Shirts and jackets from the local high schools were included in the design to encourage the feeling of ownership by the teens. The previous problems and teen input drove the new development of the library section for teens.

A good time to go to your administration and board is when they are receiving complaints about teens in the library. Maybe they will have heard about conflicts between groups of teens and staff, or teens and other patrons. Visit them right away after this kind of incident and say that your library needs a place for teens so that this will stop happening. Have prepared a list of options and steps that you are ready to take to help solve the problem. For example, maybe there is an underutilized area that could be converted into a teen space. Hand out copies of the surveys and steps you will take to find out what would be needed in the teen space. Give a reasonable timeline for collecting the information. The board and administration will see this as a positive, reasonable solution to the situation.

After you have done the research as outlined previously in this chapter with surveys and other data collection, bring teens to the next board meeting or in to meet with administration to discuss the findings. Hearing direct ideas from the teens will give your findings impact.

The administration should then be ready to give you parameters for the project. With an idea of time, space, and budget constraints, you and your teens are now ready to proceed to the most enjoyable part of this process, the creative design.

DESIGNING THE DREAM SPACE

Once you've assessed the problem areas and secured support for the project, let yourself dream. What would your ideal teen space look like if there were no spatial or financial limitations? Take the time to visualize the space in detail. Features might include a large area with many books in attractive face-out shelving, easy-to-find homework help, tutoring services, new books and magazines that are always available, state-of-the-art computers and software, and the latest music. Programming would be supported by the space. Staff would be available, friendly, and well-informed; and comfortable chairs and tables would invite teens to stay for hours. Impossible? Consider the following spaces in various locations throughout the United States:

1. The Young Adults' Services Department at the Allen County Public Library in Fort Wayne, Indiana, has a collection of approximately 40,000 volumes and a staff of eight librarians and paraprofessionals. The collection includes a thorough paperback and hardback young adult fiction selection and the entire range of the Dewey Decimal Classification system. There are also comic books; graphic novels; magazines; newspapers; videos and DVDs; music cassettes and compact discs; software; and several computers with Internet access, word processing software, and educational games. Special collections cover careers and college information, materials for pregnant and parenting teens, Cliffs Notes, science fair project information, academic bowl resources, and contemporary issues materials. Since the Allen County Public Library keeps the last existing copy of all books in the collection, staff and patrons also have access to a deep historical collection of young adult fiction materials. The library is being completely renovated, and the department will be approximately 9,000 square feet in size when the new building reopens.

2. Teen Central at the Phoenix Public Library in Arizona has books, graphic novels, comic books, compact discs, magazines, videos, a health information center, computers, study rooms, and an art gallery. There is also a dance floor with surround-sound music, a large screen television with cable, and a café area. It serves as a community center in addition to a library.

3. Teen'Scape at the Los Angeles Public Library is a 3,780-square-foot space that includes a book collection of approximately 30,000, comic books, college and career guides, classic literature, 150 magazines, and newspapers. There are several computers with Internet access and word processing software, study rooms, reading lounges, movable furniture, a living room with a fifty-inch high definition television, DVD, and CD equipment, and music listening stations. The space also has a reference desk and a staff of young adult specialists.

4. The Carmel Clay Public Library in Carmel, Indiana, has a High School Area with fiction, nonfiction, magazines, newspapers, a reading lounge, and computers. The department specifically targets high school students, whereas middle school students are served in the children's section of the library. The teen advisory board is extremely active in assisting staff with programming and collection development.

5. At the Louisville Free Public Library in Kentucky, the Young Adult OutPost is a small branch library just for teens that is adjacent to the main library facility. The branch includes library materials specifically for teens including books, magazines, and compact discs; listening stations; computers; and comfortable seating. According to Michelle Saunders, young adult librarian at the Young Adult Out-Post, "My biggest surprise is that the teens who use the space tend to be slightly older than I had imagined. I predicted we would get mostly middle school students, but we mainly see high school students and those just out of high school" (Saunders 2003, p. 116).

Dreams have come true for many libraries across the nation, and it can happen at your library, too. What are the possibilities for your library? Study what's being done at other libraries—what works and what doesn't. There are many ways to learn about features of successful teen spaces. *Voice of Youth Advocates* features a regular section on YA spaces called "YA Spaces of Your Dreams," describing teen-friendly library spaces from around the country. The teen spaces are featured in every issue of the journal complete with photographs of the spaces being described. Also, check out retail clothing, music, and bookstores that target teens or typically attract teens. Notice some of the ways they use every inch of space effectively.

Even organizing a semiprivate section of a room for older teens sends a message that they are important enough to merit a concentrated space of their own. Visit the library dream spaces nearest you, or write to them and ask for photographs. To appeal to older teens, this also means visiting college libraries. Bring decision-making staff and library directors along on visits. Take photographs and make notes of costs to help when actual decisions have to be made. Many libraries have pictures of their teen spaces on their Web sites, allowing "visits" that might not be physically feasible. Go through the catalogs of library furniture, including Demco and Highsmith. These catalogs are now trying to emulate the popular bookstores in terms of display furniture.

Considering the proposed or current space allotted to older teens will help determine which features might be practical as well as ideal:

> *Two very important action steps are the determination of where the new teen area will be located and how much physical space it will occupy. Intrinsic to these decisions is whether you want to relocate the teen area entirely, expand*

on the space you currently have, or simply improve the exist-
ing area as it stands. Regardless, remember that a successful
teen area must be easily identified, easy to get to and located
near key teen-related library areas. (Taney 2002, p. 36)

Remember that computers and music listening stations are other essential features for any area that wants to attract teens. Carefully examine the wiring and electrical situation of the space designated for the older teens.

Rewrite the list in order of importance to the teens in the area served by the library, according to the surveys, research, and teen input. Add costs and begin to determine what can be solved immediately. Discuss the results of this research with your library director and board. They will be able to advise you regarding the financial and spatial parameters of remodeling. Now you are ready to begin designing your center for older teens. The results of your surveys will show you what your priorities must be, within your budget and space parameters. Mapping out a floor plan of the current area and proposed changes, in scale, is essential. As Taney puts it, "A floor plan allows a designer to explore options before spending time and money implementing them" (2002, p. 26).

Do not fall in love with a particular element or theme within the design. Flexibility is one of the most important features of your teen space. Trends change, problems may come up with wiring or furniture, and it is best to be able to make changes easily. It is better to begin making some small changes and test reactions. For example, a great new loveseat that only fits in one corner of the teen center may look fabulous. What if no staff member can easily see that spot and it invites vandalism and/or sexual behavior? Where is it going to go now? At this stage, you are still not ready to change the area completely.

Some Quick Furniture Fixes

Furnishing your teen space doesn't have to cost a lot. Rummage through library storage. You might be surprised to find forgotten furniture and signage treasures. Can high school art students repaint any tables? Making do with items you already have on hand and stretching resources may go a long way in convincing a library director to let you have a more expensive type of chair or table or even a neon sign later.

Decide what can be fixed now. If teens do not know where to find another good book to read, buy a plastic bookmark stand or end-of-shelf holder, and make or buy bookmarks. Make signs that indicate where CD-ROM or reference tools are located. Prop a few titles on shelf tops or in other prominent spaces.

If your survey results show that the college guides are never on the shelf, see if you can afford to purchase a few more copies, and catalog one as reference so it is always available.

Too much noise from teens in one area means that a space must be designated for them to make noise. Or you can put up dividers to absorb some of the noise while keeping sight lines as open as possible. Dividers may double as bulletin boards or could be decorated by high school art students. Another solution to noise problems is to move tables farther apart, so teens will be in smaller (quieter) groups.

These quick fixes are cost effective. They allow you to save your budget for such features as new furniture or new collection items that you cannot acquire easily.

Sometimes just moving books or changing them to face-out shelving can have a tremendous impact on services. A rearrangement of shelves can provide "walls" and sound barriers or force traffic patterns of teens to acknowledge the collection they may have been missing.

Before its move to a new building in 1998, the young adult collection at the Schaumburg Township District Library in Illinois consisted of a few paperback spinner racks two feet behind an information desk. The racks were moved to a hallway near study carrels, and circulation skyrocketed. The numbers increased again (at the rate of 80 percent over the previous year) after the library moved into a new facility with a designated teen area complete with seating. The circulation of the expanded collection increased another 70 percent each year after that space was remodeled with teen and designated teen staff input.

When considering book placement, be sure to grant users some privacy. How many adults would like to pick out their romance or true crime books with a library staff member peering over their shoulders? Libraries claiming to adhere to principles of intellectual freedom need to act on this by allowing all patrons a modicum of privacy in checking out materials. Teens are especially self-conscious, and an understanding of this will help librarians design a space that welcomes and serves them.

Focusing the Collection for Older Teens

One of the major concerns in designing your space will be the collection. Where will it be situated? How large will it be? What types of materials will be in it?

Public libraries usually support the homework needs of teenagers. Your survey results will show whether teens are familiar with the research materials in your library. Beyond that, you may need to build your teen collection, either through new purchases or through relocating of materials from other parts of the library. There are three options to consider when reworking the teen collection:

1. Can the budget afford to duplicate the materials already present in the collection that teens use for homework and research purposes in other sections of the library?

2. Is there a way to effectively direct the teens to the present materials if the budget is not available for duplication?

3. Are there basic reference materials that may be housed in the teen area?

Mary Arnold, regional teen services manager of the Cuyahoga County Public Library in Ohio and YALSA past president, describes her teen services desk as also serving as the AV desk for the first floor collection. There is a ready reference collection: almanacs, dictionary, thesaurus, *Encyclopedia of Careers*, state history, *Authors and Artists for YA*, *Contemporary Musicians*, and *Shakespeare for Students*. Also, there are reference sets on the Middle Ages, Colonial America, Ancient Greece and Rome, and the environment, as well as books on science fair projects. Professional resources include lots of readers' advisory tools including *What Do I Read Next for Young Adults*, "Best Books for YAs," and the *Internet Resources Directory K–12*.

Other ready reference materials handy for teens may include name and address directories of famous people, guides on citing sources in research papers, summaries of classic titles, and guides to where to find criticism on them. If there is going to be a ready reference section at the service desk closest to the teen area, the materials should be as accessible as possible. Alternatively, a few duplicate copies may be kept in the teen area for checkout or use there only. These sources would include more sensitive health issue books, biographies of popular culture icons, and values of collectibles that are of interest to teens (e.g., baseball or basketball cards).

The future is on the minds of older teens more than anything else. They earn money for cars and college, date, think about getting serious, and try to figure out what it is they want to do for the rest of their lives. Outdated materials on career choices tell teens that the library is not the place to go for timely information. Take a good look at your collection of career guides. Identify community trends to determine popular career choices among local teens. College fairs are popular programs that bring representatives of institutions, the military, and students together. With the right resources in easy access format, your library can become a virtual continuous college fair. If your library has limited space, consider subscribing to online services to help teens search institutions. Articles on the outlook for careers, salary scales, and advertisements for colleges could be displayed on a bulletin board or in a binder. Consider featuring a different career each month, with books and articles in a display, such as morticians at Halloween, gardeners in April, firefighters and police officers in September to remember those who lost their lives on September 11, 2001, and the military in November to commemorate Veterans Day.

As older teens increasingly explore the reality of adult responsibilities through work, family, and personal situations, they may find nonfiction reading more relevant to their interests. A nonfiction section built on pleasure reading, with subjects such as self-help, poetry, spirituality, health, and biography, may be very popular with this age group. For example, materials on sexuality and dating are of interest to high school teens and should be found in the leisure area as well as in the reference and adult nonfiction areas. Teens may be embarrassed to ask for help finding these materials, and they may be intimidated by a large list, a huge building, or a confusing computer catalog.

After the materials in the collection are adjusted to meet older teens' needs, it is time to consider both the physical space in the teen center and how that space affects the other places in the library surrounding it. A wonderful collection with no comfortable seating does not invite anyone. A good teen space that invites conversation will disturb an adjoining quiet study area. Comfortable and practical aspects must be considered to make the best use of the space.

Collection Challenges

Even if every spine of every item in the teen area is clearly marked as being for teens; if the section is next to the children's area, materials challenges may occur. Parents might complain that younger children are viewing the items in your teen collection. A graphic novel collection will attract different ages from all over the library no matter where it is located. A private school or one with a conservative administration may actively discourage or prohibit graphic novel purchases. These considerations can affect your selection process and the design of your space. Clear policies and processes will help manage challenges, but this is an argument for a clear designation of a space for older teens.

Physical Space Problems with Older Teens

Older teens bring their own set of difficulties into the library with them, and to avoid conflict, a space for them should be designed with this in mind. Because of their larger size, teens may intimidate younger children, whether they mean to or not. Is your teen space clearly defined from the children's room? It must be, for the protection of both children and teens. Do older teens have areas that are separate from those of middle schoolers and younger teens? Does the furniture in your teen space accommodate a larger-sized person? Is it sturdy and durable? Older teens tend to raise the chairs on their back legs to accommodate their longer legs. Are the tables round, instead of square, to accommodate group projects, which are assigned to students more and more often?

Groups that are too large for the tables may invite conflicts between tables and often result in intimidation of single teens of any age who wander through the area in search of a book. A cramped space overloaded with furniture invites bumping and jostling, which may turn aggressive, as stronger bodies are not always caught up with maturity level at this age. Fights can easily break out if teens at tables interfere with each other's conversations or tell each other to be quiet. Having consistent policies in place to handle disruptive behavior is essential, with copies of these policies handy for all staff in an emergency. Documentation of disruptive incidents can help the library administration handle situations before they develop into a pattern or into worse behaviors.

Traffic pattern is also very important. Does the single reader coming in have a chance to select a title without running the gauntlet of tables of teen groups?

Dating becomes a concern as teens get older, and the teen center may turn into the "Dating Connection" in the evenings. Although teens deserve some privacy to select their materials, no area should be so private that it invites sexual behavior.

As changes are made toward creating the new teen space, both physical furniture changes and collection changes, keep a log and note the responses of teens. Keep the board and administration updated about these developments, both good and bad. After significant changes are made, have a "Grand Reopening" celebration and invite both the board and teens involved in the planning. Invite their comments, and note those as well.

Although the response will likely be overwhelmingly positive for a while, give teens opportunities to discuss factors they may not like as they settle in and the library gets accustomed to the space. Conduct another survey after a few months asking teens how they use the center, and what they think about it. Even though you may not be in a position to make huge changes again, the space may require adjustments. The best planning cannot anticipate every situation.

REALITY CHECK

No library is without problem areas, including meeting rooms, adult Internet stations, and front steps where smokers typically like to congregate. Every age group has its own situations and problems. Not every change to the teen space or redesign may have the intended effects. Maybe younger teens are still hanging out in the area, or perhaps parts of new displays are regularly being vandalized. Any space that hopes to continue to appeal to teens must continually reinvent itself in some way. Marketing techniques will help with a lot of this, but some changes will have to be considered as problems occur. The changes will most likely not happen quickly, and there will be elements that may not work and will have to be changed again. One of the most important tenets of successfully serving teens (or truly any target market) is to be flexible and responsive to their needs first.

KEEPING IT FRESH

Older teens are only in this age group for a few years. An area that does not change frequently can quickly become stale and bore users. Older teens may have outgrown pop icons and the trends followed by young people in junior high, but they still need age-geared displays and spaces that welcome them. Displays and promotions within the teen area can keep this area appealing and help alleviate space concerns for libraries of every size. Begin by developing a marketing plan that includes the center.

In *Young Adults and Public Libraries: A Handbook of Materials and Services*, Mary Anne Nichols outlines an example of a "Marketing Plan for a Specific YA Segment—High School Seniors" (1998, pp. 152–154). Following the outlined steps, you can apply business marketing principles to the collection, services, and programming. Nichols breaks down the elements of the collection that are of peak interest to high school teens, with specific ways to advertise them, including areas inside and outside of the library. "Price strategy," "place strategy," and "promotion strategy" are aspects of a marketing plan to help maximize the library potential to this age group. An evaluation section underscores the importance of continuous input from teens to keep the services relevant to their needs. The Nichols plan does not require the planning of a new space. Marketing techniques can help the teen services in libraries at every stage of teen services.

Virtually Expanding the Space

Small facilities or branch libraries that cannot have a separate space for older and younger teens can find ways to appeal to their different interests. Placing YA titles near children's services instead of near the adult materials and displaying only series paperbacks is sure to turn off older teens. Reading lists for teens should include adult and YA titles. For example, science fiction and fantasy, such as books by Orson Scott Card and Brian Jacques, appeal to different ages, as does Christian fiction, such as books by Robin Jones Gunn. Staff should be familiar enough with current teen books to know which are more sophisticated. Compiling teen reviews can be done in any space, such as on index cards on a ring, in a rolodex, or clipped to the shelf under a favorite author, and will make recommendations easy. Post teen reading reviews on bulletin boards. Clip signs or captions to the shelves as video stores do, indicating "teen favorites," or "if you like this author, you'll love . . . ."

Everyone knows that books on a library cart are very likely to be checked out again. If you know of a topic often assigned for reports, put pertinent materials on a cart in the teen area, with a sign indicating where the rest of the materials are located. Another space-saving measure is to create pamphlets that list databases that may be accessed from home. Virtual reference services should also be promoted in the teen area, perhaps on bookmarks. After all, who is most likely to wait until the last minute and need these services? These bookmarks may be tucked into books and distributed at the checkout desk to teen patrons.

Marketing Outside of the Space

It is important for all proponents of teen centers to sell themselves and their services as much as possible. Teen specialists must be advocates in the local and professional communities. Quotations from teens are wonderful for advocacy and should be obtained through regular surveys or input from the TAB. Having surveys with raffles or focus groups during National Library Week or Teen Read

Week annually or biannually is an efficient way to pinpoint areas to work on in the teen areas. Use these quotes in your library newsletter, as part of a press kit to the local media.

Teen-produced videos or presentations at staff meetings can help you override complaints about and challenges to your teen center. It is difficult for library directors to rationalize removing a teen space once that space has been featured in library publications and at workshops, especially on the national level. Let the library board and administration know how much teens enjoy the space, and how it has improved collection statistics or program attendance, or reading scores, at every opportunity.

CONCLUSION

Working with teens is certainly never boring! Keeping a teen area of a public library relevant and appealing to older teens is an ongoing process that will stretch the borders of your position and imagination. Even a reluctant board and administration cannot deny that inadequate attention to teen needs can cause continuing friction among that age group and other patrons. Having a positive plan with teen input for a space that meets their needs can only improve the library. The results will be increased attention to the materials and services essential to teens who are acquiring information to prepare for the future.

REFERENCES AND SUGGESTED READINGS

Aronson, Marc. 2001. *Exploding the Myths: The Truth About Teenagers and Reading*. Lanham, MD: Scarecrow Press.

Bernier, Anthony. 2000. "Los Angeles Public Library's Teen'Scape Takes on the 'New Callousness'." *Voice of Youth Advocates* 23, no. 3 (August):180–181.

Mediavilla, Cindy. 2001. *Creating the Full-Services Homework Center in Your Library*. Chicago: American Library Association.

Nichols, Mary Anne. 2002. *Merchandising Library Materials to Young Adults*. Westport, CT: Greenwood Press.

Nichols, Mary Anne, and C. Allen, eds. 1998. *Young Adults and Public Libraries: A Handbook of Materials and Services*. Westport, CT: Greenwood Press.

Saunders, Michelle. 2003. "The Young Adult OutPost: A Library Just for Teens." *Public Libraries* 42, no.2 (March/April): 113–116.

Taney, Kimberly Bolan. 2002. *Teen Spaces: The Step-by-Step Library Makeover*. Chicago: American Library Association.

United States Department of Education, National Center for Education Statistics. 1995. *Services and Resources for Children and Young Adults in Public Libraries.* Washington, DC: Government Printing Office.

Walter, Virginia A. 1995. *Output Measures and More: Planning and Evaluating Public Library Services for Young Adults.* Chicago: Public Library Association.

4

The Hip and Well-Read: The Reading Interests of Older Teens

Patrick Jones

$\mathbf{W}$hen developing a collection for teens, a librarian is faced with one central question: "What do teens want to read?" In a perfect world, all collection building starts from the answer to that question. But this is not a perfect world, and a question often asked by parents, teachers, and even some of our colleagues is, "What SHOULD teens read?" While a Venn diagram showing the intersection of those answers might be large, there are many titles, topics, and even formats that fall outside the meaty center upon which most can agree. These are books on the edge. In so many cases, the books that teens most want to read are exactly those titles that many adults don't want them to read. That is not so much where the rubber hits the road, but where the challenges hit the desk of the principal or the librarian.

For most of the past ten years, R.L. Stine's Goosebumps have been the most challenged books in America's school and public libraries, only to lose that dubious crown to the Harry Potter saga in the past few years. The essence of the argument for banning Stine's written roller coaster rides and Rowling's flights of fantasy, and one that seems the core of any materials challenge, is about protecting children. In this case, the censors think they are protecting kids from the nightmares, violence, and other stocks of the horror trade that Stine presents, or the dipping of a toe in the occult, which is the battering ram against Rowling. The most consistently challenged books for older teenagers, books like *The Color Purple* by Alice Walker and *Catcher in the Rye* by J. D. Salinger, are also based on concerns about protecting impressionable young people. Protecting them not from the horror of fictional lives, but from the shocking circumstances of their own lives and those of their peers. Protecting them from sexual content, vulgar language, and a defiant attitude. When books start to chart uncomfortable territory by being too scary, too real, too honest, or too vulgar, then many recoil. Whenever books for kids push the envelope by saying new things in a new way, often with a new attitude, there are those who think things are going "too far."

The envelope is also pushed, as it has been for years, by teens wanting to read beyond young adult fiction. Many a librarian has a story to tell about using a public library as an adolescent and being forbidden to check out adult books without a parent's permission. The essence of the adolescent reading experience thus mirrors the stuff of everyday teen life: the struggle for independence. With high school students, this becomes even more pronounced as the battle of teen independence rages hot, hotter, hottest. Many teens declare that independence by their reading choices, moving away from "kid" stuff like young adult fiction to the books they see their parents reading. It is another way of saying, "I belong at the grown up table now." Many devour popular fiction titles, including the thrillers of Thomas Harris or James Patterson, the horror novels of Stephen King and Dean Koontz, and the bestselling fare of John Grisham and Mary Higgins Clark. Genre readers move quickly into books written for adults, in particular in the areas of horror, science fiction, and fantasy. These books usually have nothing to do with adolescent concerns, and they may not even appeal to teen readers apart from the desire for teens to act, and therefore read like, adults.

There is also an interest in adult nonfiction, in particular in true crime. For a certain group of teens, reading *Helter Skelter* is almost a rite of passage. Many of that same subset of teens prefer to jump ahead just a few years and take on the reading interests of college students, devouring the works of Kurt Vonnegut, Thomas Pynchon, and the like. What was cult fiction in the 1960s in some ways remains the same several generations removed. Reading the works of the touchstones of cult books is the very crux of being hip and well-read as an older teen.

This chapter examines each of two of these reading interest areas: cutting edge young adult fiction and cult books, both fiction and nonfiction. This is not to dismiss popular reading, but the fact that it is popular means it is well known and available. Even more popular among high school students than the latest Stephen King are magazines. Magazines are a huge format, as are "practical" nonfiction such as books on financial aid, writing college essays, etc., for high school students. Homework support is not an issue here either; instead we are looking at what older teens read for pleasure.

Cutting edge fiction and cult books have much in common, and there is plenty of overlap. What books in both camps have in common is pushing the envelope. They speak to the very strong drive in older teenagers to define themselves, to be independent in thought and action, and to challenge authority. The cutting edge and cult books they choose mirror those concerns in several ways.

First and foremost, the focus of many of these titles is on the outsider. As teens grapple with identity issues, books that show young men and women disturbing the universe provide both comfort and release. Many of these titles are unconventional in terms of plot, character, and theme. Many titles go further by also presenting unusual methods of telling a story, using language, and other stylistic elements. Finally, cutting edge and cult books are primarily about acceptance of the alternative. The characters and situations that dominate these books are not standard fare; they are about hard issues, hard lives, and hard choices. They use harsh language and harsh images, and sometimes they present harsh truths about the way life really works. An edgy or cult book offers an alternative and sometimes a radical departure from books that are formal and normal.

Adults often assume that older teens don't read: because they don't have time and because they don't want to. These assumptions are backed up by some facts, but at the same time, there are lots of older teens who do read. Let us turn our attention to understanding that reading experience to learn how to bring more teens into the reading tent.

What belongs in that tent? The answer depends on the type of library, school or public. It also depends on the configuration in a public library of the young adult area, which often houses only middle grade fiction and nonfiction. In part this is because middle school fiction is the most reviewed, most available, and least controversial reading material for teens. A book like *Fallen Angels* by Walter Dean Meyers challenges the boundary between a young adult book and a book for young adults—they are not the same thing. The primary duty of any librarian building a collection for teens is to consider literature for young adults, not just young adult literature. This is not a matter of simple semantics, but instead about recognizing the wide range of reading interests of young people.

It is a tough call, but librarians have help; the three primary review journals for librarians working with teens—*Booklist, Voice of Youth Advocates,* and *School Library Journal*—also identify books of interest to older teens. In 1998 the Young Adult Library Services Association launched, not without some controversy, the Alex Awards. Alex Awards are given to ten books written and marketed to adults that have appeal to young adult readers, in particular to older teens, those hip and well-read high schoolers.

This chapter includes a series of "core collections" lists of books with cult appeal and cutting edge attraction. The lists were compiled through a variety of means, but mostly through conversations with older teens about their reading and by following the "web of lists" left by teen readers on Amazon.com. The add-a-list feature on Amazon.com is one of the most powerful tools available to librarians to learn not just *what* books readers like, but the reason for the reader's response. In general, the comments are short and to the point, normally talking a lot about a title being "cool," but annotations for titles as diverse as Francesca Lia Block's *The Hanged Man* and Orwell's *1984* demonstrate that teens respond to books that speak to them. Relevance creates reader response, even in pleasure reading.

READING RESEARCH

Research suggests that generally speaking, teens are not spending much time reading for pleasure. The Search Institute, based in Minneapolis, Minnesota, measures the "development assets" of young people. Their most recent report, based on surveys of almost 100,000 students, primarily in suburbs of Midwestern cities, finds that reading for pleasure, defined as nonschool reading of at least three hours a week, is one of the lowest rated of all the forty assets. Reading for pleasure decreases among teens as they move up in school and is closely tied to gender; research suggests that reading is a young girl thing. This makes perfect sense since as teens get older, they become busier with work, schools, clubs, and friends, and these other activities compete for their time. Nor is the gender breakdown surprising, as the research about boys and reading is well established and explained. (See Table 4.1.)

Table 4.1. Percentage of Teens Who Read for Pleasure

		Grade 6	Grade 7	Grade 8	Grade 9	Grade 10	Grade 11	Grade 12
	Percent Reporting							
All		24	33	28	24	22	22	21	23
Females		30	41	36	31	28	27	25	27
Male		19	25	20	18	17	17	17	18

Interesting is the upswing in the senior year. In personal interviews with high school seniors, I was told by some students that they found themselves reading more, in part as a reaction to the stress of that final year. They found pleasure reading comforting during the considerable changes, decisions, and pressures occurring during their final year in high school.

In October 1999, as part of the Houston Public (Texas) Library's Teen Read Week celebration, teens from across the city were surveyed on their reading interests. Students in the Alief School District, a suburban but very diverse district on the west side of the city, were encouraged by their teachers to participate in the survey, resulting in a strong sample. Over 300 students from the Hastings, Elisk, and Kerr High Schools described their reading interests and habits. If we can assume that interest in filling out the survey might be related to interest in reading, then the demographics of the survey audience mirror those of the Search Institute: Readers are female and young. (See Figures 4.1 and 4.2.)

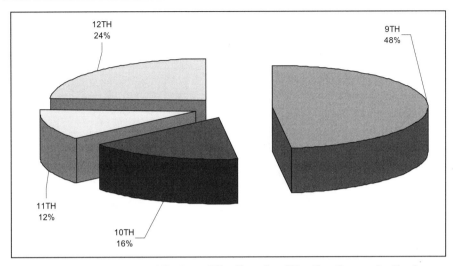

Figure 4.1. Percentage of Students Who Completed Reading Survey, by Grade

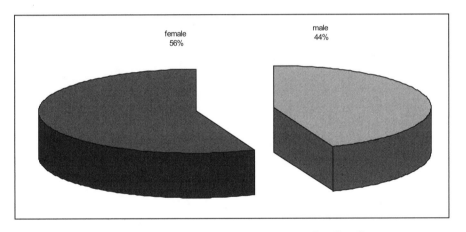

Figure 4.2. Gender of Students Who Completed Reading Survey

The first question was the most basic, and sadly missing from many reading interest surveys, which often jump into getting at favorite books. Instead, the Alief students were asked to choose one of four formats as their favorite to read. (See Figure 4.3, page 110.)

The purpose of the survey was to assist in collection development of books; thus students were next asked, "Which type of books do you prefer?" Since newspapers and magazines fall into the category of nonfiction, the answer does contradict other reading interest surveys, which put nonfiction much higher. (See Figure 4.4, page 110.)

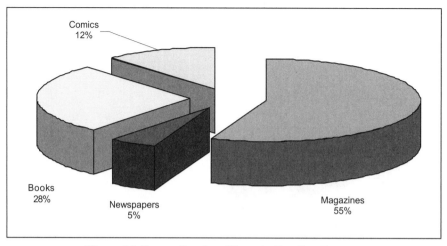

Figure 4.3. Survey Results of Favorite Reading Formats

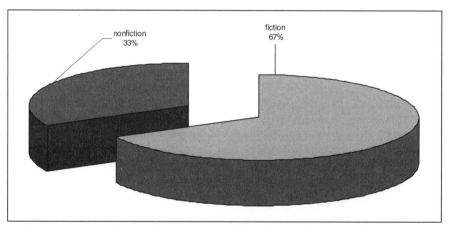

Figure 4.4. Survey Results When Asked, "Which Types of Books Do You Prefer?"

Participants were also asked what genres of fiction they enjoyed reading most. The survey was taken in the middle of the Harry Potter craze, which might explain the high number of fantasy readers, although that could also be related to demographics. The most popular formats were not surprising, both because of long-standing teen interest in mystery and horror and because both are cross-over genres. Although there are some girls who read sports books and some boys who read romances, those genres are a little more gender specific, whereas horror and mystery are not. (See Figure 4.5.)

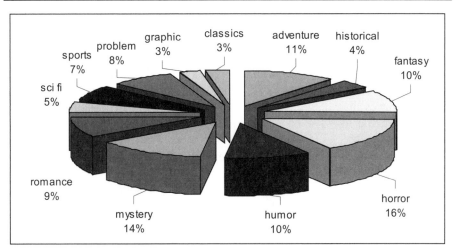

**Figure 4.5. Survey Results When Asked,
"Which Genres of Fiction Do You Enjoy Reading Most?"**

Nonfiction was much more difficult to define by genre; perhaps ranking by sex, drugs, and rock and roll would have been better. Still, there is a clear preference for things related to popular culture, although the high rating of poetry is a bit surprising. (See Figure 4.6.)

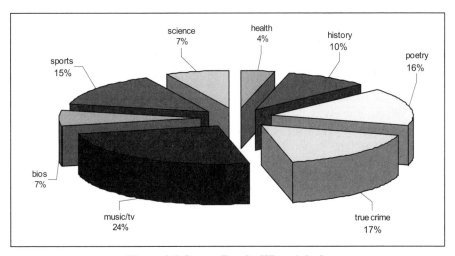

**Figure 4.6. Survey Results When Asked,
"Which Genres of Nonfiction Do You Enjoy Reading Most?"**

The most telling statistic here is that books are the choice of less than 30 percent of those surveyed, and magazines were the preferred reading material among 55 percent of high school students.

While the Houston survey was taking place, there was a national survey sponsored by the Young Adult Library Services Association at the smartgirl. com Web site. Of the 3,072 young men and women aged eleven through eighteen who were surveyed, nearly half (43 percent) said they enjoyed reading for fun but did not have time to do so. The survey results weren't as specific as the Houston survey, but no doubt kids with little time to read are more likely to grab a teen magazine like *YM* or a magazine about one of their passions (such as skateboarding) than tackle a novel.

This is best summed up by a fourteen-year-old girl who commented in the survey that, "I probably read magazines most often because you don't have to start on a certain page for reading. You can choose what you do and don't want to read."

CUTTING EDGE

Would teens read more fiction if they knew about the exciting new books in the young adult genre? Comments from students in the Houston survey suggest that teens were not aware of this new edge that is causing concern among parents, critics, and some educators, while at the same time, not surprisingly, revitalizing interest in books for older teens. Does the Hasting tenth-grade student who wrote on his survey, "sometimes the books are so old they don't make sense in today's world," know about the works of Jess Mowry or Francesca Lia Block? Excitement, in both story and style, characterizes this new edge in YA fiction. After decades of almost entirely abandoning fiction for older teens, most YA publishers are back with a vengeance, trying to turn up the heat and get back in the kitchen. Following are examples from some seminal works at this new edge in YA fiction:

- "We cut ourselves. Not by accident, we do it purposely—and regularly—because physical pain is comforting, and because now it has become a habit. Like the drugs" (*Crosses,* by Shelley Stoehr [Delacorte, 1991]).

- "Impersonating the dead is easy, but easy like swimming underwater for the first time, thinking, when it's done, how easy it was, and how ridiculous it was to be afraid" (*Calling Home,* by Michael Cadnum [Viking, 1991]).

- "Though I tried to clear my head of the effects of the fat, resiny doobie I polished off an hour before, things were still fuzzy as I stumbled into the senior counselor Jeff DeMouy's office" (*Rats Saw God,* by Rob Thomas [Simon & Schuster, 1996]).

- " 'Hey homo!' The boy tensed like a drive by target" (*Babylon Boyz,* by Jess Mowry [Simon & Schuster, 1997]).

Clearly this is not your father's Oldsmobile or young adult novel. Passing its thirtieth birthday, the YA novel is not just far from dead, as predicted just a few years ago, but buzzing with energy and enigmatic new voices, and changing our conception of what makes up a young adult novel.

The modern YA novel as we know it began when S. E. Hinton exploded with the big bang known as *The Outsiders*. This first work of realistic YA fiction was a revelation because, like the works of Thomas, Mowry, and Block, Hinton was saying new things in a new way with a new attitude. Hinton's work reflected her talent not just as a writer but as a reader. As a teen reader, Hinton couldn't find, nor could anyone else, books that reflected in subject, theme, and language the life she was living. Other breakthrough books followed, most notably the first "hard-edged" book, Robert Cormier's *The Chocolate War*. Written as an adult novel, Cormier's finely constructed yet dark, distressing vision broke new ground in a field that was breaking new ground every minute. But by the late 1970s the revolution was over and YA literature was settling into patterns, formulas, and predictability. The "problem novel" of this time would on occasion break new ground in subject matter in movie-of-the-week fashion, latching onto the next taboo topic. There was an edge, perhaps, to content and subject matter, but rarely an edge to the writing.

The literature was, to many, stagnating, so much so that just a few years back people were asking out loud: "Is the YA novel dead?" Fiction for youth seemed to have lost relevance. The teen life being reflected in YA fiction had less and less to do with the outward trappings and circumstances of many young adults' lives. As teen life had become more diverse, stressed, riskier, raucous, and rebellious, the literature didn't reflect that sheen. It's not a simple matter of characters in books, for example, not having pierced body parts, but rather living in emotional landscapes where it was out of the question to do such things. Similar to most of television in the 1960s, which was absurdly out of whack with the youth zeitgeist, fiction for teens seemed agonizingly out of focus as this next generation started coming into its own.

This has changed in the past few years, causing a whole other set of problems, along with the fear that current books are too bleak, and that many titles lack a moral center. These books are linked not by morality or subject matter or even style but rather by an attitude of honesty. These edgy books are diverse in style, from those by Chris Lynch, he of the punchy direct prose, to those of Jacqueline Woodson, she of the poetic muse. They are as dissimilar in voice as a classic coming-of-age story like Helen Kim's *The Long Season of the Rain* (published under Holt's Edge imprint) and its lunar opposite, the slam bang curse-a-thon of Shelley Stoehr's *Crosses*. They are dissimilar in setting, from Block's glittery lights and nights of Hollywood to stories set in the rough streets of Oakland by Jess Mowry. If there is one unifying theme, it is not something new or revolutionary, but rather that most of these titles are classic coming-of-age stories with new spit, polish, and paste, like Rob Thomas's *Rats Saw God*. Although many of these books are being produced by new voices, more traditional YA voices like those of Norma Fox Mazer and Cynthia Voigt fit as they dangle on the edge, presenting hard stories of true grit.

I have to admit I'm a sucker for this kind of book. I recall sitting on YALSA's Recommended Books for the Reluctant Young Adult Reader Committee a few years back as we were reading yet another story about some shy quirky girl who overcomes a problem and emerges from it a better person. Not really a coming-of-age story, not really a problem novel, more just a slice of adolescent life that wasn't the least bit interesting. I just hated those books: too slow, too languid, too ordinary, and too dishonest. Then a book like *Crosses*, in some ways one of the groundbreakers, comes out and just blows us out of the water, mainly by showing what a YA books could be if they dared to stretch (although *Crosses* stretches back to the mundane at the last minute). I know people are bothered by books with bleak endings, no hope, and the like, but that's the crux of our dilemma. Kids say they want realism, but they also want happy endings, Hollywood endings, but that tacked-on ending where characters "meet the caring adult and go to family therapy" seems boilerplate and patently false.

The one theme common to almost every teen book is that somebody grows. R. L. Stine said that one of the many reasons he is looked down upon is that his characters don't grow; they just are. And many people consider that notion, found in some ways in books like Cormier's *Tenderness*, scarier than any *Fear Street* book. A message that some kids don't change; that life does not always get better; and that taking drugs for kicks, engaging in sex, and drinking does not always ruin life, might not be the message that books for youth should send. But then again, should YA books send a message?

The popular consensus seems to be that books for youth are held to a higher standard. Books for kids must teach the good tale and send the positive message. They must be moral. (We'll move beyond the whole "whose morality" issue, sidestepping that nicely, thank you very much.) Despite the "problem" in them these books must remain positive. Perhaps the one overriding characteristic of most of these new YA novels is that the kids try to do what Pony Boy called "saying gold," but the odds are much more difficult, the landscape more treacherous. Block sums it up nicely in *Weetzie Bat:* Weetzie realizes that probably there is no happily ever after, so she is willing to settle for happily. Mazer's *When She Was Good* describes a wretched existence for her YA heroine—a broken home, an abusive family member, and back-breaking poverty—yet still there is hope.

Mazer's book also demonstrates another part of the landscape that seems different in cutting edge books—the home front. The role of parents and other adults in YA literature is always worth picking a good fight about. As the role (and number) of parents keeps changing in our society, that's reflected in these stories. What is amazing, perhaps even appalling, is that if there is a lack of morality in these books, it is not on the part of the kids, but in the parents. Scoundrels, all of them. Almost every book features a family that is not just dysfunctional, but hyper-dysfunctional. There's always an addictive personality, usually alcoholic, and there's always a missing parent: runaway, suicide. I wonder if these books are not so much commenting on the coping skills of teenagers as on the parenting skills, or lack thereof, of baby boomers. Those chickens are coming home not just to roost, but to roast. In book after book, I am stuck by the selfishness and degradation of adults: Parents unwilling to control their addictions, to parent their children, to keep their word, or to act honorably. They are drunks, bullies, abusers, rapists, and emotionally detached. These books seem to be saying that the kids had better change their lives, because if they look across the dinner table or at the photo left behind, that is the life they are heading for, which sounds like a pretty moral story to me. Maybe these books are still teaching a moral story, but using parents as anti-role models.

In many of these titles, parents are demonized or cast negatively because, as teens work out issues of independence, they become super-aware of the flaws and shortcomings of their parents. Teens are going through a stage of more or less "demonizing" their parents to break free. This is nothing new with teens or in teen literature, although the specific problems may have changed, and today's stories may be more "outspoken" about the problems. If publishers want to sell books to teen readers, painting a dark picture of parents and their problems is simply a good marketing move.

These are often not pretty stories, and they are not intended for children; they are intended for young adults. Given the circumstances of many teen lives, they are living and thinking and acting as adults, even though the emotions can't keep pace with the body.

The "grown-upness" of these books comes out in many ways, as there is more freedom in subject matter, in particular regarding sex. Sex plays a part in most of these novels. One thing Block, as well as Klause, did is to show teen characters with sex drives and lives. Maybe some people don't want to think about sixteen-year-old girls or boys having sex lives, but the reality is that many of them do. Moreover, these authors don't comment negatively on teen sexual activity: They are not getting pregnant, not contracting diseases. Instead, they are just people living their lives, which happens to include a sexual component. That's again challenging the status quo and adult perceptions of the way it ought to be.

There is change in terms not only of content but also of telling the story. Block, again, is a big threshold crosser. When *Weetzie Bat* was published, there was nothing else like it. It had a voice and a vision, and it stuck. Michael Cadnum, a successful poet and horror writer, has combined tricks from both of those trades to become one of the foremost stylists, combining a mix of poetic diction and pulp fiction. With *Calling Home,* he was among the first out of the box with this new attitude. In fact *Calling Home,* with its alcoholic haze, its vision of guilt and shame, and its shocking beginning, is really a standard-setter for this lot. Books like Adam Rapp's *Buffalo Tree* go further, being sophisticated and challenging in a way that most outside observers would never believe "kids' books" could be.

Although much of this subject matter might be new to YA books, none of it is new to young adults with cable television. The still mesmerizing talk horror shows like Jerry Springer, with its atrocity of the month, are mostly filled with teen characters. The public is overloaded with tales of incest, rape and revenge, sexual abuse, and dark secrets. It is not that these problems are new. Rather, there is just so much information about them that they burst into the national debate with a fury.

Young adult writers, even the very best of them, follow the news. Yes, they write their stories, but they are very much grounded in the daily lives of their audience. Daily life changes rather dramatically from generation to generation.

This trend has also shaken up our conception of what a young adult novel is or should be. YA is a hard sell. Bookstores, love them or hate them, stock primarily *Fear Street* and series stuff because that is what sells. The other stuff gets sold to the library market, which, thanks to budget cutting, automation, and the other usual suspects, is becoming a dying market for YA publishers. In particular, high schools—once the primary market of YA publishers—are increasingly opting to buy adult titles rather than YA titles. This is due in part to the fact that despite trying to hold the YA market in the burgeoning middle school area, YA publishers for years made twelve year olds the focus of every novel. Another part of the problem is that the mere term *young adult*, which means to most kids in the age range of twelve to eighteen, is too broad to be considered a unified group. As pointed out in every article about this issue, there are actually two markets: –ages ten to fourteen, which are the classic YA book readers, and those aged fourteen to twenty plus, who are looking for edgier books. These are books with attitude, books for the adults in young adults. This too reflects changes in the teen marketplace, where advertisements and products are pitched as reflections of an attitude. For example, the marketing strategy of the World Wrestling Federation has moved away from family entertainment aimed at middle school kids to an edgier, rawer approach with the slogan: "WWF attitude—get it."

The one big caveat here, as pointed out by YA publisher Sharyn November, is that while there's a buzz in the industry and the library world about these books, it is not yet clear if it is carrying over to the actual market: kids. In part, these books are published, pushed, and publicized because editors and librarians find them exciting (witness this chapter). It seems that editors, not surprisingly, would rather work with an author who is breaking new ground than with one who is planting turnips in dead soil. Perhaps one of the reasons for these books is to shake up the industry as a whole. They are attention-getting, look-at-me books, demanding of their audience. This seems to be working, as books like Block's Weetzie series are being cross-marketed to adult readers. Michael Cart (*My Father's Scar)* and other YA authors are looking at adult trade versions. There is talk of more cross- marketing in the future, of releasing two editions of a title, one still aimed at the library YA market, the other at bookstores and the twenty-something coffee shop hang-out crowd. Now that's a real new edge.

The bifurcation is also a by-product of a generational shift. Puberty is happening earlier in each generation. Young people are coming of age earlier on both the inside and the outside, pushed on by the circumstances surrounding them. The YA coming-of-age story is becoming less of a problem novel and more of an adventure story, even a survival story. Part of the newness of this trend is the publication by YA houses of coming-of-age stories written for adults, books like Valerie Hobb's *How Far Would You Have Gotten If I Hadn't Called You Back*. The literature is filled with first YA novels—Chris Crutcher's *Running Loose* and Terry Davis's tour de force *Vision Quest* leap to mind—that were not meant to be YA novels at all.

Some authors and publishers are also getting back to the basic premise that literature about teenagers, no matter who it is written for, is about coming of age. (They focus on significant events in the lives of young people that define, transform, and permanently mark their lives.) Just as each generation has its day of remembrance, so does every person. That singular, yet ultimately shared, changing experience is the soul of young adult fiction.

The generational shift becomes apparent when one takes a look at the creators and editors of these books. Yes, some of these books are by authors like Cormier, Voigt, and Mazer, who have been writing since in the 1970s, but some are by people who grew up in the 1970s, like Stoehr, Block, Mowry, and Thomas. Their coming-of-age experiences, of course, are going to be radically different from the Peck and even the Crutcher generation of writers. That is bound to shape their work. Perhaps the editors mirror the authors and are also *Boogie Nights* babies, as are many of the frontline YA librarians reading, reviewing, and recommending this literature.

The real genius in many of these books is the ability of the authors to capture the intensity and essence of adolescence. Perhaps Rob Thomas represents this best. In *Rats Saw God*, he portrayed these elements with a voice that was strong, sure, and yet heartbreakingly honest. It's not just the pop culture details or the slang, but the essence: the irony, the moodiness, the core stuff that make most teenagers twist and turn.

Part of the problem with many YA books is the underlying assumption that if they get the kids wearing the right shoes and listening to the right band, then they've created a realistic YA character. Wrong. For example, the language in these novels is certainly not rated G. The "f" word is used freely, not reserved for special occasions. Again, maybe since books are words, and words demonstrate the language in action, a moral book wouldn't include vulgarities. But when left without adults, lots—not all, maybe not even a majority—but lots of kids curse. It's just part of the outland: If you have a teen boy who's upset about something, he's not going to yell out "oh shoot," or to tell someone off he's not gonna say "forget you." What's real in these books, as Rob Thomas says, is honesty, so let's stop insulting the audience.

Sex, lurid "problems," and coarse language are nothing new to YA literature. Yet what occurs, after the fire burns down, is the new edge becoming the status quo as everything moves toward the center. Again, a quick look at the history of teen culture demonstrates this phenomenon. It wasn't outrageous bands like the Sex Pistols that the mass audience liked, but a tame corporate spin-offs like the Police. It was not the edgy rap of Public Enemy that dominated the airwaves, but the corporate safe soap like Vanilla Ice and Hammer. There is always a limit to the edge, and that is the desire of the audience to follow. As long as the literature accurately reflects the hopes, dreams, fears, and essence of the teen market, it will find an audience. The key to that is making the reflection accurate, which, for better or worse, doesn't always produce clear images, sparkling expectations, or a clear-cut moral tale. The crux of the problem of these books is the very same one faced by parents as they struggle with the need to provide their children with independence yet still long to protect them from harsh realities. These books send a real message, and this perhaps seems the most profound distinguishing characteristic: that life is often unkind, sometimes unfair, and never uncomplicated.

Collecting these books in libraries also sends a message. The message to teens struggling with these issues is that within books they can find stories reflecting their experience; that within libraries they can find literature relevant to their lives. Ultimately, it is the issue of relevance that drives any discussion of teenagers and reading. When teens find relevance in books, they place a value on reading. They demonstrate that value by the time they spend and the attention they pay, as well as the money they spend. Although cutting edge and cult books may not have relevance in the life of all teenagers, there is in most high schools a clique of the hip and well-read.

CULT FICTION AND NONFICTION

Almost like the remaining readers in *Fahrenheit 451*, each high school has that small, dedicated group of readers, many of them drawn not to the popular but to the cult. The idea of cult books and movies took hold in the early seventies, when it became obvious that there were creative works that were too difficult for the mainstream market and middlebrow tastes. Almost like sacred texts, these cult works were seen not just as works of art but as statements of philosophy: We're different and we don't care. A harsh, unfair world and one person's stance against it is also the mark of cult fiction and nonfiction. From the ultimate cult and YA book, J. D. Salinger's *Catcher in the Rye,* to Stephen Chbosky's contender for that title, *Perks of Being a Wallflower,* the outsider is celebrated both in young adult literature and cult books. Cult books are about life on the edge: Most of the titles are about characters on the fringes of society, which again sums up the high school experience pretty well.

The junkies who inhabit the decades-old *Naked Lunch* by William Burroughs and the new version, *Trainspotting* by Irvine Welsh, actually represent life beyond the edge. The characters in cult fiction are deviants, in the sense that they are outside of the mainstream. The high school students attracted to this literature often fit this definition as well. Some are outcast for social reasons, some intellectual; they may be smarter than those who seek to exclude them. These works are as much about psychology as they are pleasure reading. If the "story" of many of these titles—from the philosophical musing of Herman Hesse's *Steppenwolf,* to the potboiling pop culture of Stephen King's *Carrie,* to nonfiction such as the autobiographies of Maya Angelou, Richard Wright, and Malcolm X—is about search for identity; the quest is the deep heart of the adolescent experience. The books are toted around like badges, defining through defiance of the mainstream. But in some ways nothing could be less iconoclastic than reading this type of fiction. Cult books hit on all the "normal" stages of developmental growth during middle and late adolescence, the high school years. Cult books speak to the high school student's growing needs to experiment with self-image, to develop a sense of values/morality, to increase intellectual awareness, to become concerned about the world around them, and to firmly establish independence.

The late stage of adolescence is marked by the development of the intellect. The books here are the stuff of college-bound reading and English 101 at the university level. If not read in the classroom, they are passed around the dorm. High school students reading *Another Roadside Attraction* by Tom Robbins are announcing, in a subtle way, that they are done with high school.

These books speak also to the concerns about social justice and expanded views of the world developing in the older adolescent, which is intriguing given that many of the books, such as Anthony Burgess's *Clockwork Orange,* have been banned as threats against the social order. But books as simple as John Steinbeck's *Of Mice and Men,* or as complex as Robert Pirsig's *Zen and the Art of Motorcycle Maintenance,* carry a social message as well. Finding and relating to that social message is part of the intellectual experience. By reading cult books, high school students, like the characters in *Grapes of Wrath,* feel they are part of something bigger. Cult books are about the world and the reader's place in it. Or, as the late great Robert Cormier wrote in *The Chocolate War,* these books allow the characters and the readers to wonder if "they dare disturb the universe."

Cult books are not just fiction. Nonfiction, in particular biography and autobiography, asks the same questions. True crime, as evidenced in the reading surveys, has great appeal, as seen with titles like *In Cold Blood.* But a lot of nonfiction fulfills another element of culthood, which is humor. Sense of humor, who "gets it" in movies like *Monty Python and the Holy Grail,* seems to be part of this experience, in titles like *The Straight Dope.* Sometimes the humor is scatological; more often it is sophisticated. The cult experience gives teens an air of sophistication or a sense of worldly experience they might not enjoy in their social situations. The books are winks and nods, saying "we get it." And if peers push them out of the inner circle, high schoolers lugging around fiction like *Lolita* by Nabokov or nonfiction like Hunter S. Thompson's gonzo classic *Fear and Loathing in Las Vegas* are, in a way, saying, "we are outside and we like it. We have our own books, our own language, and our own sense of humor."

And "we are adults." Cult books are usually first written and marketed to adults, and reading is an adult thing. Because of that, the subject matter and language, just like edgy fiction, make some adults really nervous. The cult book includes the normal suspects of sex, drugs, and rock and roll, with the focus heavy on drugs and the "gangsta" lifestyle celebrated in music but cautioned against in books like Luis Rodriguez's *Always Running: La Vida Loca: Gang Days in L.A.* For a variety of reasons, almost all of these books have shown up on lists of banned books, which also explains their appeal. As high schoolers push toward independence, behavior becomes contrary. You don't want me to do it, I will; you tell me I can't read, so I will. Books like *On the Road* by Jack Kerouac have served that purpose for generations. It is not surprising that the whole concept of cult, and the first wide acceptance of many of these titles, came out of the rebellious 1960s. Reading these touchstone books, then, is a gentle act of rebellion for many high school students. Reading about others' rites of passage down mean streets prepares high schoolers for the journey they are about to make into adulthood.

High school students are readers. They are forced in school to read lots of novels they probably would prefer they never heard of and never have to see again. Some cult titles, like Huxley's *Brave New World*, make it as assigned reading, while others, like *Underground Education* by Richard Zacks, probably should. High school students will read and do, if they can find the time and the right materials. Magazines are certainly one answer, appealing both to broad popular interest with titles like *YM* and to niche interests with magazines like *The Source*, which is about rap music.

Similarly, cult books can be widely popular, like *Silence of the Lambs* by Thomas Harris, or certified classics like Anne Frank's *Diary of a Young Girl.* Cult books can hang out on the fringe and appeal only to special interests of genre readers (e.g., Tolkein's *The Hobbit* or the horror works of H. P. Lovecraft). Books such as *Rules of the Bone* by Russell Banks, or several nonfiction titles, such as *Autobiography of Face*, have young protagonists such as those teens find in YA fiction. By combining honesty and attitude with the everyday concerns of high school students, cutting edge YA fiction like *Rats Saw God* by Rob Thomas demonstrate the stuff of cult books.

Perhaps these types of books, both cutting edge and cult, appeal to high school readers not because of genre, subject matter, or even the big themes, but because of something else. Relevance to their lives seems to be the key, books that respond to real needs for intellectual stimulation, for a pass code to the land of cool, and for identity exploration. As high school students move into adult reading, be it with cult novels or this month's darling on the *New York Times*

Best Seller's list, librarians should learn their reading interest through conversation, respond with collections, and help teen readers carry on their reading journey.

THE BOOKS

Cutting Edge Fiction for Older Teens: A Core Collection of Fifty Books in Paperback

Alphin, Elaine Marie	*Counterfeit Son*
Anderson, Laurie Halse	*Speak*
Atkins, Catherine	*When Jeff Comes Home*
Bauer, Joan	*Rules of the Road*
Block, Francesca Lia	*The Hanged Man*
Brashares, Ann	*Sisterhood of the Traveling Pants*
Burgess, Melvin	*Smack*
Cadnum, Michael	*Calling Home*
Cole, Brock	*The Facts Speak for Themselves*
Cormier, Robert	*The Rag and Bone Shop*
Crutcher, Chris	*Staying Fat for Sarah Byrnes*
Dessen, Sarah	*Dreamland*
Draper, Sharon M.	*Darkness Before Dawn*
Ferris, Jean	*Bad*
Finn, Alex	*Breathing Underwater*
Frank, E. R.	*America*
Garden, Nancy	*Annie on My Mind*
Grant, Cynthia	*The White Horse*
Haddix, Margaret Peterson	*Don't You Dare Read This, Mrs. Dunphrey*
Howe, James	*The Watcher*
Jenkins, A. M	*Damage*
Kerr, M. E.	*Deliver Us from Evie*
Klass, David	*You Don't Know Me*
Klause, Annette Curtis	*Blood and Chocolate*
Lane, Dakota	*Johnny Voodoo*
Lynch, Chris	*Freewill*

Marsden, John	*Tomorrow, When the War Began*
Mazer, Norma Fox	*When She Was Good*
McCormick, Patricia	*Cut*
McKinley, Robin	*Beauty: A Retelling of the Story of Beauty and the Beast*
Mowry, Jess	*Babylon Boyz*
Myers, Walter Dean	*Monster*
Nolan, Han	*Born Blue*
Oates, Joyce Carol	*Big Mouth and Ugly Girl*
Orr, Wendy	*Peeling the Onion*
Plum-Ucci, Carol	*The Body of Christopher Creed*
Rennison, Laura	*On the Bright Side, I'm Now the Girlfriend of a Sex God*
Spinelli, Jerry	*Stargirl*
Stoehr, Shelley	*Crosses*
Strasser, Todd	*Give a Boy a Gun*
Tashjian, Janet	*The Gospel According to Larry*
Thomas, Rob	*Rats Saw God*
Thompson, Julian F.	*Grounding of Group Six*
Voigt, Cynthia	*When She Hollers*
Wallace, Rich	*Wrestling Sturbridge*
Weaver, Will	*Farm Team*
Williams-Garcia, Rita	*Every Time a Rainbow Dies*
Wittlinger, Ellen	*Razzle*
Wolff, Virginia Euwer	*True Believer*
Woodson, Jacqueline	*If You Come Softly*

Cult Fiction for Older Teens: A Core Collection of Fifty Books

Adams, Douglass	*Hitchhiker's Guide to the Galaxy*
Adams, Richard	*Watership Down*
Banks, Russell	*Rules of the Bone*
Block, Francesca Lia	*Dangerous Angels*
Blume, Judy	*Forever*
Bradbury, Ray	*Farenheit 451*

Burgess, Anthony	*Clockwork Orange*
Burroughs, William	*Naked Lunch*
Camus, Albert	*The Stranger*
Card, Orson Scott	*Ender's Game*
Chbosky, Stephen	*Perks of Being a Wallflower*
Cisneros, Sandra	*The House on Mango Street*
Dick, Phillip	*Do Androids Dream of Electric Sleep*
Ellison, Harlan	*I Have No Mouth and I Must Scream*
Farina, Richard	*Been Down So Long It Looks Like Up To Me*
Fitzgerald, F. Scott	*The Great Gatsby*
Gibson, William	*Neuromancer*
Goldman, William	*The Princess Bride*
Harris, Thomas	*Silence of the Lambs*
Hesse, Herman	*Steppenwolf*
Hornby, Nick	*High Fidelity*
Huxley, Aldous	*Brave New World*
Irving, John	*World According to Garp*
Kafka, Franz	*The Metamorphosis*
Kerouac, Jack	*On the Road*
Kesey, Ken	*One Flew Over the Cuckoo's Nest*
King, Stephen	*Carrie*
Koontz, Dean	*Fear Nothing*
Lamb, Wally	*She's Come Undone*
Lee, Harper	*To Kill a Mockingbird*
Lovecraft, H. P.	*At the Mountains of Madness*
Mohr, Nicholas	*El Bronx Remembered: A Novella and Stories*
Morrison, Toni	*The Bluest Eye*
Nabokov, Vladimir	*Lolita*
Noon, Jeff	*Vurt*
Orwell, George	*1984*
Plath, Sylvia	*The Bell Jar*
Price, Richard	*The Wanderers*
Pynchon, Thomas	*V*

Rice, Anne	*Interview with the Vampire*
Robbins, Tom	*Another Roadside Attraction*
Salinger, J. D.	*Catcher in the Rye*
Steinbeck, John	*Of Mice and Men*
Souljah, Sister	*The Coldest Winter Ever*
Tan, Amy	*Joy Luck Club*
Tolkein, J. R. R.	*The Hobbit*
Toole, John Kennedy	*Confederacy of Dunces*
Vonnegut, Kurt, Jr.	*Slaughterhouse Five*
Walker, Alice	*The Color Purple*
Welsh, Irvine	*Trainspotting*

Cult Nonfiction for Older Teens:
A Core Collection of Fifty Books

Adams, Cecil	*Straight Dope*
Angelou, Maya	*I Know Why the Caged Bird Sings*
anonymous	*Go Ask Alice*
Barlow, Wayne	*Barlowe's Guide to Extraterrestrials*
Bernstein, Anne D.	*The Daria Diaries*
Bitton-Jackson, Liv	*I Have Lived a Thousand Years: Growing Up in the Holocaust*
Brumberg, Joan Jacobs	*The Body Project: An Intimate History of American Girls*
Bugliosi, Vincent	*Helter Skelter: The True Story of the Manson Murders*
Capote, Truman	*In Cold Blood*
Carroll, James	*The Basketball Diaries*
DeCurits, Anthony	*The Rolling Stone Illustrated History of Rock & Roll*
Duncan, Lois	*Who Killed My Daughter?*
Edwards, Gavin	*'Scuse Me While I Kiss This Guy and Other Misheard Lyrics*
Filipovic, Zlata	*Zlata's Diary: A Child's Life in Sarajevo*
Foley, Mick	*Have a Nice Day*
Frank, Anne	*Diary of a Young Girl*

Gaines, Donna	*Teenage Wasteland*
Grealy, Lucy	*Autobiography of a Face*
Hayden, Tori	*Ghost Girl*
Hirsch, Karen	*Mind Riot: Coming of Age in Comix*
Hoff, Benjamin	*Tao of Pooh*
Hornbacher, Mary A.	*Wasted: A Memoir of Anorexia and Bulimia*
Houston, Jeanne Wakatsuki	*Farewell to Manzanar*
Junger, Sebastian	*The Perfect Storm*
Katz, Jon	*Geeks*
Kaysen, Susanna	*Girl, Interrupted*
Krakauer, Jon	*Into Thin Air*
Loewen, James	*Lies My Teacher Told Me*
Malcolm X	*The Autobiography of Malcolm X*
McCall, Nathan	*Makes Me Wanna Holler: A Young Black Man in America*
McCloud, Scott	*Understanding Comics*
Northcutt, Wendy	*Darwin Awards: Evolution in Action*
Onion	*Our Dumb Century: The Onion Presents 100 Years of Headlines from America's Finest News Source*
Patnaik, Gayatri	*The Secret Life of Teens*
Pirsig, Robert	*Zen and the Art of Motorcycle Maintenance*
Poundstone, William	*Biggest Secrets*
Preston, Richard	*The Hot Zone*
Ravencraft, Silva	*Teen Witch: Wicca For a New Generation*
Rodriguez, Luis	*Always Running: La Vida Loca: Gang Days in L.A.*
Salinger, Adriene	*In My Room: Teenagers in Their Bedrooms*
Schiller, Lori	*The Quiet Room*
Shakur, Sanyika	*Monster: Autobiography of an L.A. Gang Member*
Sikes, Gini	*8 Ball Chicks: A Year in the Violent World of Girl Gangsters*

Taormino, Tristan	*Girl's Guide to Taking Over the World: Writings from the Girl Zine Revolution*
Thompson, Hunter S.	*Fear and Loathing in Las Vegas*
Usual Gang of Idiots	*Mad Gross Book*
Vibe magazine	*Tupac Amaru Shakur 1971–1996*
Vibe magazine	*Vibe History of Hip Hop*
Wolfe, Tom	*The Electric Kool-Aid Acid Test*
Wright, Richard	*Black Boy*
Zacks, Richard	*Underground Education*

REFERENCES AND SUGGESTED READINGS

Aronson, Marc. 1997. "The Challenge and the Glory of Young Adult Literature." *Booklist* (April 15): 1418–1419.

———. 2001. *Exploding the Myth: The Truth About Teenagers and Reading.* Lanham, MD: Scarecrow Press.

Barber, Ray, and Suzanne Manczuk. 1997. "Yes, Author List: Best Adult Nonfiction For High School Libraries." *Voice of Youth Advocates* 20, no. 5 (December): 299–302.

———. 1998. "Best Adult Nonfiction For High School Libraries." *Voice of Youth Advocates* (October): 251–256.

Brown, Jennifer. 1998. "Why So Grim? Awards and Controversy Focus Attention on a Recent Burst of Dark-Themed Fiction for Teens." *Publishers Weekly* (February 16): 120–123.

Calcutt, Andrew, and Richard Shephard. 1999. *Cult Fiction: A Reader's Guide.* Chicago: Contemporary Books.

Campbell, Patty. 1997. "Rescuing Young Adult Literature." *The Horn Book Magazine* (May–June): 363.

———. 1998. "Don't Ask Alex." *The Horn Book Magazine* (September/October): 632–635.

Cart, Michael. 1997. "Not Just for Children Anymore." *Booklist* (November 15): 553.

———. 1999. "The Bleak Goes On: Realism in YA Novels." *Booklist* (September 15): 248.

Chance, Rosemary. 2000. "Smartgirl.Com Reading Survey: What Are the Messages for Librarians?" *Journal of Youth Services in Libraries* 13, no. 3 (Spring): 20–23.

Cooper, Ilene, and Stephanie Zvirin. 1998. "Publishing on the Edge." *Booklist* (January 1): 235.

Cruz, Clarissa. 1999. "No Kidding: Think All Teen Books Are Cute and Lightweight? Think Again." *Entertainment Weekly* (October 15): 19.

Diaz-Rubin, C. 1996. "Reading Interests of High School Students." *Reading Improvement* (Fall): 169–175.

Gale, David. 1999. "What Teens Are Reading: A Publisher's Perspective." *Journal of Youth Services in Libraries* (Fall): 9–12.

Jackson, Richard. 1998. "The Beasts Within: The Dark Side of Young Adult Fiction." *Booklist* (August): 1984.

Jones, Patrick. 1998. "Sex, Thugs, and Rock 'N' Roll: Magazines for Young Adults." In *Young Adults and Public Libraries.* Westport, CT: Greenwood Press, 96–110.

MacRae, Cathi Dunn. 1998. "The Myth of the "Bleak" Young Adult Novel." *Voice of Youth Advocates* 21, no. 5 (December): 325–327.

Mitchell, Terry. 1996. "The Reading Attitudes and Behaviors of High School Students." *Reading Psychology* (January–March): 65–92.

Mosle, Sara. 1998. "The Outlook's Bleak: Judging from What Teen-Agers Are Reading, They're Growing Old Before Their Time." *The New York Times Magazine,* (August 2): 34.

November, Sharyn. 1997. "We're Not 'Young Adults'—We're Prisoners of Life." *Voice of Youth Advocates* (August): 169–172.

———.1998. "Field Notes: I'm Not a Teenager—I Just Read Like One." *The Horn Book Magazine* (November/December): 775–780.

Rosen, Judith. 1997. "Breaking the Age Barrier." *Publisher's Weekly* (September 8,): 28–31.

Rosen, Julia. 1998. "Mature Young Adult Books Are Given a Bad Reputation." *Voice of Youth Advocates* (December): 347.

Search Institute. 1999. *A Fragile Foundation: The State of Development Assets among American Youth.* Minneapolis, MN: Search Institute.

Spitz, David. 1999. "Reads Like Teen Spirit: Edgy Fiction Is Making Literature Cool Again." *Time* (July 19): 79.

Stoehr, Shelley. 1997. "Controversial Issues in the Lives of Contemporary Young Adults." *ALAN Review* 24, no. 2 (Winter): 3–5.

Weeks, Lindon. 2001. "Books That May Make Parents Blush: Fiction Aimed at Teens Features Grown-Up Themes." *Washington Post,* March 11: A01.

Wilder, Ann. 1998. "Young Adult Literature in the High School." *ALAN Review* 26, no. 1 (Fall): 42.

5

Real Books for Real Teens: Realistic Fiction for Older Teens

Sheila B. Anderson

Imagine Holden Caulfield in a teen novel today. Would he befriend Steve Harmon, the incarcerated protagonist of *Monster* (Myers 1999)? Would The Tao Jones recruit Holden for the swim team in *Whale Talk* (Crutcher 2001)? Perhaps Holden would assist Martyn Pig (Brooks 2002) with covering up the evidence of an accidental homicide. Would Holden leave boarding school for an adventure in New York City, or would he stay at school and become glued to his keyboard and chat with other teens about his miserable life? Perhaps Holden would simply drop out of school and begin attending junior college, like the main character does in the book *Jesse* (Soto 1994).

Realistic fiction for teens has changed, just as life has changed.

REALISTIC FICTION: A BRIEF HISTORY

The goal of realistic fiction is to portray life as accurately as possible. This allows readers to identify with characters and to relate to their experiences. By reading realistic fiction, teens may achieve an understanding of their lives, which makes this fiction appeal to teens. Realistic fiction allows readers to try on different roles, meet people like themselves, and discover that others have conquered problems similar to their own. Well-written realistic fiction mirrors the life of real teens. After reading about negative behaviors, teens may choose not to engage in those behaviors due to the negative outcomes. Realistic fiction is also useful for healthy, well-adjusted teens needing to experience, through literature, activities in which they would not normally engage. Whatever the specific motivation, teens have an opportunity to grow as people from experiences they have read about in realistic fiction.

Realistic fiction, known as the "problem novel," "issues novel," or "bleak books," sprouted in the late 1960s when adults (particularly those in the publishing industry) realized that teenagers were not just large children after all. One of the earliest problem novels, published in 1967, was *The Outsiders*, written by S. E. Hinton. Hinton wrote the book at age sixteen in because there were no realistic books available for people her age. She believed that a book portraying real life would be more appealing to teens. Even today, decades later, most teenagers loathe the phony and artificial and are drawn to stark realities and gritty details. Excited about life and interested in solving problems to become successful adults, teens can also gain valuable insights into their own lives by reading realistic stories. Perhaps there is also an element of morbid curiosity in that teens want to read about other teens who are in the midst of problems, whether those problems relate to relationships, death, homelessness, or any of the other social problems featured in young adult literature.

Consider Holden Caulfield, sixteen, who runs away from his boarding school to return to his home in New York City in *The Catcher in the Rye* (Salinger 1951). When arriving in the city, he comes into contact with various people, including a hooker, who is annoyed when she finds out that Holden wants to talk, not have sex. Holden does not refrain from cursing, drinking, or smoking while roaming the streets of New York. This book has remained popular partly because Holden is a self-proclaimed underachiever who is frustrated with society—a bit like Bart Simpson. Teens can also easily relate to Holden's stream-of-consciousness thinking. And although Holden attempts to appear tough and apathetic, it is obvious that he has a big heart, if one considers his love for his sister, Phoebe, and his general concern for people.

The Catcher in the Rye is apparently so realistic, and Holden Caulfield is such a strong, believable character, that the book had an incredible impact on mentally ill Mark David Chapman, who shot and killed John Lennon. After the murder, Chapman wrote a letter to the *New York Times* claiming that the reason he killed Lennon could be found in *The Catcher in the Rye*. Chapman even considered changing his name to Holden Caulfield—and he believed that he would turn into Holden right after killing Lennon. The fact that Chapman identified so deeply with Holden Caulfield and related so completely to *The Catcher in the Rye* is intriguing when considering the power of realistic literature and the impact that it may have on people, whether or not they are in a healthy mental state. It is striking that Chapman was obsessed with a book portraying an angry sixteen year old, one of the most well-known books ever published about older teenagers.

My Darling, My Hamburger (Zindel 1969), another groundbreaking book for teens, presented a story about high school students confronting love, sex, and abortion. By 1976, Judy Blume's book *Forever* had emerged and was in the hands of many teens throughout the country. How many teens across America gave names to penises after reading about Ralph? This love story offered a fresh, realistic look at sex and love.

Are You in the House Alone? (Peck 1967) became another benchmark title in realism. It depicts a teenage girl raped by a wealthy boy, who gets away with his crime.

One of the most prolific authors in the 1970s and 1980s, who did not hesitate to deal with controversial topics in realistic fiction for older teens, was the late Norma Klein. Klein wrote some thirty novels for young adults. Many of her older teen characters struggle with issues surrounding their future, such as deciding which college to attend. Touching upon such problematic topics as sexuality, teen pregnancy, divorce, and religious prejudice, Klein was ahead of her time. In *Love is One of the Choices* (Klein 1978), Caroline, eighteen, begins babysitting for her chemistry teacher, Mr. Prager, and eventually they fall in love. *That's My Baby*, (Klein 1988) features Paul, a senior in high school, who begins a job as a dog walker for his married neighbor, Zoe, who is in her early twenties. Their friendship eventually turns sexual and becomes an ongoing affair, until Zoe becomes pregnant and moves out of the state with her husband. In *Beginner's Love* (Klein 1982), Joel, a shy, inexperienced seventeen year old, becomes more experienced, thanks to the help of his new girlfriend, Leda.

Throughout the 1990s and into the new century, many excellent realistic novels, portraying a multitude of problems, have been published for older teens. Some authors are exceptional at creating realistic characters. Chris Crutcher successfully portrays male characters struggling with a variety of very real problems. For example, in *Whale Talk* (Crutcher 2001), the main character struggles with racism and the conformity of high school athletics.

The late Robert Cormier, a master at character development, has also created believable teen characters, such as Eric Poole, the serial killer in *Tenderness* (Cormier 1997). Also, Paul Zindel, who passed away in 2003, was able to present realistic characters with a touch of humor. For example, in *David and Della* (Zindel 1993), the main characters live both a humorous and a sad life in New York City, without much parental contact and support.

More recently, Sarah Dessen, Laurie Halse Anderson, Sharon M. Draper, E. R. Frank, Chris Lynch, David Klass, and Alex Finn, as well as other new voices, have emerged in the genre of realistic fiction. Dessen and Anderson have mainly focused on the lives of teenage girls and the struggles that they face while growing up. David Klass and Chris Lynch, like Dessen and Anderson, also focus on difficulties with reaching adulthood, but with a slant toward the specific difficulties that males tend to encounter. Sharon M. Draper, a high school teacher who is very much in touch with older teens, has continued to explore issues relating to suicide, drunk driving, racism, and violence in her novels.

Some publishers have made great attempts to attract teens to reading realistic fiction. Scholastic, for instance, has focused on the genre of realistic fiction for teens in recent years. Scholastic began publishing a new imprint called Push, featuring new authors who typically write realistic fiction. On their Web site at www.thisispush.com, the publishing imprint is described as follows: "PUSH is dedicated to new authors and new voices. These writers tell it like it really is. No preaching. No false endings. No stereotypes or contrivance. Just an honest dose of reality. These books are funny, observant, heartbreaking, and heartstopping. Just like life." As of May 2003, the Push imprint had published a total of ten books for teens. Two that were especially noteworthy, and featured older teens, were *Pure Sunshine* by Brian James and *Kerosene* by Chris Wooding, both published in 2002. *Pure Sunshine* tells the tale of two teens in Philadelphia who spend forty-eight hours tripping on acid. *Kerosene* features Cal, and eleventh grader, who is obsessed with fire. Another publisher that has been producing a lot of teen paperbacks, many featuring realistic stories, is Simon & Schuster, under the Simon Pulse imprint. This publisher also has a Web site geared for teens, which features a discussion board, information about a monthly book club for teens, and a magazine describing new books called *Check Your PULSE*.

There has been some debate throughout the years about what older teens are really reading. Some experts in the field of young adult literature have claimed that many older teenagers do not read young adult fiction. Instead, they are more likely to read adult books. Just like the adults around them, older teens read books by popular adult authors, such as John Grisham, Stephen King, and Sue Grafton. Young adult novels intended for older teens are actually read by younger teens:

> *From a publishing standpoint, "young adult" really applies to middle-school students, ages 13 to 15. By 16, most teens prefer adult fiction. Again, the reasons are multiple. Kids want to emulate older ones; thus, the rule of thumb is that a character should be two years older than the target age. (Dunnewind 2002, p. E4)*

In addition, young adult literature is typically not assigned in high schools, and most high school students are only reading the classics. Dunnewind continues, "Some schools discourage high-school students from reading contemporary young-adult novels by emphasizing adult classics, despite widespread agreement about the high quality of new young-adult fiction" (2002, p. E4).

Young adult librarians and educators may not necessarily agree with all of these comments about older teens not reading young adult literature. Many librarians regularly promote young adult fiction to older teens. They see older teens checking out and reading young adult fiction. Large bookstores typically carry more of a variety of young adult fiction novels, and chances are you might see older teens searching for that perfect realistic fiction novel.

Realistic fiction can surprise, shock, or even disgust readers. It can open your eyes, make you smile, and make you cry. Whatever its effect, good realistic fiction is always compelling. Listen to what the characters in realistic fiction tell us. To better serve older teens, learn from their voices.

Older Teen Tidbits: Disco and Polyester! Realistic Fiction for Older Teens from the 1970s

1. *Deathwatch*, by Robb White (1972)
2. *The Man Without a Face*, by Isabelle Holland (1972)
3. *If Beale Street Could Talk*, by James Baldwin (1974)
4. *Forever*, by Judy Blume (1975)
5. *Rumble Fish*, by S. E. Hinton (1975)
6. *Are You in the House Alone?*, by Richard Peck (1976)
7. *One Fat Summer*, by Robert Lipsyte (1977)
8. *Gentlehands*, by M. E. Kerr (1978)
9. *Killing Mr. Griffin*, by Lois Duncan (1978)
10. *The Last Mission*, by Harry Mazer (1979)

Older Teen Tidbits: Big Hair Days! Realistic Fiction for Older Teens from the 1980s

1. *Annie On My Mind*, by Nancy Garden (1982)
2. *In Country*, by Bobbie Ann Mason (1985)
3. *Beyond the Chocolate War*, by Robert Cormier (1985)
4. *The Catalogue of the Universe*, by Margaret Mahy (1986)
5. *Midnight Hour Encores*, by Bruce Brooks (1986)
6. *The Crazy Horse Electric Game*, by Chris Crutcher (1987)
7. *Fallen Angels*, by Walter Dean Myers (1988)
8. *Weetzie Bat*, by Francesca Lia Block (1989)
9. *Shabanu: Daughter of the Wind* by Suzanne Fisher Staples (1989)

Older Teen Tidbits: Ending the Century! Realistic Fiction for Older Teens from the 1990s

1. *White Peak Farm*, by Berlie Doherty (1990)
2. *The Brave*, by Robert Lipsyte (1991)
3. *When She Hollers*, by Cynthia Voigt (1994)

4. *Deliver Us From Evie,* by M. E. Kerr (1994)

5. *The Squared Circle,* by James Bennett (1995)

6. *Ironman,* by Chris Crutcher (1995)

7. *Swallowing Stones,* by Joyce McDonald (1997)

8. *Rules of the Road,* by Joan Bauer (1998)

9. *Beauty Queen,* by Linda Glovach (1998)

10. *Monster,* by Walter Dean Myers (1999)

Older Teen Tidbits: So Far, So Good! Realistic Fiction for Older Teens; 2000–2003

1. *Dreamland: A Novel,* by Sarah Dessen (2000)

2. *Playing Without the Ball: A Novel in Four Quarters,* by Rich Wallace (2000)

3. *Damage,* by A. M. Jenkins (2001)

4. *Every Time a Rainbow Dies,* by Rita Williams-Garcia (2001)

5. *America,* by E. R. Frank (2002)

6. *Home of the Braves,* by David Klass (2002)

7. *Big Mouth & Ugly Girl,* by Joyce Carol Oates (2002)

8. *10th Grade,* by Joseph Weisberg (2002)

9. *Second Summer of the Sisterhood,* by Ann Brashares (2003)

10. *Alt Ed.,* by Catherine Atkins (2003)

Older Teen Tidbits: Insightful Quotations

1. "In 1962, at John Muir High School, seniors could attend the J-Hop. Mike Mahoney threw a party before the J-Hop at his house and served frozen daiquiris. Deborah Staples had three of them and got sick in the backseat of Ralph Pacini's car en route to the prom. George Irwin walked her up and down the parking lot for an hour before entering the gym." (*The Quartzsite Trip,* by William Hogan, p. 75).

2. "So I knew better than to expect sixteen to be the time of my life, but I never imagined it would be like this. Whoever coined *"sweet* sixteen" must have had some Norman Rockwell delusion of poodle-skirted girls rocking around the clock with boys who used words like *swell.* All before their nine o'clock curfew, of course." (*Love and Other Four-Letter Words,* by Carolyn Mackler, p. 11).

3. "Everyone at school is freaked out about the senior curse. For the past eight years, a member of the senior class has died before graduation, which is now only two weeks away. Nobody has died yet, but I can think of a few candidates." (*Downers Grove,* by Michael Hornburg, p. 16).

4. "High school students are notoriously a tough crowd. They're suspicious of fancy rhetoric and sensitive to the slightest sign of self-importance. Raised on sitcoms, commercials, and MTV, their attention span for the spoken word is next to nonexistent. They arrange themselves in rowdy clusters and set their bullshit detectors on Red Alert." (*Election: A Novel,* by Tom Perrotta. p. 29).

5. "Seventeen, a high-school senior, nearly a man: he'd been ready for years and he'd never had sex. What was wrong with him? He loved girls. He couldn't stop thinking about them, watching, wanting, lusting. Twelve-year-old boys did it. What was wrong with him? There was a wall that divided the world, and it wasn't the Chinese Wall, or the Iron Curtain, or even the Wailing Wall in Jerusalem, though sometimes he thought it was most like that wall. The wall he was talking about divided childhood from adulthood. It was first-time sex, and the sex thereafter." (*I Love You, Stupid,* by Harry Mazer, p. 2).

6. "Man, is this lame or what? A seventeen-year-old guy writing a journal. I don't even know how to start. The whole thing is Mrs. Robinson's idea. She's making us write a practice essay for our college applications at the end of this quarter, because we have to write one for real next fall when we're seniors. She's making a big deal out of it because she says it's getting harder and harder to get into college, and colleges are even more interested in essays these days than in the SATs. So, anyhow, she came up with this journal idea." (*The Falcon,* by Jackie French Koller, p. 3).

7. "Like most New York City schools, we've got thousands of kids flooding the place, which is one reason it's hard to make any really close, lasting friendships. Lots of the kids have professional experience in show business. There's always some kid from GW High showing up on a TV commercial pretending she loves eating Eggo frozen waffles or swilling a Diet Pepsi while bouncing on a trampoline." (*David and Della,* by Paul Zindel, p. 6).

8. "Like the night I announced to my family at dinner that I was going to apply to West Point. My dad didn't even bother to lift his eyes from his lumpy mashed potatoes. 'No daughter of mine is going into the military' was his only reply. 'Only sluts and whores go into the service.' His words stung worse than when my mother smacked me

across the mouth, so I never brought up West Point again. But my mother did. She was never one to pass up a bargain, and West Point was a big one. A $250,000 education for nothing. And the only payback—five years in the Army after graduation. Armed with that information, my mother easily convinced my dad that maybe West Point, in spite of all its sluts and whores, would make a wonderful place for his daughter to get an education, after all." (*Battle Dress* by Amy Efaw, p. 8).

9. "See, one thing you have to understand from the start—faceless, suffering teenagers—is that our story is going to have a lot to do with sex. I mean there is sex, out-and-out, straight-talk sex on every page you're about to read. But you also have to understand that we intend to handle all this sex very delicately. With this big flap about censorship in the schools, we've got to say right up front that we believe the only kind of censorship we can support in the United States is self-censorship. So Jess and I will censor ourselves, but only up to a point. And then you've got to just censor yourself. If you don't think you can handle this book, if straight-talk about sex offends you, then put this book down right now." (*The Mayday Rampage,* by Clayton Bess, p. 9).

10. "The thing is, Brady and I had made this plan. First, he psyched out his mom. He refused to get a summer job, and lay around the house all day with the stereo blaring. He got drunk every night. It worked like a charm. When the first of August rolled around and he told her that he wanted to get an apartment for his senior year, she thought it was a great idea and talked his dad into paying for it. Our senior year was going to be so cool. 'The beginning of the end,' Brady said when we talked about it. The apartment would be a place where all our friends could hang out, one place they'd always feel welcome. Where, he assured me, one way or another, both of us would get laid ourselves before the lease was up." (*Wish You Were Here,* by Barbara Shoup, p. 4).

WHY READ AND PROMOTE REALISTIC FICTION?

If you serve teenagers, you must be willing to learn about contemporary teenagers instead of relying on your own experiences of adolescence. After all, have you actually experienced drug addiction, running away from home, teen parenting, being suicidal, participating as a gang member, shoplifting, alcoholism, incest, rape, bulimia, physical challenges, and mental challenges, all in your teenage years? Through realistic fiction, you can get a glimpse of what it's like.

Realistic fiction can also help you expand your knowledge of other cultures, ethnicities, sexual preferences, and geographical locations. If you assist teens of different ethnicities, you learn about their cultures and traditions by reading realistic fiction.

So, do you think that you are young, hip, and with-it, perhaps just like a teenager? Remember that most teenagers want adults to act like adults, not regress into being like them. If you are younger, fresh out of graduate school, making lots of "Dewey need more books" jokes, and carrying the AACR2 everywhere, listen to this: Being younger should not be an excuse for refraining from reading realistic literature to learn about teens. Even if you are not a day over age twenty-three, keep in mind that life for older teens is different compared to five years earlier when you were in high school. Five years may seem like a short period of time to you, but pop culture changes quickly, dramatically, and constantly. Fiction produced for teens changes on a regular basis, and there are new materials published all of the time. New authors are becoming popular with teens, and books by those authors are quickly making their way onto the shelves of libraries and bookstore shelves.

Unlike younger teenagers, who are more likely to be attending middle school, older teens may be more difficult to reach because they may be scattered in high schools, at colleges, in the military, at jobs, in prison, or on the streets. Delving into their worlds through literature may be more practical for librarians who serve teens but who do not have a lot of casual interaction with them. In addition to reading nonfiction—such as news stories, informative books, Web pages, and journal articles—consider reading realistic fiction to learn about teens.

You can use realistic fiction in your profession and with others who are youth service advocates. Reading realistic fiction will help you recommend titles not only to teens but also to adults who have contact with youth. Educators, school media specialists, and school counselors have a lot of contact with teenagers, and they may seek literature that portrays teens confronting problems. Counselors and medical personnel sometimes use literature to help people cope with problems. This is called bibliotherapy. Bibliotherapists use literature in a therapeutic setting, and they may find booklists of realistic fiction useful in working with teens. To find out more about bibliotherapy, consider using the series Using Literature to Help Troubled Teens, published by Greenwood Press. This series focuses on literature relating to issues of health, society, identity, end-of-life, and family.

Physicians, alcohol and drug abuse counselors, psychologists, psychiatrists, and juvenile detention center workers may also have a need for literature exploring problems faced by youth. Faith-based agencies, social workers, and employees at youth service organizations are other audiences for realistic literature. Parents may also want to read about teens to feel more in touch with their own sons and daughters, so be prepared to recommend books to parents. These are just a few of the possibilities you have for promoting realistic fiction.

RECOMMENDED REALISTIC FICTION

The following thematic lists include fiction in which the main characters are mostly ages sixteen through nineteen or in grades ten through twelve. Not all of the titles listed were specifically published for young adults. Since older teens are almost adults, and since many teens are already reading books intended for adults, the adult titles sometimes may be even more appropriate for older teens, depending on the reading and maturity level of the reader. Most of the annotations were derived from the Library of Congress. These lists only include titles published after 1994. The lists can be used to recommend books, to create booklists, to build your realistic fiction collection, or to identify books to use in reading programs. Many of the books listed could fit into more than one category, but an attempt was made to classify titles according to their most significant subject, thus organizing the titles in a practical form that will be useful for teenagers, librarians, and youth service workers.

Abuse

Atkins, Catherine. **When Jeff Comes Home.** New York: Putnam, 1999.

Jeff, sixteen, returning home after having been kidnapped and held prisoner for three years, must face his family, friends, and school and the widespread assumption that he engaged in sexual activity with his kidnapper.

Dessen, Sarah. **Dreamland: A Novel.** New York: Viking, 2000.

After her older sister runs away, Caitlin, sixteen, decides that she needs to make a major change in her own life and begins an abusive relationship with a boy who is mysterious, brilliant, and dangerous.

Draper, Sharon M. **Darkness Before Dawn.** New York: Atheneum, 2001

Recovering from the recent suicide of her ex-boyfriend, senior class president Keisha Montgomery finds herself attracted to a dangerous older man.

Flinn, Alex. **Breathing Underwater.** New York: HarperCollins, 2001.

Sent to counseling for hitting his girlfriend and ordered to keep a journal, Nick, sixteen, recounts his relationship with his girlfriend, examines his controlling behavior and anger, and describes living with his abusive father.

Glovach, Linda. **Beauty Queen.** New York: HarperCollins, 1998.

Samantha, nineteen, struggles with her addiction to heroin.

Haddix, Margaret Peterson. **Don't You Dare Read This, Mrs. Dunphrey.** New York: Simon & Schuster, 1996.

In the journal she is keeping for English class, Tish, sixteen, chronicles the changes in her life when her abusive father returns home after a two-year absence.

McNamee, Graham. **Hate You.** New York: Delacorte, 1999.

Nursing hatred for the father who choked her and damaged her voice as a child, Alice, seventeen, writes songs she feels she cannot sing and seeks to reconcile her feelings for herself and her father.

Reynolds, Marilyn. **Baby Help.** Buena Park, CA: Morning Glory Press, 1997.

Because her partner continues to abuse her, Melissa, seventeen, takes their young child and goes to a shelter for battered women, where she begins the healing process.

Alcoholism and Drug Use

Bauer, Joan. **Rules of the Road.** New York: Putnam, 1998.

Jenna, sixteen, gets a job driving the elderly owner of a chain of successful shoe stores from Chicago to Texas to confront the son who is trying to force her to retire; along the way Jenna hones her talents as a saleswoman and finds the strength to face her alcoholic father.

Deaver, Julie Reece. **Chicago Blues.** New York: HarperCollins, 1995.

Lissa, seventeen, an art student living on her own in Chicago, must raise her eleven-year-old sister when their alcoholic mother becomes incapable of caring for her.

James, Brian. **Pure Sunshine.** New York: Scholastic, 2002.

Three teenagers describe their experiences in Philadelphia while tripping on acid.

Keizer, Garret. **God of Beer.** New York: HarperCollins, 2002.

To complete a class assignment at his high school in rural Vermont, Kyle and his friends Quake and Diana do a social protest project involving alcohol.

Moore, Peter. **Blind Sighted.** New York: Viking, 2002.

Kirk, sixteen, a creative misfit who is in trouble at high school because he is bored with his classes, learns to deal with his alcoholic mother, new friends, and life with the help of a blind young woman who hires him to read to her.

Murray, Jaye. **Bottled Up.** New York: Dial Books, 2003.

Pip, sixteen, who is usually high, faces an ultimatum from his school principal, forcing him to decide whether he should follow in his father's destructive path.

Qualey, Marsha. **One Night.** New York: Dial Books, 2002.

Kelly, nineteen, the ex-addict niece of a nationally renowned Minnesota talk show host, has an unexpected adventure with the visiting prince of a war-torn Eastern European country.

Rottman, S. L. **Stetson.** New York: Viking, 2002.

Stetson, seventeen, meets the sister he never knew he had, and together they try to make sense of their pasts.

Death, Grief, and Depression

Abelove, Joan. **Saying It Out Loud.** New York: DK Publishing, 1999.

With the help of her best friend, Mindy, sixteen, sorts through her relationships with her solicitous mother and her detached father as she tries to come to terms with the fact that her mother is dying from a brain tumor.

Hawes, Loise. **Rosey in the Present Tense.** New York: Walker, 1999.

Unable to accept the sudden death of his Japanese American girlfriend Rosey, Franklin, seventeen, finds that she has come back to him as a spirit and eventually realizes that he must let her go.

Hurwin, Davida Wills. **A Time for Dancing.** Boston: Little, Brown, 1995.

Samantha and Juliana, seventeen, tell their stories in alternating chapters after Juliana is diagnosed with cancer.

Jenkins, A. M. **Damage.** New York: HarperCollins, 2001.

Football hero Austin tries to understand the inexplicable depression that has drained his interest in life. He thinks he has found relief in a girl who seems very special.

Lynch, Chris. **Freewill.** New York: HarperCollins, 2001.

A teenager trying to recover from the tragic death of his father and stepmother believes himself to be responsible for the rash of teen suicides occurring in his town.

Mahy, Margaret. **24 Hours.** New York: Margaret K. McElderry Books, 2000.

During the first twenty-four hours after finishing high school, Ellis, seventeen, becomes part of an inner-city world far different from his comfortable life, which helps him deal with his best friend's recent suicide.

McDonald, Joyce. **Swallowing Stones.** New York: Delacorte, 1997.

Dual perspectives reveal the aftermath of seventeen-year-old Michael MacKenzie's birthday celebration, during which he discharges an antique Winchester rifle and accidentally kills the father of high school classmate Jenna Ward.

Picoult, Jodi. **The Pact.** New York: Quill Books, 1999.

Emily and Chris have known each other practically since birth, and when Emily dies, Chris is reluctant to talk to family members about issues surrounding her death.

Qualey, Marsha. **Thin Ice.** New York: Bantam Doubleday, 1997.

Arden, seventeen, has been raised by her older brother, Scott, since their parents died when she was just six years old. When Scott is presumed drowned in a snowmobile accident, Arden is convinced he's really run away.

Rodowsky, Colby F. **Remembering Mog.** New York: Farrar, Straus & Giroux, 1996.

After graduating from a private high school in Baltimore, Annie comes to terms with the loss of her sister, who was murdered two years earlier.

Wild, Margaret. **Jinx.** New York: Walker, 2002.

Jen has difficulty coping after her boyfriend commits suicide.

Willey, Margaret. **Facing the Music.** New York: Delacorte, 1996.

Through her love of music and membership in her brother's band, Lisa, sixteen, learns to deal with her feelings of abandonment following her mother's death.

Williams-Garcia. Rita. **Every Time a Rainbow Dies.** New York: HarperCollins, 2001.

After seeing a girl raped and becoming obsessed with her, Thulani, sixteen, finds motivation to move beyond his interest in his pigeons and his grief over his mother's death.

Delinquency and Violence

Draper, Sharon M. **Battle of Jericho.** New York: Simon & Schuster, 2003.

Jericho, sixteen, finds that life is becoming more difficult as a result of his decision to pledge for the Warriors of Distinction, one of the most exclusive gangs in school.

Draper, Sharon M. **Romiette and Julio.** New York: Simon & Schuster, 1999.

After falling in love on the Internet, Romiette, an African American girl, and Julio, a Hispanic boy, discover that they attend the same high school, but they are harassed by a gang whose members object to their interracial dating.

Ferris, Jean. **Bad.** New York: Farrar, Straus & Giroux, 1998.

In an attempt to please her friends, Dallas, sixteen, goes along with their plan to rob a convenience store. When her father refuses to allow her to come home, she is sentenced to six months in the Girls' Rehabilitation Center.

Hewett, Lorri. **Soulfire.** New York: Dutton, 1996.

A rift develops in the closeness shared by Todd and Ezekiel, two African American cousins, when Ezekiel tries to single-handedly end the problem of gang violence in his Denver neighborhood.

McDonell, Nick. **Twelve.** New York: Grove Press, 2002
>Mike, seventeen, a high school dropout, sells drugs to affluent teenagers in Manhattan.

Mikaelsen, Ben. **Touching Spirit Bear.** New York: HarperCollins, 2001.
>After his anger erupts into violence, Cole, to avoid going to prison, agrees to participate in a sentencing alternative.

Myers, Walter Dean. **Handbook for Boys: A Novel.** New York: HarperCollins, 2002.
>Jimmy, sixteen, on probation for assault, talks about life with three senior citizens in a Harlem barbershop and hears about the tools he can use to succeed in life.

Myers, Walter Dean. **Monster.** New York: HarperCollins, 1999.
>While on trial as an accomplice to a murder, Steve, sixteen, records his experiences in prison and in the courtroom in the form of a film script, as he tries to come to terms with the course his life has taken.

Randle, Kristen D. **Breaking Rank.** New York: Morrow Junior Books, 1999.
>Casey, seventeen, has some of her preconceived notions challenged when she begins to tutor Baby, a member of a ganglike, nonconformist society called the Clan.

Strasser, Todd. **Give a Boy a Gun.** New York: Simon & Schuster, 2000.
>Gary and Brendan hold their classmates hostage at a Middletown High School dance.

Watt, Alan. **Diamond Dogs.** Boston: Little, Brown, 2000.
>Neil Garvin, seventeen, the quarterback of the high school football team, accidentally commits a terrible crime.

Wooding, Chris. **Kerosene.** New York: Scholastic, 2002.
>Cal, a junior in high school, discovers that lighting matches helps him cope with life. His obsession with fire gets out of control when he meets Abby.

Eating Disorders and Weight Control

Bennett, Cherie. **Life in the Fat Lane.** New York: Delacorte, 1998.
>Lara, sixteen, winner of beauty pageants and Homecoming Queen, is distressed and bewildered when she starts gaining weight and becomes a fat girl.

Eliot, Eve. **Insatiable: The Compelling Story of Four Teens, Food and Its Power.** Deerfield Beach, FL: Health Communications, 2001.
>Describes four girls who worry about their body image.

Eliot, Eve. **Ravenous: The Stirring Tale of Teen Love, Loss, and Courage.** Deerfield Beach, FL: Health Communications, 2002.

This sequel to *Insatiable: The Compelling Story of Four Teens, Food and Its Power* continues the saga of four girls as they deal with issues such as body image, college, and sexuality.

Going, K. L. **Fat Kid Rules the World.** New York: Putnam, 2003.

Troy, seventeen, who is depressed, suicidal, and weighs nearly 300 pounds, finds that his life is changing when he meets a homeless teen who wants Troy to be the drummer in his rock band.

Hall, Liza H. **Perk! The Story of a Teenager with Bulimia.** Carlsbad, CA: Guzre Books, 1997.

Unhappy about boys, her parents, and her body, Perk, a high school student, becomes a victim of bulimia and resorts to binge eating and forced vomiting to gain control of her life.

Hanauer, Cathi. **My Sister's Bones.** New York: Delacorte, 1996.

Billie Weinstein tries to help her older sister, Cassie, who has become withdrawn and who has stopped eating after leaving home for college.

Strasser, Todd. **How I Changed My Life.** New York: Simon & Schuster, 1995.

Overweight high school senior Bo decides to change her image while working on the school play with a former star football player who is also struggling to find a new identity for himself.

Emotional Problems

Chambers, Aidan. **The Toll Bridge.** New York: Laura Geringer Book, 1995.

Taking a job as a toll-bridge collector to escape family pressures and discover who he is, Jan, seventeen, meets and befriends Adam and Tess. The three test their friendship as each faces a turning point in his and her life.

Clarke, Judith. **Night Train.** New York: Henry Holt, 1998.

His family, peers, and teachers despair of Luke, eighteen, who seems to have turned himself into a loser: failing at school, paralyzed with fear and indecision, and losing touch with reality.

Frank, E. R. **America: A Novel.** New York: Atheneum, 2002.

America, a part-black, part-white, part-anything boy who has spent many years in institutions for disturbed, antisocial behavior, tries to piece his life together.

Mazer, Norma Fox. **When She Was Good.** New York: Arthur A. Levine Books, 1997.

The death of her abusive, manipulative older sister prompts Em, seventeen, to remember their unpleasant life together with their parents and then later on their own.

Werlin, Nancy. **The Killer's Cousin.** Thorndike, ME: Thorndike, 1999.

After being acquitted of murder, David, seventeen, goes to stay with relatives in Cambridge, Massachusetts, where he finds himself forced to face his past as he learns more about his strange young cousin Lily.

Family Problems

Caletti, Deb. **The Queen of Everything.** New York: Simon Pulse, 2002.

Jordan MacKenzie lives with her predictable father rather than her erratic mother after her parents' divorce. Things are rather normal until Gayle D'Angelo moves next door and Jordan's father starts having an affair with Gayle, who is married. When Gayle's husband is missing and Jordan's father is a suspect in the disappearance, Jordan feels her life is going out of control.

Cart, Michael, ed. **Necessary Noise: Stories About Our Families As They Really Are.** New York: HarperTempest, 2003.

Features stories about today's families, whether they are nuclear, fractured, blended, at-risk, or not considered to be traditional.

Deuker, Carl. **High Heat.** Boston: Houghton Mifflin, 2003.

When sophomore Shane Hunter's father is arrested for money laundering at his Lexus dealership, the star pitcher's life of affluence and private school begins to fall apart.

Hamilton, Jane. **Disobedience: A Novel.** New York: Doubleday, 2000.

Henry Shaw, seventeen, stumbles upon his mother's e-mail and discovers that she is having an extramarital affair.

Korman, Gordon. **Son of the Mob.** New York: Hyperion, 2002.

Vince Luca, seventeen, whose family is in the mob, has problems when he begins dating the daughter of an FBI agent.

Mackler, Carolyn. **Love and Other Four-Letter Words.** New York: Delacorte, 2000.

When she and her mother move to an apartment in New York City after her parents decide on a trial separation, Sammie, sixteen, learns to deal with her mother's fragile mental state, her best friend's self-centeredness, several new friendships, and her own budding sexuality.

Malloy, Brian. **The Year of Ice.** New York: St. Martin's Press, 2002.

After learning the truth about his mother's death two years earlier, high school senior Kevin struggles to maintain a good relationship with his father.

Wallace, Rich. **Playing Without the Ball: A Novel in Four Quarters.** New York: Alfed A. Knopf, 2000.

Abandoned by his parents, who have gone their separate ways and left him behind in a small Pennsylvania town, Jay, seventeen, finds hope for the future in a church-sponsored basketball team and a female friend.

High School Life

Anderson, Laurie Halse. **Catalyst.** New York: Viking, 2002.

Kate, eighteen, who sometimes chafes at being a preacher's daughter, finds herself losing control in her senior year as she faces difficult neighbors and the possibility that she may not be accepted by the college of her choice.

Atkins, Catherine. **Alt Ed.** New York: Putnam, 2003.

To avoid expulsion after committing various offenses, six very different high school students are required to meet with the school counselor, in a group, every Wednesday afternoon for a semester.

Bennett, James W. **Plunking Reggie Jackson.** New York: Simon & Schuster Books for Young Readers, 2001.

High school baseball star Coley Burke tries to deal with an ankle injury, back spasms, a pregnant girlfriend, academic failure, pressure from his father, and the legacy of his dead older brother.

Cappo, Nan Willard. **Cheating Lessons.** New York: Atheneum, 2002.

When her team is announced as finalists in the state Classic Bowl contest, Bernadette suspects that cheating may have been involved.

Crutcher, Chris. **Whale Talk.** New York: Greenwillow Books, 2001

Intellectually and athletically gifted, T. J., a multiracial, adopted teenager, shuns organized sports and the gung-ho athletes at his high school, then agrees to form a swimming team and recruits some of the school's less popular students.

Dygard, Thomas J. **Running Wild.** New York: Morrow, 1996.

When Coach Wilson and Officer Stowell encourage him to join the high school football team, Pete no longer believes that "nobody does anything for nothing."

Giles, Gail. **Shattering Glass.** Brookfield, CT: Roaring Brook Press, 2002.

When Rob, the charismatic leader of the senior class, turns the school nerd into Prince Charming, his actions lead to unexpected violence.

Hornburg, Michael. **Downers Grove.** New York: William Morrow, 1999.

Chrissie Swanson, seventeen, finds it difficult to be a unique person in her ordinary town.

Howe, Norma. **Blue Avenger Cracks the Code.** New York: Henry Holt, 2000.

In his new identity as Blue Avenger, David, sixteen, visits Venice, Italy, and continues to pursue various crusades, including trying to solve the mystery of who really wrote Shakespeare's works.

Klass, David. **Home of the Braves.** New York: Farrar, Straus & Giroux, 2002.

Joe, eighteen, captain of the soccer team, is dismayed when a hotshot player shows up from Brazil and threatens to take over both the team and the girl whom Joe hopes to date.

Koja, Kathe. **Buddha Boy.** New York: Foster Books, 2003.

Justin spends time with Jinsen, the unusual and artistic new student whom the school bullies torment and call Buddha Boy, and ends up making choices that affect Jinsen, himself, and the entire school.

Nelson, Blake. **New Rules of High School.** New York: Viking, 2003.

High school student Max is tired of doing what he is supposed to do, such as having the perfect girlfriend and worrying about college applications, so he decides to let go and not be dependable and reliable for a while.

Nodelman, Perry. **Behaving Bradley.** Simon & Schuster, 1998.

Recruited by his best friend to gather input for the proposed Code of Conduct at his high school, Brad encounters obstinate faculty members, monstrous bullies, spineless student leaders, and personal agendas.

Oates, Joyce Carol. **Big Mouth and Ugly Girl.** New York: Harper Tempest, 2002.

When Matt, sixteen, is falsely accused of threatening to blow up his high school and his friends turn against him, an unlikely classmate comes to his aid.

Perrotta, Tom. **Election: A Novel.** New York: Putnam, 1998.

From the point of view of four high school students and a teacher, this soap opera tale tells how a teacher ended up as a car salesman after rigging a high school election, how another teacher was fired for sleeping with his student, and how friends who are really lovers can become enemies.

Plum-Ucci, Carol. **The Body of Christopher Creed.** San Diego: Harcourt, 2000.

Torey Adams, a high school junior with a seemingly perfect life, struggles with doubts and questions surrounding the mysterious disappearance of the class outcast.

Powell, Randy. **Three Clams and an Oyster.** New York: Farrar, Straus & Giroux, 2002.

During their humorous search to find a fourth player for their flag football team, three high school juniors are forced to examine their long friendship, their individual flaws, and their inability to try new experiences.

Randle, Kristen D. **The Only Alien on the Planet.** New York: Scholastic, 1995.

> After moving to the East Coast, Ginny enters her senior year of high school and uncovers the secret behind a new friend's refusal to speak.

Seymour, Tres. **The Revelation of Saint Bruce.** New York: Orchard Books, 1998.

> When high school senior Bruce Wells inadvertently snitches on his friends, he learns painful lessons about being true to himself and different from his classmates.

Sheldon, Dyan. **My Perfect Life.** Cambridge, MA: Candlewick Press, 2002.

> Ella has no interest in running for class president at her suburban New Jersey high school, but her off-beat friend Lola tricks her into challenging the rich and overbearing Carla Santini in a less-than-friendly race.

Shoup, Barbara. **Stranded in Harmony.** New York: Hyperion Books for Children, 1997.

> While struggling with the changes he faces during his senior year in a small Indiana town, Lucas gains insight through a friendship with a former Vietnam War protester.

Spinelli, Jerry. **Stargirl.** New York: Alfred A. Knopf, 2000.

> In this story about the perils of popularity, the courage of nonconformity, and the thrill of first love, an eccentric student named Stargirl changes Mica High School forever.

Thomas, Rob. **Doing Time: Notes from the Undergrad.** New York: Simon & Schuster, 1997.

> Each of these ten short stories focuses on a high school student's mandatory 200 hours of community service and the student's response to the required project.

Thomas, Rob. **Rats Saw God.** New York: Simon & Schuster, 1996.

> By his senior year in high school, Steve York has lived through the worst two years of his life. His parents have divorced, and his girlfriend has betrayed him. Steve's only hope to graduate on time and avoid summer school is to write a 100-page paper for his guidance counselor.

Von Ziegesar, Cecily. **You Know You Love Me: A Gossip Girl Novel.** Boston: Little. Brown, 2002.

> Blair and Serena, who go to an exclusive private school in Manhattan, are no longer best friends but are still both consumed with thoughts of boyfriends and college.

Weisberg, Joseph. **10th Grade: A Novel.** New York: Random House, 2002.

> Jeremiah chronicles his sophomore year in high school, when he tries to fit in with others and make a move on Renee.

Homosexuality and Bisexuality

Bauer, Marion Dane, ed. **Am I Blue? Coming Out from the Silence.** New York: HarperCollins, 1995.

    Presents sixteen short stories about sexuality by young adult writers.

Benduhn, Tea. **Gravel Queen.** New York: Simon & Schuster, 2003.

    All Aurin wants to do the summer before her senior year in high school is hang out with her friends Kenny and Fred, but when she falls in love with Neila, everything changes.

Boock, Paula. **Dare Truth or Promise.** Boston: Houghton Mifflin, 1997.

    Louie Angelo, a Woodhaugh High student who plans to be a lawyer, falls in love with a girl who lives in a pub and just wants to get through her exams so she can be a chef.

Ferris, Jean. **Eight Seconds.** San Diego: Harcourt, 2000.

    John, eighteen, must confront his own sexuality when he goes to rodeo school and finds himself strangely attracted to an older boy who is smart, tough, complicated, gorgeous, and gay.

Gantos, Jack. **Desire Lines.** New York: Farrar, Straus & Giroux, 1997.

    When Walker, sixteen, gets caught up in a witch hunt against homosexuals, he is left to stand by and watch as a tragedy unfolds.

Garden, Nancy. **The Year They Burned the Books.** New York: Farrar, Straus & Giroux, 1999.

    While trying to come to terms with her own lesbian feelings, Jamie, a high school senior and editor of the school newspaper, finds herself in the middle of a battle with a group of townspeople over the new health education curriculum.

Hartinger, Brent. **Geography Club: A Young Adult Novel.** New York: HarperCollins, 2003.

    Russel, a high school sophomore, and three other gay students set up a club for gay and lesbian students.

Kerr, M. E. **"Hello," I Lied.** New York: HarperCollins, 1997.

    Summering in the Hamptons on the estate of a famous rock star, Lang, seventeen, tries to decide how to tell his longtime friends that he is gay, while struggling with an unexpected infatuation for a girl from France.

Levithan, David. **Boy Meets Boy.** New York: Alfred A. Knopf, 2003.

    Paul, a sophomore, finds that he is attracted to another boy, Noah.

Myracle, Lauren. **Kissing Kate.** New York: Dutton, 2003.

    Lissa feels alone after she and her best friend, Kate, share a kiss.

Quinn, Jay. **Metes and Bounds.** New York: Harrington Park Press, 2001.

    The summer after graduating from high school, while living on the coast of North Carolina, Matt, eighteen, reminisces about Chris, his former boyfriend, and engages in sexual encounters with new acquaintances.

Reynolds, Marilyn. **Love Rules.** Buena Park, CA: Morning Glory Press, 2001.

    Lynn, seventeen, experiences surprise, discomfort, and a new awareness of prejudices and stereotyping when her best friend Kit comes out as a lesbian.

Ryan, Sara. **Empress of the World.** New York: Viking, 2001.

    While attending a summer institute, Nic, fifteen, meets another girl named Battle, falls in love with her, and finds the relationship to be difficult and confusing.

Sanchez, Alex. **Rainbow Boys.** New York: Simon & Schuster, 2001.

    Three gay teens describe their life experiences during their senior year in high school.

Stoehr, Shelley. **Tomorrow Wendy: A Love Story.** New York: Delacorte, 1998.

    Cary, seventeen, seems to have it all—gorgeous body, cool boyfriend, wealthy family, and a great sense of style—but she also has a serious problem.

Storandt, William. **The Summer They Came: A Novel.** New York: Villard Books, 2002.

    Anthony, eighteen, a waiter in the seaside town of Long Spit in Rhode Island, comes to terms with his sexuality when his formerly sleepy town is transformed into a gay hot spot.

Wersba, Barbara. **Whistle Me Home.** New York: Henry Holt, 1997.

    Noli, seventeen, feels as if she has found her soul mate when handsome, sensitive TJ moves to Sag Harbor, but even as their feelings deepen, individual secrets threaten their relationship.

Interpersonal Relationships

Barry, Lynda. **Cruddy: An Illustrated Novel.** New York: Simon & Schuster, 1999.

    Roberta Rohbeson, sixteen, tries to cope with her cruddy neighborhood, her annoying sister, and her angry mother.

Bennett, James W. **Blue Star Rapture.** New York: Simon & Schuster, 1998.

    While attending a high-profile basketball camp, T.J. begins to rethink both his motivations and his actions in guiding his learning-disabled but athletically gifted friend through the college recruitment process.

Bernardo, Anilu. **Loves Me, Loves Me Not.** New York: Pinata Books, 1998.

While trying to win the attention of a high school basketball player who already has a girlfriend, Maggie, a Cuban American, learns painful lessons about romantic young love.

Brashares, Ann. **The Second Summer of the Sisterhood.** New York: Delacorte, 2003.

Bridget, Lena, Carmen, and Tiby embark on their sixteenth summer. Sequel to *The Sisterhood of the Traveling Pants* (Delacorte, 2001), in which the four best friends experienced magic through an ordinary pair of pants.

Brooks, Kevin. **Lucas: A Story of Love and Hate.** New York: Scholastic, 2003.

When Lucas is accused of a crime that he did not commit, his friend Caitlin has to make a difficult choice.

Brooks, Martha. **True Confessions of a Heartless Girl.** New York: Farrar, Straus & Giroux, 2003.

While spending time in a small town after driving off in her boy-friend's truck and ending up at a rundown café, Noreen, seventeen, who has led a life filled with conflict, reflects on her past.

Cann, Kate. **Ready?** New York: HarperTempest, 1996.

Intrigued by a gorgeous boy she sees at the swimming pool, Coll, six-teen, begins a relationship with him but is dismayed to find him both more experienced and more forceful than she is.

Crutcher, Chris. **Ironman.** New York: Greenwillow Books, 1995.

While training for a triathlon, Bo, seventeen, attends an anger man-agement group at school that leads him to examine his relationship with his father.

Dessen, Sarah. **This Lullaby.** New York: Viking, 2002.

Raised by a mother who's had five husbands, Remy, eighteen, be-lieves in short-term, no-commitment relationships, until she meets Dexter, a rock band musician, during the summer after her senior year.

Gauthier, Gail. **Saving the Planet and Other Stuff.** New York: Putnam, 2003.

Michael, sixteen, agrees to work for an ecology magazine in Vermont after losing his summer job with his uncle.

Henson, Heather. **Making the Run: A Novel.** New York: Joanna Cotler Books, 2002.

Lu, eighteen, is set on leaving her Kentucky home town after high school graduation, but her plans are complicated by friends and family, old grief, and new love.

Heynen, Jim. **Cosmos Coyote and William the Nice.** New York: HarperTempest, 2000.

When sent to live on a farm in Iowa as an alternative to juvenile detention, Cosmos, seventeen, falls in love with a religious girl and reconsiders his values and beliefs.

Lubar, David. **Dunk.** New York: Clarion, 2002.

While hoping to work as the clown in an amusement park dunk tank on the New Jersey shore the summer before his junior year in high school, Chad faces his best friend's serious illness, hassles with police, and the girl that got away.

McCafferty, Megan. **Sloppy Firsts.** New York: Crown, 2001.

Jessica Darling, sixteen, learns to cope when her best friend moves away.

Nolan, Han. **Born Blue.** San Diego: Harcourt, 2001.

Janie was four years old when she nearly drowned due to her mother's neglect. Through an unhappy foster home experience and years of feeling that she is unwanted, she keeps alive her dream of some day being a famous singer.

Okimoto, Jean Davis. **To JayKae: Life Stinx.** New York: Tor, 1999.

Jason, sixteen, feels alone and misunderstood when his best friend moves away, his father plans to remarry, and his step-brother-to-be is a high school basketball star, until he starts an online relationship with a girl from Hawaii.

Plum-Ucci, Carol. **What Happened to Lani Garver.** San Diego: Harcourt, 2002.

Claire, sixteen, is unable to face her fears about a recurrence of her leukemia, her eating disorder, her need to fit in with the popular crowd on Hackett Island, and her mother's alcoholism, until the enigmatic Lani Garver helps her get control of her life at the risk of his own.

Reynolds, Marilyn. **If You Loved Me.** Buena Park, CA: Morning Glory Press, 1999.

Racially mixed Lauren, seventeen, the daughter of drug users, is pressured to have sex with her boyfriend and questions her promise to herself to stay a virgin until she is married.

Strasser, Todd. **Girl Gives Birth to Own Prom Date.** New York: Simon & Schuster Books for Young Readers, 1996.

When Brad asks someone else to the senior prom, Nicole resorts to a desperate measure: She decides to make her next-door neighbor over into a dream date.

Sweeney, Joyce. **Players.** Del Ray Beach, FL: Winslow Press, 2000.

Corey, eighteen, sees a threat to his dream of winning the basketball championship when he discovers that the new player on his team is a girl-stealing, friend-framing, team-destroying force of evil.

Wittlinger, Ellen. **Hard Love.** New York: Simon & Schuster, 1999.

After starting to publish a zine in which he writes his secret feelings about his lonely life and his parents' divorce, John, sixteen, meets an unusual girl and begins to develop a healthier personality.

Young, Ronder Thomas. **Objects in Mirror.** Brookfield, CT: Roaring Brook Press, 2002.

In a maze of school assignments and interpersonal relationships, Grace, sixteen, tries to decide who she is.

Mental Challenges

Deaver, Julie Reece. **The Night I Disappeared.** New York: Simon Pulse, 2002.

After moving to Chicago, Jamie, seventeen, fears that she is slowly losing her mind when she is plagued by freaky mind-slips.

Dewey, Jennifer Owings. **Borderlands.** New York: Marshall Cavendish, 2002.

After attempting suicide, Jamie, seventeen, is admitted to a psychiatric ward, where she must come to terms with the abusive, neglectful family relationships that have brought her to this and where she meets a young man whose problems are much worse than her own.

Fraustino, Lisa Rowe. **Ash: A Novel.** New York: Orchard Books, 1995.

Ash's change of behavior and its disruptive effects on his family are recounted by younger brother Wes.

Harrar, George. **Not As Crazy As I Seem.** Boston: Houghton Mifflin, 2003.

High school student Devon Brown tries to cope with his preoccupation with rituals, cleanliness, and orderliness.

Marsden, John. **Checkers.** Boston: Houghton Mifflin, 1996.

Speaking from a mental hospital, a teenage girl recounts the tremendous media pressure that preceded the breaking scandal of her father's unethical business dealings.

Rosenberg, Liz. **Seventeen: A Novel in Prose Poems.** Chicago: Cricket Books, 2002.

Stephanie, seventeen, journeys from fall to spring and from childhood to womanhood as she experiences first love and deals with her fear of inheriting her mother's mental illness.

Rottman, S. L. **Head Above Water.** Atlanta, GA: Peachtree, 1999.

> Skye, a high school junior, tries to find the time for both family obligations and personal interests, which include caring for her brother, who has Down syndrome, dating her first boyfriend, and swimming competitively.

Thompson, Julian F. **Brothers.** New York: Alfred A. Knopf, 1998.

> When his idolized older brother leaves college for a mental health facility and then disappears, Chris, seventeen, follows him to the compound of an antigovernment militia group and tries to rescue him.

Trueman, Terry. **Inside Out.** New York: HarperCollins, 2003.

> Life becomes chaotic when schizophrenic Zach, sixteen, does not get his medications on time.

Physical Challenges

Fleischman, Paul. **Mind's Eye.** New York: Henry Holt, 1999.

> A novel in play form in which Courtney, sixteen, paralyzed in an accident, learns about the power of the mind from an elderly blind woman, who takes Courtney on an imaginary journey to Italy using a 1910 guidebook.

Johnson, Scott. **Safe at Second.** New York: Philomel, 1999.

> Paulie Lockwood's best friend Todd Bannister is destined for the major leagues until a line drive to the head causes him to lose an eye, and they both must find a new future for themselves.

Jordan, Sherryl. **The Raging Quiet.** New York: Simon & Schuster, 1999.

> Suspicious of Marnie, sixteen, a newcomer to their village, the residents accuse her of witchcraft when she discovers that the village madman is not crazy but deaf and she begins to communicate with him through hand gestures.

Koertge, Ron. **Stoner & Spaz.** Cambridge, MA: Candlewick Press, 2002.

> Ben, who is sixteen and has cerebral palsy, struggles toward self-acceptance with the help of a drug-addicted young woman.

Koller, Jackie French. **The Falcon.** New York: Atheneum, 1998.

> While running from the truth to escape painful memories of losing his eye, Luke, seventeen, gets himself into a series of dangerous situations.

Lewis, Catherine. **Postcards to Father Abraham.** New York: Atheneum Books for Young Readers, 2000.

> When Meghan, sixteen, loses her leg to cancer and her brother to the Vietnam War, she expresses intense anger in postcards, which she writes to her idol, Abraham Lincoln.

Pregnancy and Teen Parenting

Bauer, Tricia. **Shelterbelt.** New York: St. Martin's Press, 2000.
> After deciding that she cannot tell her father and his pro-life girlfriend that she wants an abortion, Jade, a pregnant teenager in Paradise, Nebraska, drops out of school, becomes a nanny, and has her baby.

Bechard, Margaret. **Hanging on to Max.** Brookfield, CT: Roaring Brook Press, 2002.
> When his girlfriend decides to give their baby away, Sam, seventeen, is determined to keep him and raise him alone.

Bennett, James. **Faith Wish.** New York: Holiday House, 2003.
> Upset with the course her life has taken, popular senior Anne-Marie is drawn to Brother Jackson, the leader of a cult-like Christian group, becomes pregnant by him, and runs away to figure out what the Lord wants her to do.

Casely, Judith. **Losing Louisa.** New York: Farrar, Straus & Giroux, 1999.
> Lacey, sixteen, worries about the effect of her parents' divorce on her family, especially her mother, and about her older sister's sexual activity, which may have made her pregnant.

Dessen, Sarah. **Someone Like You.** New York: Viking, 1998.
> Halley's junior year of high school includes the death of her best friend Scarlett's boyfriend, the discovery that Scarlett is pregnant, and Halley's own first serious relationship.

Fienberg, Anna. **Borrowed Light.** New York: Delacorte, 2000.
> While struggling with the difficult decisions surrounding her unplanned pregnancy, a sixteen year old feels alienated from her family.

Grant, Cynthia. **The White Horse.** New York: Atheneum, 1998.
> In her writing for a concerned teacher, Raina, sixteen, reveals her troubles with a dysfunctional family, life on the streets, drug abuse, and an unplanned pregnancy.

Hobbs, Valerie. **Get It While It's Hot—or Not: A Novel.** New York: Orchard Books, 1996.
> When she learns that her friend is pregnant, Megan, a high school junior, begins to question some of the promises that she has made to others and to herself.

Horniman, Joanne. **Mahalia.** New York: Alfred A. Knopf, 2003.
> Chronicles a teen father's struggle to be a good parent.

Hrdlitschka, Shelley. **Dancing Naked.** New York: Orca Books, 2002.
> Kia, sixteen, who is pregnant, learns how to confront her own fears and those of her parents and her friends from her church youth group.

Johnson, Angela. **The First Part Last.** New York: Simon & Schuster, 2003.
   Bobby's life changes forever on his sixteenth birthday when his girl-friend, Nia, announces that she is pregnant.

Letts, Billie. **Where the Heart Is.** New York: Warner, 1995.
   After being abandoned by her boyfriend, Novalee Nation, who is seventeen and pregnant, lives in Wal-Mart and also gives birth to her baby in the store.

McDonald, Janet. **Chill Wind.** New York: Farrar, Straus & Giroux, 2002.
   Afraid that she will have nowhere to go when her welfare checks are stopped, high school dropout Aisha, nineteen, tries to figure out how she can support herself and her two young children in New York City.

Pennebaker, Ruth. **Don't Think Twice.** New York: Henry Holt, 1996.
   Anne, seventeen and pregnant, lives with other unwed mothers in a group home in rural Texas, where she learns to be herself before giving her child up for adoption.

Picoult, Jodi. **Plain Truth: A Novel.** New York: Pocket Books, 2000.
   In the small town of Paradise, Pennsylvania, Katie Fisher, eighteen, an unwed Amish woman, gives birth to a live baby in a barn, but suspicions arise when the baby is found dead.

Waddell, Martin. **Tango's Baby.** Cambridge, MA: Candlewick Press, 1995.
   Even though friends struggle to help him, Tango, seventeen, has little hope of supporting Crystal, fifteen, and their son.

Prejudice and Ethnicity

Bell, William. **Zack.** New York: Aladdin Paperbacks, 2000.
   The son of a Jewish father and black mother, high school senior Zack has never been allowed to meet his mother's family, but after doing a research project on a former slave, he travels from his home in Canada to Natchez, Mississippi, to find his grandfather.

Desai Hidier, Tanuja. **Born Confused.** New York: Scholastic, 2002.
   Dimple, seventeen, whose family is from India, discovers that she is not Indian enough for the Indians and not American enough for the Americans, as she sees her hypnotically beautiful, manipulative best friend taking possession of both her heritage and the boy she likes.

Lee, Marie G. **Necessary Roughness.** New York: HarperCollins, 1996.
   Korean American Chan, sixteen, moves from Los Angeles to a small town in Minnesota, where he must cope not only with racism on the football team but also with the tensions in his relationship with his strict father.

Martin, Nora. **A Perfect Snow.** New York: Bloomsbury USA Children's Books, 2002.

Ben, seventeen, must deal with a violent white-supremacy hate group in his small Montana town because his father and his friends are involved with it.

Myers, Walter Dean. **Slam!** New York: Scholastic, 1996.

"Slam" Harris, sixteen, is counting on his noteworthy basketball talents to get him out of the inner city and give him a chance to succeed in life, but his coach sees things differently.

Runaways and Homelessness

Cormier, Robert. **Tenderness.** New York: Delacorte, 1997.

A psychological thriller told from the points of view of an eighteen-year-old serial killer and the runaway girl who falls in love with him.

Grant, Cynthia. **Mary Wolf.** New York: Atheneum, 1995.

Mary, sixteen, tries to keep her family together as they aimlessly travel the country after her father's business fails and he starts to change.

Moriarty, Jaclyn. **Feeling Sorry for Celia.** New York: St. Martin's Press, 2000.

Elizabeth Clarry's best friend has run away again, her absent father has reappeared, and her dialogue with her mother consists of notes left on the fridge.

Paulsen, Gary. **The Beet Fields: A Sixteenth Summer.** New York: Delacorte, 2000.

The author recalls his experiences as a migrant laborer and carnival worker after he ran away from home at age sixteen.

Pedersen, Laura. **Beginner's Luck.** New York: Ballantine, 2003.

After dropping out of school and running away from home, Hallie, sixteen, accepts a job doing yard work for the quirky Stockton family.

Rapp, Adam. **33 Snowfish.** Cambridge, MA: Candlewick Press, 2003.

A homeless boy, running from the police with a drug-addicted prostitute, gets the chance to make a better life for himself.

Wyss, Thelma Hatch. **Ten Miles from Winnemucca.** New York: HarperCollins, 2002.

When his mother and her new husband take off on a long honeymoon and his new stepbrother throws his belongings out the window, Martin, sixteen, takes off in his Jeep and settles in Red Rock, Idaho, where he finds a job, enrolls in school, and suffers from loneliness.

Universities and Colleges

Bennett, James W. **The Squared Circle.** New York: Scholastic, 1995.
  Sonny, a university freshman and star basketball player, finds that the pressures of college life, NCAA competition, and an unsettling relationship with his feminist cousin bring up painful memories that he must face before he can decide what is important in his life.

Brownrigg, Sylvia. **Pages for You.** New York: Farrar, Straus & Giroux, 2001.
  Flannery, seventen, a student at an Ivy League school, falls in love with a teaching assistant who is eleven years older.

Efaw, Amy. **Battle Dress.** New York: HarperCollins, 2000.
  As a newly arrived freshman at West Point, Andi, seventeen, finds herself gaining both confidence and self-esteem as she struggles to get through the grueling six weeks of training for new cadets, known as the Beast.

Frank, Hillary. **Better Than Running at Night.** Boston: Houghton Mifflin, 2002.
  During Ellie's first year of college, she loses her virginity, gains more confidence in herself as an artist, and learns about the social transition from high school to college.

Perrotta, Tom. **Joe College.** New York: St. Martin's Press, 2000.
  As a junior at Yale, Danny tries to juggle affairs with two women while being involved with his father's business during school breaks.

Soto, Gary. **Buried Onions.** San Diego: Harcourt Brace, 1997.
  When Eddie, nineteen, drops out of college, he struggles to find a place for himself as a Mexican American living in a violence-infested neighborhood of Fresno, California.

CONCLUSION

Realistic fiction can provide you with valuable tools for understanding and reaching teen readers. If your library has a dearth of realistic fiction for teens, make it a priority to add to the collection. And if you haven't read realistic YA fiction, try it—you'll like it. You may even find yourself recommending titles not just to teens, but to your peers and colleagues as well. Some library staff members have mock elections for the Michael L. Printz Award, and many of the books discussed are realistic fiction. These discussions are sometimes on a more formal basis, with participation from library patrons, both teens and adults. In other cases, the discussions are held informally, either at the library after hours or in the homes of librarians who love to talk with others about their favorite books.

REFERENCES AND SUGGESTED READINGS

Allen, Janet, ed. 2002. *Using Literature to Help Troubled Teens Cope with End-of-Life Issues*. Westport, CT: Greenwood Press.

Bess, Clayton. 1993. *Mayday Rampage*. Sacramento, CA: Lookout Press.

Blume, Judy. 1975. *Forever*. New York: Simon & Schuster.

Bowman, Cynthia Ann, ed. 2000. *Using Literature to Help Troubled Teens Cope with Health Issues*. Westport, CT: Greenwood Press.

Brooks, Kevin. 2002. *Martyn Pig*. New York: Scholastic.

Carroll, Pamela S., ed. 1999. *Using Literature to Help Troubled Teens Cope with Societal Issues*. Westport, CT: Greenwood Press.

Cormier, Robert. 1997. *Tenderness*. New York: Delacorte.

Crutcher, Chris. 2001. *Whale Talk*. New York: Greenwillow Books.

Donelson, Kenneth L., and Alleen Pace Nilsen. 2000. *Literature for Today's Young Adults*. 6th ed. New York: Addison Wesley Longman.

Dunnewind, Stephanie. 2002. "Teen Reading Gets Real: Increasingly, Books for Teenagers Mirror World As They Know It." *Seattle Times,* September 28: E4.

Efaw, Amy. 2000. *Battle Dress*. New York: HarperCollins.

Hinton, S. E. 1967. *The Outsiders*. New York: Viking.

Hogan, William. 1980. *The Quartzsite Trip*. New York: Avon.

Hornburg, Michael. 1999. *Downer's Grove*. New York: William Morrow.

James, Brian. 2002. *Pure Sunshine*. New York: Scholastic.

Kaplan, Jeffrey S, ed. 1999. *Using Literature to Help Troubled Teens Cope With Identity Issues*. Westport, CT: Greenwood Press.

Klein, Norma. 1978. *Love Is One of the Choices*. New York: Fawcett Juniper.

———. 1982. *Beginner's Love*. New York: Fawcett Juniper.

———. 1988. *That's My Baby*. New York: Fawcett Juniper.

Koller, Jackie French. 1998. *The Falcon*. New York: Atheneum.

Mackler, Carolyn. 2000. *Love and Other Four-Letter Words*. New York: Delacorte.

Mazer, Harry. 1981. *I Love You, Stupid!* New York: Avon.

Myers, Walter Dean. 1999. *Monster*. New York: HarperCollins.

Peck, Richard. 1967. *Are You in the House Alone?* New York: Viking.

Perrotta, Tom. 1998. *Election: A Novel*. New York: Putnam.

Salinger, J. D. 1951. *Catcher in the Rye.* Boston: Little, Brown.

Shoup, Barbara. 1994. *Wish You Were Here.* New York: Hyperion.

Soto, Gary. 1994. *Jesse.* San Diego: Harcourt Brace.

Wooding, Chris. 2002. *Kerosene.* New York: Scholastic.

Zindel, Paul. 1969. *My Darling, My Hamburger.* New York: HarperCollins.

———. 1993. *David & Della.* New York: HarperCollins.

6

Off the Page and Onto the Stage: Booktalking to Older Teens

Kristine Mahood

Your library can boast the world's greatest collection of books for teens, but unless teens know about them, the books will sit on the shelves. Displays, genre shelving, and an array of bookmarks and booklists can help to promote the collection. However, one of the most effective ways to connect teens with books is through booktalks—and booktalking to older teens can be a lot of fun.

IT'S FUN TO BOOKTALK TO OLDER TEENS

Following are four reasons why I've found it so much fun to booktalk to older teens in classrooms, school libraries, and public libraries.

First of all, booktalking to older teens opens up the entire world of books to you as a booktalker, because your audience is open to the entire world of books as readers. Older teens are reading, talking with friends about, and hearing about a cornucopia of books. They're reading nonfiction to get information they need for life issues, personal interests, and school projects. They're reading popular young adult fiction and realistic young adult fiction. They're reading popular adult fiction—before or after seeing the movies—as well as realistic adult fiction. And they're reading classics, as school assignments, as a jump-start on college reading, or because their best friend just read this *great book*.

Second, while older teens tend to be more familiar with a greater variety of books than younger teens, they also tend to possess a broader and deeper grasp of popular culture, current events, trends, and ideas. They are more likely to understand allusions and references to national and world politics, economics, and social circumstances. They are also more inclined to have a direct understanding of the personal dilemmas explored in teen and adult books than they had as younger teens. This is because they and their friends have encountered more personal dilemmas in their lives. High school offers teens a larger and more complex arena than middle school, with more specialized classes, after-school activities, and relationships. Because they can drive, their world is expanding beyond home, neighborhood, and school, with more possibilities for risk, experience, and growth. Older teens are more likely than younger teens to assume more responsibilities at home and to hold jobs, bringing them into contact with a wider range of adults beyond the more controlled worlds of relatives and school personnel.

Third, older teens get the jokes. Having discovered jokes and riddles as children and sarcasm and satire as younger teens, many older teens now use humor as a communication medium, and they continue to flex and build their linguistic muscles through slang, catch phrases, rhythm, and rhyme (Elkind 1998, pp. 32–33). After teething on the parodies and satires of *Mad* magazine, teens go on to devour such conventional wisdom-tweaking Web sites as *The Onion*, just as they graduated from howling at fast and funny cartoons to howling at standup comedy. Communicating via humor, keeping up with pop culture and current events, older teens can pick up innuendoes and allusions, and they can understand jokes. Their appreciation of humor and a humor-based performance style thus allows booktalkers to have fun with their audiences, because they are all working from a large number of shared reference points.

Fourth, older teens are more likely than younger teens to have reached a degree of rapprochement with the simultaneous bombardment of hormones and social hyper-awareness, first launched in their younger teen years. Although physical and social self-consciousness are still big issues for many teens, they are no longer the revolutionary forces that took them by surprise as younger teens. The "imaginary audience" (Elkind 1998, pp. 40–43) that younger teens believe is focusing exclusively on their physical flaws and social struggles recedes a bit, as, with experience, older teens gain more trust in their own choices. And so while some older teens may have decided that it's uncool to display overt interest in your performance, it can be equally if not even more uncool to squirm, giggle, snicker, preen, or otherwise show off for each other—the kind of behavior they may have indulged in as younger teens. The appearance of indifference that some older teens assume during a booktalk program may have little to do with your presentation. It could be that teens expected to look lively in class all day finally get a chance simply to sit back, relax, and listen! And as many booktalkers have counseled, do not assume that dead silence means nobody's taking in your performance. They are listening. Besides, more often than not, the older teens I've booktalked to show overt interest: listening intently, muttering "whoa!" at intervals, asking questions, wanting to look at the books immediately after each booktalk, etc.

There is a special magic that can happen when a savvy, live-wire booktalker lands in a classroom or small teaching auditorium and his or her mind combines with the minds of older teens—minds that are open, curious, capable of expanding into ever more abstract thought and scooping up ever more detailed information. You can booktalk a wide variety of books, you can wander about happily in a wider frame of reference, and you can pull up and offer a colorful vocabulary in a complex syntax.

Be wary, however, of affecting teen slang; even if you could keep current—which you probably can't—nobody expects you to act and speak like a teen, and for sure nobody wants you to. You can be whimsical, you can be serious, but never a buffoon, never heavy-handed, and always in control of yourself, your material, and your performance. You are a harbinger of the great big world of ideas, the enthralling world of stories, tossing out handfuls of sparkly stardust, Scheherazade in glasses (or contacts). Enjoy yourself! And if you love your books, you won't have to say so: Your passion will shine through.

The sections that follow discuss the types of literature you can booktalk to older teens: young adult and adult nonfiction, popular young adult fiction, realistic young adult fiction, adult fiction, and classics. I include sample booktalks and end with some tips on booktalking performance. You've seen how much fun it can be to booktalk to older teens. Now you'll see how very many books there are that you can bring into teens' lives.

NONFICTION

Nonfiction is a great genre to promote to teens. It appeals to their hunger for knowledge. As their inner and outer worlds expand, as their minds grow, as they encounter more life issues and challenges, as their need to understand themselves and others expands, their appetite for answers and insights explodes. And like adults, teens are looking for those answers and insights in a variety of places: magazines, Web sites, and nonfiction books. Nonfiction directly provides answers and insights, unlike fiction, which addresses issues symbolically.

If teens are already reading nonfiction, why include it in a booktalk performance? Because they *are* reading it. By including nonfiction, you validate and encourage teens' interests and reading choices while letting them know that the library has books to meet their interests. By booktalking nonfiction you are expanding the definition of reading to include nonfiction, liberating teens labeled "nonreaders" and "reluctant readers" from the idea that if they don't like to read fiction, there's nothing for them to read. Nonfiction can appeal to nonreaders and reluctant male readers (Abramson 2001) and/or new English speakers (Jones 2001). The popularity of magazines among girls suggests that girls also enjoy reading nonfiction.

Each of the following subjects of informational, personal interest, and school-related nonfiction has a particular appeal to teen readers. By appeal, I mean the answer to the questions that pop into a reader's mind when he or she hears about a book: "What's in it for me? Why should I want to read this book?"

Informational Nonfiction

Inspiration, Self-Help, and How-To

High School

- **Appeal:** Teens are looking for answers to questions such as "Who am I? What do I want out of life? What's the right thing to do in this situation?" Heading for independence, they also want to learn how to do things for themselves.

- **Examples:** *Chicken Soup for the Teenage Soul* (Canfield 1997), *Goosehead Guide to Life* (Power 2001), and *Clueless in the Kitchen* (Raab 1998).

Beyond High School

- **Appeal:** Teens are looking down the road ahead, to jobs, living on their own, college, the military, and other life choices. Practical guides can help clear the haze off the road.

- **Examples:** *Campus Life Exposed* (Cohen 2000), *201 Best Questions to Ask on Your Interview* (Kador 2002), and *Peterson's Vocational and Technical Schools: West* (2001).

Personal Interest Nonfiction

Personal Care

- **Appeal:** Like fashion and health magazines, books on makeup, hair, grooming, health, and fitness answer the question on many teen minds, "How can I look good?"

- **Examples:** *Fighting the Freshman Fifteen* (Flipse 2002) and *The Teenage Body Book* (McCoy 1999).

Hobbies, Interests, and Pastimes

- **Appeal:** Teens spend time and money on music, movies, hobbies, and sports, and they can find plenty of books to meet and nourish those interests at the library.

- **Examples:** *You Can Write Song Lyrics* (Cox 2000), *Gotta Hike B.C.* (Nomad 2001), and *Skateboarding: New Levels* (Werner and Badillo 2002).

School-Related Nonfiction

The appeal of school-related nonfiction is basic: Topics in a subject area have been assigned by a teacher, and teens need to find books! Some subject areas may offer an additional appeal to teens.

Biography

- **Appeal:** Trying to figure out their own lives, teens can find inspiration in the lives of others, particularly people who have overcome adversity. The closer a person is to teens' interests and concerns, the more appealing his or her biography is.

- **Examples:** *Sheryl Crow* (Buskin 2002), *Geeks* (Katz 2000), and *On Writing: A Memoir of the Craft* (King 2000).

Current Events and Issues

- **Appeal:** Teens have long been made aware of illegal drugs and other teen-associated problems. Booktalking titles on other topics can expand teens' (and teachers') definition of current events and issues to include legal, financial, community health, political, and communication issues.

- **Examples:** *911: The Book of Help* (Cart 2002), *Bias* (Goldberg 2001), and *Fast Food Nation* (Schlosser 2001).

History

- **Appeal:** Looking for something a little different from the same old history subject? Try books about a lesser-known aspect of an event, time, or place, or books that put a new spin on an old story, or books that tell a story for the first time.

- **Examples:** *Secret Soldiers* (Gerard 2002) and *The Answer Is Never* (Weyland 2002).

Social and Cultural Studies

- **Appeal:** Older teens can see how social, economic, political, racial, and cultural phenomena can affect them. They may also be looking for ideas for term projects that differ from the same old topics.

- **Examples:** *Nickel and Dimed* (Ehrenreich 2001), *What Are You? Voices of Mixed-Race Young People* (Gaskins 1999), and *Inside Islam* (Miller and Kenedi 2002).

Science

- **Appeal:** Books on scientific exploration—of a continent, a disease, the universe, and more—mirror the curiosity of teens about their own lives and the world around them. And there's always that term project . . .

- **Examples:** *Shipwreck at the Bottom of the World* (Armstrong 1998), *The Secret Family* (Bodanis 1997), and *Seeing in the Dark* (Ferris 2002).

Finding Nonfiction Titles

This is a great time to be booktalking nonfiction. Young adult nonfiction has expanded beyond the educational market to meet the informational needs and personal interests of teens. The format of many young adult nonfiction titles resembles teen magazines, with page layouts broken up with sidebars and other floating text blocks. The writing style is often punctuated by humor and direct appeals to the reader.

It's easy to find titles. Think of some subjects with high teen-appeal, and just go out and look on the shelves, on the returned book trucks, and around the young adult area of the library. That's how I found *California Dreaming* (Donegan 2002), an immigrant Scot's harrowing and hilarious account of his five months as a used car salesman in Silicon Valley.

Other resources include the Young Adult Library Services Association's booklists, "Best Books for Young Adults," "Quick Picks for Reluctant Young Adult Readers," and the "Alex Awards," which recognize adult books with high teen appeal. Reviews in library journals such as *Booklist, School Library Journal,* and *Voice of Youth Advocates* indicate adult books of interest to older teens. Check the teen pages of booksellers' Web sites, such as Amazon.com, which features teen best sellers, "top ten" book lists compiled by teens, and book reviews written by teens.

A good source for adult nonfiction is C-SPAN TV's "Book TV" broadcast. This cable station devotes every weekend to programming about nonfiction books: author presentations in bookstores and at conferences, panel discussions of books and publishing, and author interviews. Book subjects include biography, cultural studies, economics, finance, history, true adventure, science, politics, humor, language, social policy, the arts, and social commentary. Authors who know how to present their work in an appealing style—extracting and polishing their gems—can give booktalkers ideas on how to write and perform booktalks.

Sample Nonfiction Booktalks

What Are You? Voices of Mixed-Race Young People,
edited by Pearl Fuyo Gaskins

What kind of name is that? Where are you from? Is that a perm? Do you wear colored contacts? What *are* you?

Mixed-race teens and young adults talk about what it's like to be asked these and other questions, by friends, people at school, and others. They talk about what it's like to be made to feel as though they have to explain their identity. Race is one of the first things we notice about people. When a person's name, skin, hair, and eyes don't all match up according to our perception of his or her race, we're confused. We can't make sense of our first impression.

Anybody here ever been asked any of those questions? I have. "Mahooooood—what kind of a name is that?" people have asked me—even before the terrorist attacks on September 11, 2001. So then I explain that it's an old Scottish name, and I can see their faces relax. My name, my skin, my hair, my eyes . . . *now* they all match. This book makes you think about those questions, and about what it is that truly identifies a person.

On Writing: A Memoir of the Craft, by Stephen King

How does he do it?

How does Stephen King write that stuff?

Where do his ideas come from, and once he's got them, how does he shape them into the books that are read by millions all over the world?

Stephen King answers these and many other questions in *On Writing: A Memoir of the Craft*. He writes first about his childhood, teen years, low-paying jobs, and years as a struggling young English teacher and short story writer. Next he shares what he's learned about the craft of writing. Finally, he describes his ongoing recovery from the horrifying accident that almost killed him. King was out for a walk when a man driving a van hit him, breaking his pelvis and turning one of his legs into what King's doctor called a sack of marbles.

So how does he write?

To be a writer, King says, you must read a lot, and you must write a lot. Reading builds up your own personal collection of words. It helps you to absorb the structure and code of language. You must write a lot, because as with anything else, practice helps. To start a book, King doesn't outline a plot. He starts with a situation, a problem, a dilemma. Situations arise when two or three ideas come together in a new way. What turns a situation into a story are characters. Like many writers, King lets the characters do the talking and take the story where it needs to go.

And like anything else, King notes, "the scariest moment is just before you start." For this book, that moment came six weeks after the accident. He had to decide that the excruciating pain of sitting at a desk for more than forty minutes would not stop him from writing. Writing had gotten him through other terrible times in his life. He gambled that it would help him again.

It did. The proof is this book, and the books that Stephen King has written ever since that moment when he sat down at his desk once again . . . to write.

POPULAR YOUNG ADULT FICTION

By booktalking popular young adult fiction, you acknowledge that like everybody else, sometimes teens want a story that is instantly gratifying and familiar, with enough surprises to keep turning the pages. In popular young adult fiction, the scene is set, the characters take their places, the plot begins, and the writing style doesn't get in the way of a smoothly unfolding story and characters who all seem to know what to do. Although plot-driven, the best popular young adult fiction is well written, interwoven with character development and social commentary.

Popular fiction for older teens differs from that for younger teens by offering older protagonists (from sixteen to the twenties), more complex plots with more serious consequences, and more sophisticated vocabulary and syntax. Here's an example. *Sammy Keyes and the Search for Snake Eyes* (Van Draanen 2002) is a mystery for younger teens, featuring a thirteen-year-old heroine who looks for the mother of an abandoned baby—and risks her spot on a softball team. *Locked Inside* (Werlin 2000) is a mystery for older teens, featuring an older teen heroine who has been kidnapped and must examine her tragic past to find out why and by whom—and risks her life.

Each genre sports its own story and appeal. The story is the basic plotline. The appeal is the reason why a teen would want to read the book.

Popular Young Adult Fiction Genres

Adventure

- **Story:** Take-charge teens overcome the elements/adversity, survive, and rescue others.

- **Appeal:** The message that teens are strong, not helpless. Fast pacing and plenty of action appeal to many teen readers.

- **Examples:** *The Maze* (Hobbs 1998) and *Rising Water* (Peterson 2002).

Mystery

- **Story:** There's a problem to be solved.

- **Appeal:** The message that teens are smart and resourceful. Teens enjoy solving problems.

- **Examples:** *Thin Ice* (Qualey 1997) and *For Mike* (Sykes 1998)

Suspense

- **Story:** There's a problem to be solved, and it's getting dark and creepy around here.

- **Appeal:** The message that teens are smart, resourceful, and brave. Teens enjoy solving problems and facing their fears.

- **Examples:** *Haunted Sister* (Littke 1998) and *The Body of Christopher Creed* (Plum-Ucci 2000).

Horror

- **Story:** There's a problem to be solved, it's getting dark and creepy around here, and I just slipped in a pool of blood.

- **Appeal:** Teens love to be scared spitless.

- **Examples:** *Thirsty* (Anderson 1997) and *Blood and Chocolate* (Klause 1997).

Fantasy

- **Story:** Anything is possible in another time and place.

- **Appeal:** Teens enjoy visiting other worlds where the rules are fairly clear, in contrast to the uncertainty of their own lives and the unpredictability of this world. They enjoy using their imaginations to envision other worlds and consider alternatives.

- **Examples:** *The Hunting of the Last Dragon* (Jordan 2002) and *Treasure at the Heart of the Tanglewood* (Pierce 2001).

Science Fiction

- **Story:** Science can save or destroy the universe.

- **Appeal:** Teens can deal with any challenge, whether it's alien invasion, post-apocalyptic chaos, mutants escaping from a sinister research facility, etc. Imagination and problem-solving skills are tested.

- **Examples:** *Turnabout* (Haddix 2000) and *The Night the Heads Came* (Sleator 1996).

Romance

- **Story:** Teens fall in, out of, and back in love.

- **Appeal:** Teens' emotions are valid.

- **Examples:** *Truth or Dairy* (Clark 2000) and *Both Sides of Time* (Cooney 1995).

Historical Fiction

- **Story:** Teens lived through great events in other times and places.

- **Appeal:** Teens can imagine what it would be like to live in other times and places and how they would meet challenges and make positive contributions.

- **Examples:** *Anna of Byzantium* (Barrett 1999) and *Soldier X* (Wulffson 2001).

Humor

- **Story:** Smart teens offer wry, sarcastic commentary on life.

- **Appeal:** Teens question the status quo in every arena—family, friends, school, and the world—and one of the joys of teen life is eyeball-rolling sarcasm. Humor offers stress release and a different take on life's problems.

- **Examples:** *Cheating Lessons* (Cappo 2002) and *A Fly Named Alfred* (Trembath 1997).

Realistic Young Adult Fiction

At its best realistic young adult fiction is good literature, blending powerful subjects with compelling, beautiful writing. Reading realistic fiction allows teens to explore issues and ideas affecting their lives. Many of these novels are written in the first person, as though speaking just to the teen reading the book. This intimacy gives the protagonist an authenticity for and an immediate connection with the reader. Another choice is a third-person narration style that focuses almost exclusively on the protagonist—rather than on the wider cast of characters featured in an omniscient third-person narrative style—making a connection between the protagonist and the reader that is almost as close.

Realistic young adult fiction shows teens that they are not alone in their thoughts, feelings, and the circumstances of their lives. Finding out that other teens have similar problems and joys can help ameliorate feelings of isolation and uncertainty. Realistic young adult fiction also shows teens that as human beings, they have within them the intelligence, humanity, courage, and resilience not only to survive but to prevail.

First known as the "problem novel" in the 1960s and 1970s, realistic young adult fiction presented a view of teen life that was not limited to boys tossing footballs and girls waiting for boys to stop tossing footballs. Writers such as Robert Cormier, S. E. Hinton, M. E. Kerr, Norma Klein, Robert Lipsyte, Norma Fox Mazer, Walter Dean Myers, Richard Peck, Marilyn Sachs, and Todd Strasser took on such issues as family problems, racism, violence, poverty, illness, alcoholism, sexual experiences, pregnancy, drugs, and criminal behavior.

In the 1980s, 1990s, and 2000s, other issues that affect teens have been explored by such writers as Francesca Lia Block, Chris Crutcher, Sarah Dessen, Sharon Draper, Jean Ferris, Sherry Garland, Cynthia Grant, Lorri Hewett, David Klass, Joyce McDonald, Maureen Wartski, Rita Williams-Garcia, and Jacqueline Woodson. These and other writers have depicted teens encountering AIDS; homelessness; immigration; alienation, illiteracy; violent mental illness; incest; parental neglect; school violence; and sexual orientation, harassment, abuse, and assault. Teens in real-life crises are often faced with more than one dilemma, driving one-issue problem fiction to evolve into multi-issue realistic fiction, sometimes known as "bleak fiction."

Writers of realistic young adult fiction have experimented with formats, interspersing first- or third-person narratives with diary entries or other writing. In *Letters to Julia* (Holmes 1997), Liz begins with first-person narration. Then she writes a diary entry about the same events described in her narration. Then she writers a chapter of an autobiographical novel based on those events. This is the chapter she sends to Julia, a New York editor, along with a cover letter explaining that her English teacher suggested she send Julia her writing. Julia writes back. And all writing forms—narrative, diary entries, chapters, letters—continue to tell the story. Walter Dean Myers employs a similar mix of narrative, diary entries, letters, and screenplay scenes to tell Steve's story in *Monster* (Myers 1999).

Popular young adult fiction glides into genres. Realistic young adult fiction, like classic fiction and realistic adult fiction, delves below the surface of issues, problems, and events to explore their emotional, psychological, social, and philosophical effects on teens. Whatever the issues and problems, what emerges are themes, that is, ways in which teen characters respond to issues and problems. For example, Chris Crutcher's novels examine problems as disparate as cheating in athletics, illness, parental abuse, racism, death, incest, anger management, and disabilities. What they share as a theme is their depiction of a great teen guy in crisis.

Several recurring themes in realistic young adult fiction are described below.

Great Guys or Gals in Crisis

- **Appeal:** These stand-up teen heroes and heroines are immediately likable and sympathetic, the kind of people teens are drawn to as friends or leaders.

- **Examples:** *Staying Fat for Sarah Byrnes* (Crutcher 1993), *Eight Seconds* (Ferris 2000), and *Big Mouth and Ugly Girl* (Oates 2002).

Not So Great Guys and Gals in Crisis

- **Appeal:** Like their readers, teen heroes and heroines are faced with very real challenges, and it's good to see that you don't have to be great to meet them. In fact, you can be very flawed.

- **Examples:** *Rundown* (Cadnum 1999), *Dreamland* (Dessen 2000), *Breathing Underwater* (Flinn 2001), and *Fast Talk on a Slow Track* (Williams-Garcia 1991).

Outsiders

- **Appeal:** Is there a teen who hasn't felt like an outsider?

- **Examples:** *On the Fringe* (Gallo 2001) and *What Happened to Lani Garver* (Plum-Ucci 2002).

Becoming an Individual—While Trying to Fit In

- **Appeal:** One of the many challenges teens are discovering about becoming an adult is how to balance being oneself with acceptance by peers and the larger society.

- **Examples:** *Lives of Our Own* (Hewett 1998) and *Shattering Glass* (Giles 2002).

Shouldering Responsibilities Beyond One's Years

- **Appeal:** Get good grades, stay involved in activities, stay out of trouble, help out around the house, don't hang out with bad teens, etc., etc., etc. Are there any teens out there who *don't* feel overloaded?

- **Examples:** *Define "Normal"* (Peters 2000) and *A Door Near Here* (Quarles 1998).

Finding Fiction Titles

When looking for young adult fiction to booktalk to older teens, focus on titles featuring older protagonists (from sixteen to the twenties), more serious plots and themes, and more mature treatments. Study your returned-books trucks to learn not only what specific titles teens are reading but also what genres and themes appeal to them. Then look for more titles within those genres. Avoid being driven solely by apparent popularity, however. Maybe you're seeing a lot of fantasy on the trucks because your library owns a lot of fantasy, and readers are always looking for it and finding it. Maybe you're not seeing a lot of romance on the trucks because your library doesn't own a lot of romance, and the romance readers have read out your collection.

Library circulation doesn't tell the entire story, either. That's why it's a good idea to focus on the issues affecting teens in your community. Ask teens what *they* see as important issues. Talk with school librarians, high school counselors, and social service agency staff. Look for local news stories about teens. If you find an announcement of a public meeting or workshop on a teen-related topic, that's an indication of an issue in your community. Keep up with what's going on and select realistic young adult fiction titles accordingly. This is not to say that you'd begin a booktalk on *Mary Wolf* (Grant 1995) by glibly prattling about how homelessness, shoplifting, and mental illness affect the community. Just be aware of what's going on in your community.

Good resources for popular young adult fiction titles include the Young Adult Library Service Association's annual "Quick Picks for Reluctant Young Adult Readers" and "Popular Paperbacks" booklists. Realistic young adult fiction titles can be found on YALSA's annual "Best Books for Young Adult Readers" booklist. YALSA also presents an annual Michael L. Printz Award, which is given to the outstanding young adult novel of the year. *What Do Young Adults Read Next?* (Spencer 1999), one of numerous excellent print reference resources; indexes young adult fiction titles by time period; location; subject; and the characters' names, descriptions, and ages. *Teen Genreflecting* (Herald 1997) describes fiction genres, details subgenres, and lists representative authors and titles.

The Internet offers many resources for titles, including the mega site Internet Public Library, public and high school library Web pages, and teen reading sites such as Reading Rants and Favorite Teen Angst Books. These sites include everything from genre and theme booklists to book reviews by teens. Check out the teen pages of booksellers' Web sites. Amazon.com's teen page, for example, features teen bestseller lists, "top ten" book lists chosen by teens, and book reviews by teens.

Finally, outstanding realistic young adult fiction titles are easy to spot as starred review journals—*Booklist, Kliatt, Library Journal, School Library Journal, Voice of Youth Advocates,* and others—and with good reason. These books are the stars of young adult literature.

Young Adult Fiction Booktalks

Dunk, by David Lubar

The Bozo sits on a bench over a tank of slimy water, dressed like a clown in a bright red wig and grinning like a fiend with a bright red mouth.
DUNK THE BOZO
3 BALLS FOR $2

Chad rolls his eyes. What kind of a dope would fall for *that* old boardwalk come-on? Chad's lived on the Jersey shore his whole life. He's seen the summer tourists come and go, and he's seen the hope of winning a worthless stuffed toy triumph over common sense, time after time. Dunk the Bozo? Nobody's going to waste money on *that*.

Then the Bozo opens his mouth, and his voice cuts the air like a chain saw.

"Hey! Where'd you get that wig?" he yells at a tourist. "Scrape it off a poodle?"

The crowd laughs. The guy turns red. He's insulted. He's angry. But he doesn't want to spend the $2.

"What's the matter? Get *glue* in your ears when you pasted on that wig?"

The guy is furious. He reaches into his wallet. He spends the $2, the $4, whatever it takes to dunk the Bozo.

Chad hangs around to watch. The Bozo is a master. He doesn't just yell at the crowd to get their attention. He picks out targets, hurls insults, and reels in the suckers on a line of anger.

Chad cannot believe how good the Bozo is. And he knows, instantly, what he wants to do this summer. He wants to yell out insults and strike back at every person who's ever called him a dork and a dweeb and worse—if they even noticed him at all. He wants to let out the anger churning inside at Dad's leaving him and Mom, at Mom's cluelessness, at the creeps at school who treat him like dirt. Chad didn't have any plans for the summer, but he has a plan now.

Chad wants to be the Bozo.

Tomorrow, When the War Began, by John Marsden

The dogs all lay dead in Ellie's front yard.

That's the first thing that Ellie, Homer, and their five friends notice when they turn up at Ellie's farmhouse after a week-long camping trip. Ellie and her friends go into the house. It's empty. All the food is rotten. The electricity is off. Where is everybody?

Ellie's family, like everybody's family in the farm district, went into town for Commemoration Day, a big celebration that's like a county fair, only for the whole country of Australia. For some reason, though, they didn't come home.

The seven friends drive to Corrie's house. Nobody's home. They go to Homer's house. Nobody. They go into town. The streets are deserted. It's as though Ellie and her friends are the only seven people left on earth.

Only . . . they're not.

Because in the next instant Ellie and her friends see and hear something that proves a wild, terrifying guess to be true. They see soldiers in strange uniforms, carrying big guns, and talking in a language they don't understand.

Australia has been invaded.

And these seven teens have to run for their lives.

Tomorrow, When the War Began is the first book in a series of seven books about teens who are forced to transform themselves into guerrilla fighters to survive and to save their families, their friends, and their country.

Big Mouth and Ugly Girl, by Joyce Carol Oates

"I didn't do it! How many times do I have to tell you?!"

"He didn't do anything! This whole thing is ridiculous!"

Big Mouth. And Ugly Girl.

Around their high school, Matt is known as Big Mouth, the guy who'll say anything for a laugh.

Ursula is known as Ugly Girl: tall, strong, and tough, the girl nobody messes with.

One day Matt is taken out of class by the principal and two police detectives. "Witnesses" have reported that at lunch in the cafeteria that day, Matt talked about blowing up the school. Matt tries to explain that he and his friends had just been joking around about what he could do if the play he'd written for a school arts festival were rejected. He'd said, "so like what could I do, blow up the school?" That was reported as a real threat, and Matt is in big, big trouble.

Until Ursula marches into the principal's office a few days later and tells him the whole story, in context . . . and Matt is exonerated.

Matt's no longer in trouble, but his troubles aren't over. All of his friends fade away, afraid to be seen with him or to reply to his e-mail, and they don't come running back. Matt has enemies, too, jocks and creeps who beat him up. And so Matt shuts his Big Mouth and withdraws from everyone.

Only one person talks to Matt, somebody he's never talked to before, someone who's never had a friend, who's never opened her heart. Ursula. And is she ugly? No way.

ADULT FICTION

Many older teens are drawn to adult fiction for the same reasons that they enjoy movies and TV shows featuring adult characters, settings, plots, and themes. Older teens are looking ahead to the adult world, and teen flicks and TV series notwithstanding, the majority of entertainment choices are adult-centered. Like young adult fiction, adult fiction includes genre fiction and realistic fiction. Like young adult fiction, the various genres and themes exert various appeals.

Popular Adult Fiction

Adult fiction genres with high appeal for teens include adventure, fantasy, mystery/suspense, horror, and science fiction. All of these genres are characterized by *action*, throwing their heroes and heroines into exciting situations and forcing them to make decisions and act quickly. Titles from these genres are most likely to be made into big budget, heavily promoted movies, reinforcing their prominence in readers' minds as good stories. When I ask older teens to recommend books for me to read, they often mention authors rather than specific titles. Many adult popular fiction authors have written six to a dozen or more books in their genres, and their names function as reliable brands.

Tom Clancy and Michael Crichton top the list of adventure novelists. Fantasy authors popular with teens include Orson Scott Card, Raymond Feist, Terry Goodkind, Robert Jordan, Mercedes Lackey, Anne McCaffrey, and Margaret Weis. The mystery/suspense genre benefits from its dominance of movies and TV. Mystery/suspense authors popular with teens include Edna Buchanan, Mary Higgins Clark, Harlan Cohen, Janet Evanovitch, John Grisham, Carl Hiaasen, Tony Hillerman, Barbara Michaels, Ridley Pearson, and Elizabeth Peters. Clive Barker, Stephen King, Dean Koontz, and Anne Rice hold the horror concession, keeping teens scared spitless. Science fiction authors popular with teens include Lois McMasters Bujold, Orson Scott Card, Dennis Danvers, Robert Silverberg, and Connie Willis.

Other genres read by teens are retold Arthurian and other tales, romance, inspirational fiction, graphic novels, and historical fiction. I usually confine my presentation of these genres to quick show-and-tells of a few titles so that teens know the library has books in those genres.

Realistic Adult Fiction

Realistic adult fiction of interest to older teens runs the gamut from thoughtful, literate fiction to spunky contemporary tales. Of particular appeal are novels featuring teens, college students, or twenty-something adults. These novels play on one of the strongest bonds between teens and books: to read about someone who, like them, is working out the story of his or her life, weathering challenges and seeking happiness.

Popular authors include Tracy Chevalier, Jane Hamilton, Barbara Kingsolver, and Nicholas Sparks. *The Lovely Bones* (Sebold 2002) allows the spirit of fourteen-year-old Susie to watch her family and friends as their lives continue after she was raped and murdered. *Where the Heart Is* (Letts 1995) finds Novalee, seventeen, who is seven months pregnant, abandoned in a Wal-Mart parking lot. *The Secret History* (Tartt 1992) follows the fates of several super-smart college students in the wake of a crime. And remember, humor is a major communication medium for teens. *Bridget Jones's Diary* (Fielding 1998) leads the new wave of contemporary tales dubbed "Chick Lit," featuring young women who are just trying to make a living, keep their friends, and find a mate—only everything keeps getting in their way!

Finding Adult Fiction Titles

Bestseller lists—print and electronic—are good sources for adult fiction. What's playing at your local movie theater? Chances are that you have the book on your shelves, and many more like it. YALSA's "Alex Awards," mentioned in the section on nonfiction, recognize both adult nonfiction and fiction, as do *Booklist, School Library Journal*, and *Voice of Youth Advocates* when indicating adult books of interest to older teens. These journals may also feature articles highlighting adult books, such as mysteries (Charles and Morrison 2002).

Reader advisory sources have proliferated in the past fifteen years. Following are just a few. Now in its fifth edition, the one-volume *Genreflecting* (Herald 2000) breaks down popular adult fiction into genres, subgenres, and sub-subgenres. In recent years, a new Genreflecting reader advisory series has devoted entire volumes to such genres as fantasy, science fiction, adventure/suspense, romance, horror, Christian, and contemporary mainstream fiction. Volumes in the series include *Fluent in Fantasy: A Guide to Reading Interests* (Herald 1999), *Now Read This II: A Guide to Mainstream Fiction, 1990–2001* (Pearl 2002), *Romance Fiction: A Guide to the Genre* (Ramsdell 1999), and *Strictly Science Fiction: A Guide to Reading Interests* (Herald and Kunzel, 2002). The *What Do I Read Next?* (Gale Group, 1991–present) series has expanded into genre advisory titles for fantasy, horror, mystery, and science fiction. One of the useful features of these resources is their inclusion of "Teenager" in their character indexes.

National chain booksellers maintain Web sites. So also do many independent booksellers, such as Powell's City of Books. Looking at the Web sites of locally owned bookstores, you can get a sense of what people in your area are reading. You'll also find author interviews, "best books" lists, and ideas for book displays. Many reading groups publish their booklists on the Web and are excellent sources for realistic adult fiction. Toss "Reading Groups" into an Internet search engine and pick out something like The Book House of Stuyvesant Plaza, a clearinghouse for book reading groups in New York State. Looking for books? Click on What the Reading Groups are Reading to get a list of adult fiction, nonfiction, and classics.

Adult Fiction Booktalk

Jenna Starborn, by Sharon Shinn

Jenna was an orphan, raised by her wealthy aunt and despised by her creepy cousin. Jenna was never quite sure what her aunt wanted her to be, and finally she was sent far away to school. Jenna stayed in school for ten years—and stayed on as a teacher. But a restless spirit inspired her to look for employment elsewhere, and she found it, at a remote old house.

Jenna's new job was easy. But the house was strange. It was cut off from the rest of the world, and some of the other people who worked there were deeply weird. And the sounds, the odd laughter in the night, the moans, the screams, all made Jenna wonder if she'd made the right choice. Until Mr. Ravenbeck, the owner of the house, arrived on the scene. A man with a terrible secret, he challenged Jenna with his intelligence, his wit, and his stormy good looks. To her amazement, Jenna fell in love.

Sound familiar?

Orphan, long years at school, new job in a remote place, strange sounds in the night, man with a terrible secret . . .

Could this book be . . . *Jane Eyre*, by Charlotte Bronte?

Well, yes . . . and no.

Yes, the house is remote, the owner is fascinating, and his secret is indeed terrible.

But no. Jenna is not an orphan, she was harvested from the human generation tanks on a faraway planet. She was purchased by a woman who wanted a child but rejected her when her own child was born, sending Jenna to school to study astronomy, physics, and force fields.

If you like science fiction, and if you enjoy tales of independence and passionate love, fast-forward hundreds of years and travel from the English countryside out into the new worlds of the universe. And if you like *Jenna Starborn*, you'll love *Jane Eyre*.

CLASSICS

By booktalking classic literature, you are paying older teens the ultimate compliment: They are smart. They can read and enjoy books that handle the big themes: becoming an individual, finding one's place in the world, love, betrayal, sacrifice, death, redemption. Unlike other books you may be booktalking, classics are often assigned rather than discretionary reading. Classics may be assigned during the school year or as required reading over the summer. Graduating seniors may have received suggested reading lists from their colleges or universities. And there may be some older teens who enjoy reading classics for their depth, their power, their intensity, and the time they take to tell a story really well.

Booktalking classics thus answers the "what's in it for me?" question, giving older teens a sneak preview of something they know they have to read anyway, so they might as well listen up. It's a good deal for everybody, including teachers, who may be looking to sell their students on the classics.

Finding Classics

There are many sources for classics titles. Your high school English department may use a classics reading list. Get it. Look for titles you can booktalk, and find out if students can read additional titles to expand the pool. For example, if the high school list includes *The Stranger* (Camus [1942] 1946), booktalk *The Plague* (Camus [1947] 1991). And go regional. If you live in Nebraska, booktalk *My Antonia* (Cather [1918] 1996). If you live in New Mexico, booktalk *Death Comes for the Archbishop* (Cather [1927] 1993). If it's okay with the teachers, booktalk classic plays by Ibsen, Shaw, Chekhov, Lorca, and Baldwin. Booktalk Homer.

An excellent source for classics is *Outstanding Books for the College Bound* (Lewis 1996). Over 1,000 classic titles, selected by the Young Adult Library Services Association from 1959 to 1994, are drawn from the categories of arts, biography, fiction, nonfiction, current issues, and poetry. The current list appears as "Outstanding Books for the College Bound" on YALSA's Web site, as one of its booklists. *Reading Lists for College Bound Students* (Estell et al. 2000) contains actual reading lists from the freshman English classes of over 100 colleges and universities. An annotated list of the 100 titles most often recommended by schools is a good place to start when looking for high-profile books.

Look for ways to connect teens with classics. One way is to booktalk titles relevant to times and places they're studying in history classes. Emphasize the relevance and timelessness of classics by tying them to current events, trends, problems, ideas, or interests. Conflicts between fathers and sons are explored in *Go Tell It on the Mountain* (Baldwin [1953] 1963) and *Brothers Karamazov* (Dostoevsky [1880] 2002). *The Plague* (Camus [1947] 1996) can be linked to AIDS and other contemporary disasters. If teens think their town is full of weirdos, they need to stroll through *Winesburg, Ohio* (Anderson [1919] 1960). *Kristin Lavransdatter* (Undset [1922] 1955) begins on Kristin's wedding day, when she's already pregnant (in fourteenth-century Norway). This novel, like other works set in medieval times, may appeal to fantasy readers familiar with created worlds of knights, armor, and connection with nature. Teens can hang out with slackers lounging around nineteenth-century German spa resorts in *Smoke* (Turgenev [1867] 1995). *The Dream of the Red Chamber* (Tsao [18th century] 1977) draws readers into an eighteenth-century Chinese world as far away as any fantasy novel, and yet its family problems and tale of undying love span the centuries. *Madame Bovary* (Flaubert [1856] 1957) coolly skewers small-town life, medical experimentation, romance without love, and credit card debt.

And here's something else. Many "classics" started out as popular fiction. These books feature exciting plots, colorful characters, and solid writing. One example of this type of classic is *Michael Strogoff* (Verne [1876] 1997), a robust adventure novel about a courier for the Russian Tsar which, like adventure novels today, was made into a movie (twice!).

Classics Booktalk

The House of Mirth, by Edith Wharton

You know how it is. It always looks so easy for them, the popular people. They wear the cool clothes, they go to the cool parties, they've got the cool cars, and they've got cool places to go. Beautiful, smart, funny, Lily fits right in with the popular people, and they accept her as one of them. It's the world Lily knows, the world where she thinks she belongs.

Not that it isn't kind of difficult sometimes. Unlike her friends, Lily has no money. Her father went bankrupt and her parents died. She lives with her aunt, who gives her a tiny allowance. It's barely enough to buy enough of the right clothes so that Lily can keep up with the crowd. It costs a lot to keep up with the popular people, but for Lily, it's an investment in the only future worth having.

Her friend Lawrence also hangs out with the popular people sometimes, but he can't take very much of it. How can you stand it? he asks Lily. They're boring, they're stupid, they think that having money makes them better than anyone. Guys like Gus are sexual harassers and women like Bertha are back-stabbing witches. Why do you care about them so much?

Lily just smiles. Lawrence obviously doesn't get it. He has a career, and he can afford to be independent. One hundred years ago in New York City, a woman like Lily had no education, no career, no money, and she could not afford to be independent.

And yet, deep down, Lily agrees with Lawrence about the shallowness and cruelty of the popular people. She dreams of another way of life, a life where long talks about ideas and long walks under the autumn trees are more important than the latest fashion, the latest scandal, the latest gadget. But if she wants a life of security and luxury, Lily has no choice: She has to set her dreams aside, and keep on the good side of people like Gus and Bertha. And she'll do whatever it takes to get the security she craves.

BOOKTALKING PERFORMANCES

Booktalking performances for older teens resemble those for younger teens, with a few differences, as outlined in the first section of this chapter. Here's what has worked for me.

I send a letter to the high school's media specialist, containing an outline of my presentation and my available dates. I follow up with a phone call and arrange a date and a schedule.

I usually speak to at least two classes at once. There are three reasons for this. One, it allows me to see more students in a shorter period of time. Two, my booktalking style is more theatrical than conversational and works better with larger groups. And three, combining two classes destabilizes the group dynamic of each class. The "host" class is no longer completely at "home," and the "visitor" class is no longer on its home turf. The group is thus organized around an event—a booktalking performance—rather than its familiar everyday routine.

I bring a box to the school containing books, magazines, books on cassette and CD, videos, DVDs, handouts with annotations of the books I'm booktalking, booklists, bookmarks, and library card applications. I also bring bookstands so I can stand up books without having to worry about them falling on their faces.

I introduce myself with my name, title, what I do, and where I work. The first thing I talk about is the library's electronic databases and Internet connection, which quickly imparts a positive first impression of the library as a place of gleaming twenty-first-century hardware—rather than dimly lit, dust-choked shelves. Next, I do a quick show-and-tell about library materials, plus updates on library services, teen events, and volunteer opportunities. When show-and-telling books, I include them all, so that teens can see more than the titles I'll soon be booktalking in more detail.

Next I'm ready to booktalk. I'll begin by saying something like this: "Today I'm going to show you a mix of books for life, fun, and school. Oh, yeah, and some fiction." As booktalkers know, there are numerous ways to put together booktalk programs. Using nonfiction, you can assemble a mélange of books from all subjects. For fiction, you can focus on high-appeal genres and themes, or focus on one genre or theme. You can also booktalk in a sequence that builds to a thematic whole. These and other methods are described in materials about booktalking on YALSA's Professional Development Center Web site (Young Adult Library Services Association 2002).

Now, this last part is really important. Reserve five to ten minutes at the end of your presentation to say something like this: "Okay, I've told you about some good books. What are you reading? What do you think *I* should read?" At first there's total silence. Nobody wants to say anything. A little cajoling ensues.

Then a hand goes up, and a book is suggested. And then another hand goes up. Write down titles. If you've heard of a title, ask, "is that the one where . . .?" so that the teen can tell you (and the rest of the group) more about the book. Alert for reader advisory opportunities, suggest another title. If you haven't heard of the title, ask, "what's that about?" so that the teen can talk about it. More hands go up, more books are suggested, and then faster and faster, like popcorn taking off in a microwave, even more hands go up, more books are suggested, I'm walking up and down the rows between the chairs, writing down books, suggesting more books, stirring up a hurricane of books whirling around the classroom. Brains on fire for reading, teens are raving about books, to each other, to me, to their teachers.

And that is the *fifth* reason why it's so much fun to booktalk—to all teens!

REFERENCES AND SUGGESTED READINGS

Abramson, Marla. 2001. "Why Boys Don't Read." *Book.* (January/February): 86–88.

Anderson, M. T. 1997. *Thirsty.* Cambridge, MA: Candlewick Press.

Anderson, Sherwood. [1919] 1960. *Winesburg, Ohio.* Reprint. New York: Viking.

Armstrong, Jennifer. 1998. *Shipwreck at the Bottom of the World: The Extraordinary True Story of Shackleton and the* Endurance. New York: Crown.

Baldwin, James. [1953] 1963. *Go Tell It on the Mountain.* Reprint. New York: Dial Press.

Barrett, Tracy. 1999. *Anna of Byzantium.* New York: Delacorte Press.

Bodanis, Richard. 1997. *The Secret Family: 24 Hours Inside the Mysterious World of Our Minds and Bodies.* New York: Simon & Schuster.

Book House of Stuyvesant Plaza. Available: http://www.bhny.com/front/readgrp.html. (Accessed December 9, 2002).

Booklist. American Library Association (50 E. Huron St., Chicago, IL 60611).

Buskin, Richard. 2002. *Sheryl Crow: No Stranger to This Game.* New York: Billboard Books.

Cadnum, Michael. 1999. *Rundown.* New York: Viking.

Camus, Albert. [1942] 1946. *The Stranger.* Translated by Stuart Gilbert. Reprint. New York: Vintage Books.

———. [1947] 1991. *The Plague.* Translated by Stuart Gilbert. Reprint. New York: Vintage Books

Canfield, Jack. 1997. *Chicken Soup for the Teenage Soul: 101 Stories of Life, Love, and Learning.* Deerfield Beach, FL: Health Communications.

Cappo, Nan Willard. 2002. *Cheating Lessons.* New York: Atheneum Books for Young Readers.

Cart, Michael, ed. 2002. *911: The Book of Help.* Chicago: Cricket Books.

Cather, Willa. [1918] 1996. *My Antonia.* Reprint. New York: Alfred A. Knopf.

———. [1927] 1993. *Death Comes for the Archbishop.* Reprint. New York: Modern Library.

Charles, John, and Joanna Morrison. 2002. "Clueless: Adult Mysteries with Young Adult Appeal 2002." *Voice of Youth Advocates* 25, no. 5 (December): 335–339.

Clark, Catherine. 2000. *Truth or Dairy*. New York: HarperTempest.

Cohen, Harlan. 2000. *Campus Life Exposed: Advice from the Inside: Eye-Opening True Stories and Advice*. Princeton, NJ: Peterson's/Thomas Learning.

Cooney, Caroline. 1995. *Both Sides of Time*. New York: Delacorte.

Cox, Terry. 2000. *You Can Write Song Lyrics*. Cincinnati, OH: Writer's Digest Books.

Crutcher, Chris. 1993. *Staying Fat for Sarah Byrnes*. New York: Greenwillow Books.

Dessen, Sarah. 2000. *Dreamland*. New York: Viking.

Donegan, Lawrence. 2002. *California Dreaming: A Smooth-running, Low-mileage, Best-priced American Adventure*. New York: Atria Books.

Dostoevsky, Fyodr. [1880] 2002. *Brothers Karamazov*. Reprint. New York: Farrar, Straus & Giroux.

Ehrenreich, Barbara. 2001. *Nickel and Dimed: On (Not) Getting by in America*. New York: Metropolitan Books.

Elkind, David. 1998. *All Grown Up and No Place to Go: Teenagers in Crisis*. Reading, MA: Perseus Books.

Estell, Doug, Michele L. Satchwell, Patricia S. Wright, and Tim Padgett. 2000. *Reading Lists for College Bound Students*. New York: Arco.

Favorite Teen Angst Books. Available: http://www.grouchy.com/angst/. (Accessed December 9, 2002).

Ferris, Jean. 2000. *Eight Seconds*. San Diego, CA: Harcourt.

Ferris, Timothy. 2002. *Seeing in the Dark: How Backyard Stargazers Are Probing Deep Space and Guarding Earth from Interplanetary Peril*. New York: Simon & Schuster.

Fielding, Helen. 1998. *Bridget Jones's Diary*. New York: Viking.

Flaubert, Gustav. [1856] 1957. *Madame Bovary*. Translated by Francis Steegmuller. Reprint. New York: Random House.

Flinn, Alex. 2001. *Breathing Underwater*. New York: HarperCollins.

Flipse, Robyn, M.S., R.D. 2002. *Fighting the Freshman Fifteen: A College Woman's Guide to Getting Real About Food and Keeping the Pounds Off*. New York: Three Rivers Press.

Gallo, Don, ed. 2001. *On the Fringe*. New York: Dial Books.

Gaskins, Pearl Fuyo. 1999. *What Are You?: Voices of Mixed-Race Young People.* New York: Henry Holt.

Gerard, Philip. 2002. *Secret Soldiers: The Story of World War II's Heroic Army of Deception.* New York: Dutton Books.

Giles, Gail. 2002. *Shattering Glass.* Brookfield, CT: Roaring Brook Press.

Goldberg, Bernard. 2001. *Bias: A CBS Insider Exposes How the Media Distorts the News.* Washington, DC: Regnery Publishing.

Grant, Cynthia. 1995. *Mary Wolf.* New York: Atheneum Books for Young Readers.

Haddix, Margaret Peterson. 2000. *Turnabout.* New York: Simon & Schuster.

Herald, Diana Tixier. 1997. *Teen Genreflecting.* Englewood, CO: Libraries Unlimited.

———. 1999. *Fluent in Fantasy: A Guide to Reading Interests.* Englewood, CO: Libraries Unlimited.

———. 2000. *Genreflecting: a guide to reading interests in genre fiction.* Englewood, Colo.: Libraries Unlimited.

Herald, Diana Tixier, and Bonnie Kunzel. 2002. *Strictly Science Fiction: A Guide to Reading Interests.* Englewood, CO: Libraries Unlimited.

Hewett, Lorri. 1998. *Lives of Our Own.* New York: Dutton Children's Books.

Hobbs, Will. 1998. *The Maze.* New York: Morrow Junior Books.

Holmes, Barbara Ware. 1997. *Letters to Julia.* New York: HarperCollins.

Internet Public Library. *TeenSpace: Books and Writing.* Available: http://www.ipl.org/div/teen/browse/bw2000/. (Accessed December 9, 2002).

Jones, Patrick. 2001. "Nonfiction: The Real Stuff." *School Library Journal* 47, no. 4 (April): 44–45.

Jordan, Sherryl. 2002. *The Hunting of the Last Dragon.* New York: HarperCollins.

Kador, John. 2002. *201 Best Questions to Ask on Your Interview.* New York: McGraw-Hill.

Katz, Jon. 2000. *Geeks: How Two Lost Boys Rode the Internet Out of Idaho.* New York: Villard Books.

King, Stephen. 2000. *On Writing: A Memoir of the Craft.* New York: Scribner.

Klause, Annette Curtis. 1997. *Blood and Chocolate.* New York: Laurel Leaf.

Kliatt (Kliatt Publishing, 33 Bay State Rd., Wellesley, MA 02481).

Letts, Billie. 1995. *Where the Heart Is*. New York: Warner Books.

Lewis, Marjorie, ed. 1996. *Outstanding Books for the College Bound: Choices for a Generation*. Chicago: American Library Association.

Littke, Lael. 1998. *Haunted Sister*. New York: Henry Holt.

Lubar, David. 2002. *Dunk*. New York: Clarion Books.

Mad. E.C. Publications (1700 Broadway, New York, NY 10019).

Marsden, John. 1995. *Tomorrow, When the War Began*. Boston: Houghton Mifflin.

McCoy, Kathy, et al. 1999. *The Teenage Body Book*. New York: Perigee.

Miller, John, and Aaron Kenedi, eds. 2002. *Inside Islam: The Faith, the People, and the Conflicts of the World's Fastest-Growing Religion*. New York: Marlowe.

Myers, Walter Dean. 1999. *Monster*. New York: HarperCollins Children's Books.

Nomad, Skye, and Lake Nomad. 2001. *Gotta Hike B.C.* Riondel, BC: Voice in the Wilderness Press.

Oates, Joyce Carol. 2002. *Big Mouth & Ugly Girl*. New York: HarperTempest.

The Onion. Available: http://www.theonion.com. (Accessed December 9, 2002).

Pearl, Nancy. 2002. *Now Read This II: A Guide to Mainstream Fiction, 1990–2001*. Englewood, CO: Libraries Unlimited.

Peters, Julie Anne. 2000. *Define "Normal."* Boston: Little, Brown.

Peterson, P. J. 2002. *Rising Water*. New York: Simon & Schuster.

Peterson's Vocational and Technical Schools: West. 2001. Princeton, NJ: Peterson's Guides.

Pfetzer, Mark, and Jack Galvin. 1998. *Within Reach: My Everest Story*. New York: Dutton Books.

Pierce, Meredith Ann. 2001. *Treasure at the Heart of the Tanglewood*. New York: Viking.

Plum-Ucci, Carol. 2000. *The Body of Christopher Creed*. San Diego, CA: Harcourt.

———. 2002. *What Happened to Lani Garver*. San Diego, CA: Harcourt.

Powell's City of Books. Available: http://www.powells.com. (Accessed December 9, 2002).

Power, Ashley. 2001. *Goosehead Guide to Life*. New York: Hyperion.

Qualey, Marsha. 1997. *Thin Ice.* New York: Delacorte.

Quarles, Heather. 1998. *A Door Near Here.* New York: Delacorte.

Raab, Evelyn. 1998. *Clueless in the Kitchen.* Buffalo, NY: Firefly Books.

Ramsdell, Kristin. 1999. *Romance Fiction: A Guide to the Genre.* Englewood, CO: Libraries Unlimited.

Reading Rants. Available: http://tln.lib.mi.us/~amutch/jen/index.html. (Accessed December 9, 2002).

Rinaldi, Ann. 1997. *An Acquaintance with Darkness.* San Diego, CA: Harcourt.

Santrock, John W. 1997. *Life-Span Development.* Madison, WI: Brown & Benchmark.

Schlosser, Eric. 2001. *Fast Food Nation: The Dark Side of the All-American Meal.* Boston: Houghton Mifflin.

School Library Journal (Cahners Publishing, 360 Park Avenue South, New York, NY 10010).

Sebold, Alice. 2002. *The Lovely Bones.* Boston: Little, Brown.

Shinn, Sharon. 2002. *Jenna Starborn.* New York: Ace Books.

Sleator, William. 1996. *The Night the Heads Came.* New York: Dutton's Children's Books.

Spencer, Pam. 1999. *What Do Young Adults Read Next? Volume 3: A Reader's Guide to Fiction for Young Adults.* Detroit: Gale Group.

Sykes, Shelley. 1998. *For Mike.* New York: Delacorte.

Tartt, Donna. 1992. *The Secret History.* New York: Alfred A. Knopf.

Trembath, Don. 1997. *A Fly Named Alfred.* Victoria, BC: Orca Book.

Tsao, Hsueh-Chin. [18th century] 1997. *The Story of the Stone (aka the Dream of the Red Chamber), volumes 1–5.* Translated by David Hawkes et al. Reprint. New York: Viking.

Turgenev, Ivan. [1867] 1995. *Smoke.* Translated by Constance Garnett. Reprint. New York: Turtle Point Press.

Undset, Sigrid. [1922] 1955. *Kristin Lavransdatter.* Translated by C. Archer and J. S. Scott. Reprint. New York: A. A. Knopf.

Van Draanen, Wendelin. 2002. *Sammy Keyes and the Search for Snake-Eyes.* New York: Alfred A. Knopf.

Verne, Jules. [1876] 1997. *Michael Strogoff.* Translator not given. Reprint. Simon & Schuster Children's Books.

Voice of Youth Advocates (Scarecrow Press, Inc., 4720A Boston Way, Lanham, MD 20706).

Werlin, Nancy. 2000. *Locked Inside*. New York: Delacorte.

Werner, Doug, and Steve Badillo. 2002. *Skateboarding: New Levels: Tips and Tricks for Serious Riders*. Chula Vista, CA: Tracks Publishing.

Weyland, Jocko. 2002. *The Answer Is Never: A Skateboarder's History of the World*. New York: Grove Press.

Wharton, Edith. [1905] 1997. *The House of Mirth*. New York: Simon & Schuster.

What Do I Read Next? 1991–present. Detroit: Gale Research.

Williams-Garcia, Rita. 1991. *Fast Talk on a Slow Track*. New York: Dutton.

Wulffson, Don. 2001. *Soldier X*. New York: Viking.

Young Adult Library Services Association. *Winning Titles*. Available: http://www.ala.org/yalsa/booklists/index.html (Accessed December 9, 2002).

Young Adult Library Services Association: Professional Development Center. *Professional Development Topics: Booktalking*. Available: http://www.ala.org/yalsa/profdev/booktalking.html. (Accessed December 9, 2002).

7

Thinking Outside the Book: Nonprint Collections for Older Teens

Robyn Lupa

I tell my friends it's a cool place to hang out and that they have the same magazines the stores have, CDs, DVDs—and recent ones too! Kids think we only have books. We are more than books.—Myers (2001, p. 46)

This quotation was the description a young woman gave her peers to convince them to try the library. It is no mystery that many librarians, especially those who work with teens, were originally drawn to the library profession because they love books and reading. It is unlikely that many library students planning to work with teens are thinking, "I can't wait to graduate so I can help teens check out DVDs, promote music by Limp Bizkit, and show teens Web sites about video games." Librarians serving teens, however, should aspire to create and promote an appealing nonprint materials collection because teens will be looking for music, movies, and Web sites, and if the public library does not provide them, teenagers, especially older ones who drive and may have money to spend, will go elsewhere to satiate their need for nonprint materials.

IMPORTANCE OF NONPRINT MATERIALS

Children and teens born in or after 1982 have been dubbed the "Millennials" (Howe and Strauss 2000). This racially and ethnically diverse generation was the hottest media growth market in the 1990s. They were raised on MTV, the Internet, and educational environments that have fully incorporated technological as well as print learning tools. How can the public library attract and keep these library users? First, accept that technology is necessary and a reality in these patron's lives. Be aware that older teens, faced with time-consuming academics, extracurricular activities, first jobs, and family responsibilities, may be using the library more for academic reasons than for leisure. High school students are faced with great pressure to succeed in academics and athletics. Post-graduation plans are being solidified. They are investigating employment opportunities, career goals, and decisions on whether to enter college, trade school, or the military. The public library can meet needs of older teens by providing educational and life-skills videos and DVDs and recorded books. The library staff can also entice older teens into becoming recreational lifelong library users by purchasing music and feature films and computer software and by offering Internet access.

Public libraries can learn from retailers such as Old Navy and the Gap, which generate loyal customers with hip displays and constantly rotating and updated merchandise. Offering popular materials such as DVDs and CDs will likely entice teens to take a look at the print collection as well. Librarians who take the time to make themselves aware of teen interests and technology will greatly enhance their communication with these patrons who need to be hooked.

Nonprint materials should not be considered mere supplements to a young adult book collection. Informational and recreational materials are not limited to print. For many teen-oriented subjects, the best presentation of the material is on film. A video on smoking or drunk driving complete with graphics, real-life scenarios, and well-presented facts and statistics can have much more of an emotional impact than text and may be the best resource on the topic. Learning how to repair a car or balance a checkbook is very effective via a video presentation rather than perusing a manual. Listening to a recorded book for an assignment in a car on the way to school or work is the solution for a busy teen who juggles multiple projects and welcomes an alternative to more reading.

Providing popular materials will bridge the gap between haves and have-nots—those teens who cannot afford to buy many entertainment materials for their private collections. Not all teens fit the Millennial stereotype of having unlimited disposable income. Similarly, there is much national concern about the digital divide. Although today's youth have been dubbed the 'Net Generation, not every family owns a home computer. Knowledge of computers, however, is an expectation for teens today. Many have learned to multitask using computers, and it is not unusual to find that teens are chatting, researching, listening to music, and shopping all at once via the Internet.

An informal survey of public librarians conducted using the PUBYAC, PUBLIB, and YALSA-BK mailing lists indicates that librarians around the country recognize the value of nonprint collections for their teen patrons. One comment reiterated repeatedly is that these materials are purchased because teens want them and, since teens are valued library patrons, they should be provided with a selection that interests them. Several respondents similarly indicated that nonprint items attract teens who may not otherwise use the library.

LEARNING ABOUT DIFFERENT TYPES OF NONPRINT MATERIALS

To effectively purchase nonprint materials for teens, it is essential to find out what teens are currently watching on television and on the big screen, listening to on the radio or on headphones that may be hooked up to a computer or a CD player, and surfing for on the Internet. Consider the following suggestions to help with staying current:

- Read reviews from newspapers and magazines. Browse through *Teen People, Entertainment Weekly,* and *Rolling Stone.*

- Make a list of future video purchases based on current box office popularity. Look for those five-star rated CDs. Notice which entertainers are featured on the cover of young adult-oriented magazines. Check local newspapers to find out what is happening in the immediate community.

- Walk around and unobtrusively observe which sites are viewed at computer terminals.

- Check circulation and reserve statistics to see if there are any topical interest patterns that can be applied to nonprint media.

- Check the return cart before compact discs are reshelved to find out which ones seem to be constantly moving.

- Put the teen advisory board to work, discussing and making selection decisions for nonprint materials. What novels are being read in area high schools? Purchase them on tape or compact disc. Have them poll their friends on favorite artists and authors. What nonfiction video subject areas have appeal? Ask them to discuss curriculum-related needs and personal interests so that video selections can be tailored to the broader community.

- Stash comment cards or suggestion slips near AV sections of the library. Send the message to teens that their input is crucial for selection decisions. Talk to the teens who regularly hang out at the library and ask them to jot down a few titles or artists that they know to be popular.

- If outreach is offered in high schools, ask teens in the classroom for suggestions before or after giving booktalks.

- Get copies of reading lists from teachers and purchase books on tape and/or CD accordingly.

- If the budget is slim, attempt to start a collection with items donated by teens. These materials not only bring young adults into the library but give a boost to overall circulation figures.

- When building a nonprint collection, selection methods for many of these items will not be found in the usual sources, and traditional collection development methods will have to be re-thought. Whereas print collection development concentrates on quality as much as popularity, the selection criteria for nonprint materials place more emphasis to popularity. Library-specific standards must be created for these purchases. Monitoring the movement of the collection and soliciting teen suggestions will be just as important as using review sources.

- Shelve nonprint materials with YA books whenever possible, to create a true YA space. Make the area busy with face-out shelves and different formats placed near one another.

- If no separate YA audiovisual space is available, it may be better to shelve nonprint YA items with the adult collection rather than the juveniles to establish a clear age differentiation.

- Designate teen materials with a YA shelf code, a YA label, or a colored dot affixed on all items for that audience.

- Establish a separate popular music area for both juveniles and young adults, apart from the adult compact disc collection.

- Be a rebel! This is counter to traditional library ethics, but consider housing compact discs haphazardly. Put them in random order in bins or baskets that beg to be browsed. Teens who only love the music of Mozart might learn to appreciate the screams of Ozzy Osbourne, whereas mellow Pink Floyd fans might end up grooving to "No Woman No Cry" by Bob Marley.

- Realize that change is constant, especially regarding technology. Librarians will need to constantly learn about new technologies as they emerge. Some teens are accustomed to reading e-books instead of books in print. One cannot guess what the technology will be like ten years from now; who would have thought, ten years ago, that virtual reference would be so prominent throughout the United States, or that video streaming would be possible through the Internet?

DISPLAYING NONPRINT MATERIALS

Make teens aware of offerings via fliers, by scattering random compact discs on tables, or by purchasing simple display racks to advertise current acquisitions. Consider using the following merchandising techniques. First, learn from retailers. Teens like dynamic environments. Target stores use colorful advertising to tell teens that the store is fun, and Target is one of the most popular retailers for teens (White-Sax 2002). Also, showcase recreational topics or school subjects by grouping items of diverse formats together. Put a copy of *Into Thin Air* in a recorded book format next to the printed book and add the *Everest* video or DVD to the mix. Display a couple of PBS's In the Mix series videos on a shelf along with several contemporary young adult novels.

VIDEOS AND DVDs

Library videos and DVD collections are composed of three basic types: recreational (such as music, sports, and feature films), informational, and educational. Educational and informational programs are heavily reviewed in traditional selection journals including *School Library Journal* and *Booklist* and are readily found in publisher and distributor catalogs. Recreational videos are described in specialized journals such as *Video Librarian*. Some teens may also be interested in video streaming, a topic that is discussed in the December 2002 issue of *Voice of Youth Services*. As with any type of collection development, the patron community must be studied to determine subject demand. Video and DVD topics with teen appeal include the following:

- Older teens are planning their immediate future, so information about college and vocations will be in demand. Local colleges often produce recruitment videos. Documentaries give teens and their parents a first-hand look at academic life. *Inside America's Military Academies: Surviving the First Year*, for example, is a dramatic insider look at the first-year experience in military academies.

- Alternative forms of transportation are important to teens. Programs on roller blading, skateboards, scooters, and mountain bikes that both glorify the sport as well as offer practical tips on purchasing and maintaining equipment will surely be welcome.

- Examinations of social concerns (e.g., homelessness, AIDS, sexual harassment, abuse) are relevant. Read magazines and watch the news to learn about these issues. Well-produced videos that address these topics may help teens or their parents, teachers, and mentors begin to discuss their realities.

- Real-life survival skills are effectively presented on videos and DVDs: dorm life, first apartments, grocery shopping, laundry, budget planning, managing checking and saving accounts, and responsible use of credit cards.

- Driving tips and car repair basics are a concern for this age group.

- Curriculum ties for literature classes including Shakespeare productions and other classics are winners for older teens.

- PBS's In the Mix (http://www.pbs.org/inthemix) is a hip documentary series that highlights timely subjects such as the drug Ecstasy, school violence, sexuality, and gangs in a choppy, MTV style featuring familiar celebrities as hosts.

- Music videos, live concert performances, and biographies in the style of VH-1's *Behind the Music* will attract teen patrons.

- Today's hot topic is anime! A multitude of online catalogs offer the moving image equivalent of graphic novels, including http://www.rightstuf.com/ and http://www.animenmore.com/. *Sailor Moon, Dragonball Z, Ranma ½,* and *Ah My Goddess* are just a few of the popular series.

Video and DVD Selection Tools

Following are some of the professional resources that can help you build and maintain your collection:

- *Video Librarian.* In addition to the print publication, this journal and its database of searchable reviews may also be accessed online at www.videolibrarian.com.

- *Voice of Youth Advocates* has a regular column, "Teen Screen: Video Reviews," in which Sarah Flowers recommends products for teens.

- An annotated list of videos, mostly feature films, is included in "Connections: Recent Films for Young Adults" by Alan Teasley and Ann Wilder in the Winter 2003 issue of *Young Adult Library Services.* Several of the videos listed are about older teens, including some who are already out of high school.

- Library Video Company at www.libraryvideo.com can be used to select and order videos, DVDs, and CD-ROMs from reviews, recommendations, and lists of award-winning titles. The easy-to-use database allows the user to create shopping carts and also to save orders for future reference.

- Internet Movie Database at www.imdb.com allows members to rate movies within age and gender categories.

- Screen-It at www.screenit.com will help determine whether a movie fits into a library's collection development policy, with its information about violence, nudity, sex, and blood/gore contents, complete with specific examples from the films.

- The annual "Selected DVDs and Videos for Young Adults" list of the Young Adult Library Services Association (YALSA) is useful. Librarians who work with teens create the list after critiquing videos and DVDs throughout the year. The list is published immediately after the ALA Midwinter conference on YALSA's Web site and in the March issues of *School Library Journal* and *Booklist.* The Winter 2003 issue of *Young Adult Library Services* includes several articles about experiences of librarians who were part of the committee that selects the winners for the list.

Video and DVD Purchasing Decision Issues

What should you, as a librarian serving older teens, base your purchasing decisions on? Following are some things to consider:

- The decision whether to include R-or even X-rated (think of the nonedited version of *Last Tango in Paris*) items is less of a concern for the older teen group than it is for their younger counterparts. Library collections should reflect communities, and each community may be different. Community standards should be considered when building collections. In some libraries, the patron records of teens aged sixteen and over are confidential and not under parental control. Other libraries require permission forms from parents for any audiovisual borrowing by patrons under eighteen or sixteen years old, and some libraries still do not allow anyone under the age of eighteen to check out videos or DVDs. Some libraries purchase R-rated films on a case-by-case basis, if the teen appeal or patron demand strongly justifies their inclusion. Movies specifically marketed to teens that happen to be R-rated may be obvious candidates for purchase. Despite readily purchasing R-rated films, some libraries do not shelve them in a young adult section at all but store them on the adult video shelves, catering to cross-over interest for both age groups. YA labels that may be affixed to video and DVD cases to clearly identify teen materials to patrons are available from suppliers such as Brodart and Demco. Designating some videos as YA neatly separates out PG-rated materials from children's video collections. Because of the high cost of many videos, selection decisions will take much deliberation. Ideally, a collection will be balanced among informational, educational, and recreational materials.

• Should videos or DVDs be purchased? Are many patrons buying DVD players as they become more affordable? Or does VHS remain the preferred format, for now? Similar to cassette tapes and compact discs, this is a format in transition. It might be wise to purchase according to a ratio; that is, for every two copies of a VHS production, one DVD of the same title will also be acquired. Remember that as more DVD players are purchased, especially around the holidays when they are on sale, library patrons are more likely to donate videotapes to the library. It would be a waste of money to purchase a multitude of videotapes that might be donated in the near future, and the money would be better spent on DVDs.

• Should multiple copies be purchased? Clearly, this decision must be based on what your budget allows. Some productions are too costly to warrant more than one or two copies. Others, if they are affordable, might be justified because of their certain popularity. It may be advantageous to partner with neighboring library systems or state consortiums and divvy up purchases so that more videos and DVDs may be acquired and interlibrary loaned for patrons.

• Checking waiting or holds lists for popular new titles will give a good indication of which format seems to have the slighter edge. DVDs may have the greater appeal since tech-savvy teens will be able to play the discs on their Playstations and Xbox's as well as on their home PCs.

• Should Hollywood films be purchased for the public library? Many libraries limit their video buying to educational and life skills topics rather than attempting to compete with video stores or the Netflix service at www.netflix.com, from which DVDs are mailed to customer's homes. Library policies on this issue run the gamut, with some libraries opting not to match Blockbuster's selection, and others purchasing feature films only if they appear on "best of" lists such as the following:

  - National Film Registry, http://lcweb.loc.gov/film/filmnfr.html

  - Academy of Motion Picture Arts and Sciences, http://www.oscars.org/

  - American Film Institute, http://www.afi.com/tv/lists.asp

  - Sundance, http://www.sundance.org

• Some libraries opt to collect art films and documentaries that may not be readily available in chain stores. Others restrict their Hollywood purchases to films that are literary adaptations, including classic films as well as more recent ones such as *Princess Diaries* and *Tuck Everlasting*.

MUSIC

Music is essential for any popular materials collection. With teens, it is the key component of your collection. This, above all, is the one item that will lure them into the library and keep them coming back for more. Although tastes change, music itself will probably never go out of demand. One caution about musical compact discs is the likelihood that the disc or case may be broken or the liner notes ripped. Of all materials in the public library, compact discs are typically the most frequently stolen or never returned. On the other hand, shelf space is rarely an issue with compact disc collections for teens. These items will be so popular with patrons that they will undoubtedly be in constant circulation and rarely on the shelf. Library staff may never see the compact discs again after they have been purchased; not necessarily because the compact discs have been stolen, but because they are so popular that they will be listened to by teens for years, in the privacy of their bedrooms, in their cars, or by use of a portable compact disc player at practically any location.

Should materials that are labeled with Parental Advisory stickers be purchased for public library collections? In 1985, reacting to all types of explicit lyrics in popular music, Tipper Gore founded the Parents Music Resource Center (PMRC) to promote responsibility and self-policing in the recording industry. At the urging of the PMRC, the Recording Industry of America agreed to the voluntary labeling of albums. By 1990, the RIIA had developed a uniform label to be used by all of its members. This label is to be affixed on recordings that contain explicit lyrics dealing with sex, violence, suicide, drug use, bigotry, and Satanism. Some artists, such as Eminem, are selling two versions of the same musical work, one self-censored and considered the "clean" version. Stores are not permitted to sell recordings with the Parental Advisory label to people less than eighteen years old. This is not a foolproof system, however, since judgment by various record labels about the definition of "explicit" is not uniform. The absence of a Parental Advisory sticker does not guarantee the absence of profanity. Parental Advisory labels give no true indication of content and should not necessarily be considered as a selection criterion for libraries. The decision to provide Parental Advisory-labeled compact discs, similar to the decision to purchase R-, X-, or NA-rated films, depends on selection policies, the library board and administration, and community climate.

Some libraries opt for a tiered card system: full versus limited access to the collection of videos and music, based on parental consent. In a YALSA-BK mailing list poll, librarians expressed much concern that buying edited versions equates to censorship. The assumption that parents must supervise their own children's library use extends to nonprint materials: movies, the Internet, and music. However, the reality is that some library systems are under citizen or board pressure to maintain a more conservative collection. It may be a good idea to survey parents, young users, and teen advisory boards before deciding whether to purchase compact discs with the Parental Advisory label.

John Berry reminds the profession that libraries deemed "unsafe" are doing their jobs. Good libraries, he says, have similar policies about free expression: "They all warn, like good libraries anywhere, that the library 'does not limit access to materials or attempt to protect users' " (1999, p. 6). Ultimately, if librarians are politically able, they must trust teens to think critically about the media. Ironically, compact discs that have been affixed with the Parental Advisory label are probably the most popular with teens—alternative rock, rap, and heavy metal. Some library systems will purchase only Parental Advisory versions of compact discs since teens looking for appealing music will respect library staff for providing this level of access. Some libraries shelve compact discs with Parental Advisory stickers in the adult collection, to separate them from younger browsers. Music compact disc vendors will often offer alternate cover art when the original is controversial. This may be an option in more conservative communities.

Learning About Teen Music Interests

Teen musical interests cover a wide spectrum. There are several different approaches to take for music collection development. Watch MTV, especially the popular *Total Request Live,* VH-1, BET, and listen to the radio. Local record stores may be helpful to find out what is popular in the immediate area. Browse music chain stores and department stores to view displays and quickly learn what is current and hot. Above all, ask teens what they are listening to for the purpose of generating collection development ideas. Music teacher Joe Stuessy is director of the division of music at the College of Fine Arts and Humanities at the University of Texas at San Antonio. He gives some great tips on staying informed:

> *Encourage students to share their favorite cassettes with you. They are usually delighted to do so. Listen to the first and last songs on each side, only about ten to fifteen minutes of your time—perhaps the time it takes to drive to and from school. These will usually give you the typical style of the group in question. Assign yourself to watch a minimum of thirty minutes of MTV per week. Usually this will give you a general impression of what is happening. Finally, browse through Rolling Stone magazine in your school library. (1994, pp. 28–32)*

Stop teens who are listening to a headset and chat about the artist. Ask teens using the Internet to show you the latest music sites. Ask library staff members who are teenagers about musical interests to help with generation gap problems between librarians and teen patrons. Coordinate purchases with other library departments. In some libraries young adult staff order the more popular materials while the adult staff concentrate on older rock, blues, and jazz recordings.

With music, general print selection policies may cause a dilemma. Popular music will not always be well-reviewed or the "best" of what is available. If the broader goal is to serve the recreational and entertainment needs of patrons, then highly regarded material may not always be what you should buy since it is not what teens really want to hear. Both "good" and "popular" must be part of a music selection policy. Longevity is not necessarily a goal for a teen collection. Whether this wave of teen pop stands the test of time doesn't invalidate it for now—it is *relevant* now. On the other hand, many teens listen to the groundbreaking music of their parents' or even grandparents' generations, including Led Zeppelin, the Beatles, and the Doors. When buying music for teens, there is no one definitive genre on which to focus.

Music Selection Tools

Besides talking to teens and listening to music, there are a few other ways to maintain awareness of new trends and releases, including the following:

- Subscribe to commercial and librarian-oriented mailing lists to find out about new titles.

- *Rolling Stone* remains as relevant as always, and now current and retrospective compact disc reviews, quips on what is new and trendy, and quick information on featured artists may be found on its Web site at www.rollingstone.com.

- Not only may the standard *Billboard* charts be viewed at www.billboard.com, but *Hits of the Web* music charts from various Web sites including CDNOW.com, MP3.com, and emusic.com may be viewed to sample what computer users are really listening to. Specialized charts such as *Independent Albums, R&B/Hip-Hop Albums, Country Albums, Electronic Albums, Billboard Latin 50*, and *Heatseekers* will provide more specific information on the pulse of listeners than the *Billboard 200* chart. *Billboard* deals with national popularity but does not cover regional interests. Age preferences are not reflected on its charts.

- *Spin* magazine at www.spin.com is especially popular with older teens and college students.

- The latest music magazine, *Blender*, at www.blender.com, salutes " the unique brilliance of rock & roll in all its forms" and reviews games and DVDs in addition to music.

- VH-1's Web site, www.sonicnet.com, contains reviews and lists of current popular music that is usually edgier than the content of other sites.

- At Barnes and Noble stores and on their Web site at www.barnesandnoble. com, check out top bestseller lists in music categories such as alternative, country, dance and DJ, pop, R&B, and hip-hop to find out what is currently popular.

- Media Play's Web site at www.mediaplay.com includes music, videos, DVDs, and computer software. Bestseller lists and new releases are featured in all categories.

- An invaluable selection tool for all library materials, www.amazon.com, lists new releases in various categories and the option to subscribe to an online music newsletter. Amazon indicates whether compact discs contain explicit lyrics.

- CDNOW at www.cdnow.com is a comprehensive music site that includes buying guides, best-of lists, and categorized reviews. CDNOW includes world music and Christian/gospel along with the usual categories. Its DVD and video lists are also very useful and are broken down into specific categories such as anime.

- A definitive one-stop source is the All-Music Guide at www.allmusic. com. Look here for maps of various musical genres and styles.

- A comprehensive site on which the catalogs of specific artists in 716 music genres may be browsed is found at www.artistdirect.com. It contains lists of online magazines and e-zines in those genres, useful for concentrated collection development.

- Music for young adults is featured on http://teenmusic.about.com, a site that offers a pulse on mainstream music.

- Epinions at www.epinions.com is a source that, based on unbiased consumer reviews, "helps people make informed buying decisions." Read here the opinions of fans on music grouped into various categories.

COMPUTER SOFTWARE

As older teens prepare for the future, the necessity for word processing software is a given. Older teens also need software that provides preparation for the SAT, PSAT, and other standardized tests. College, financial aid, and scholarship information will also be in demand. A multitude of software on educational topics and practical skills is available: career exploration, typing, resume writing, computer training, foreign language learning, childbirth, reading comprehension, street atlases, guitar tutorials, vocabulary practice, and high school and college-prep curriculum titles. CD-ROM reviews are published monthly in *School Library Journal* and in online catalogs such as Crimson Multimedia at www.crimsoninc.com.

Games will be a sure hit with teens, and as with other formats, should be purchased according to local demand and popularity. They will boost circulation and attract a loyal patron base. Types of games to buy include the enduring arcade style, simulation scenarios, tycoon adventures, TV tie-ins such as *Who Wants to Be a Millionaire,* and board game spin-offs, including *Monopoly*, *Scrabble*, and *Trivial Pursuit.* Find reviews in print and online gaming magazines such as *PC Gamer* at www.pcgamer.com, Nintendo Power at www.nintendo.com, and *Electronic Gaming Monthly* at gamers.com. Online reviews of computer games are also found at the following sites:

www.happypuppy.com

www.gamespot.com

www.gamezilla.com

www.pcgameworld.com

www.allgame.com

www.gamezone.com

Web sites of individual gaming systems are helpful for learning more about the products and quickly determining best-selling software. View Microsoft's Xbox at www.xbox.com, Sony's Playstation 2 at www.us.playstation.com, and Nintendo Game Cube at www.gamecube.com. With ever-changing technology and a multitude of new products released monthly, it may be wise to wait one year after a new game system is released to determine which software will remain popular and to let the initial high prices of the games decrease.

COMPUTER HARDWARE

Consider the importance of upgrading and maintaining computers, as well as increasing the number of computers available as demand also escalates. Without up-to-date equipment, teens will quickly become discouraged. They will not use library computers that are slow, if they constantly freeze, or if the waiting list is too long to access the machine. Many teens have computers at home and labs at school. State-of-the art PCs that allow access to sound bytes and video clips, headphones plugged into jacks, and swift connections to the Internet are ideal. Create full communication stations with both word processing and the Internet where teens can download files and e-mail attachments such as resumes for job searches or college correspondence. Librarians should provide teens as much free public access to computers as possible with the best equipment possible.

Due to the Supreme Court's decision in 2003 regarding the Children's Internet Protection Act (CIPA), librarians need to be especially in tune with older teens who need computer access. The decision states that people aged seventeen and over are allowed to ask for unfiltered Internet access in public libraries. It is likely that some older teens may be embarrassed to ask for filters to be turned off, even though the filters may block important information that they may desperately need.

WEB PAGES

Internet provision is now a given in most public libraries across the country. Teens use the Internet for e-mail, search engines, music, television and movie sites, general research, games, chat rooms, personal Web pages, and sports sites. Beyond providing computer terminals, libraries can create Web pages with selected sites that cater to their own teen communities, reflect collection development policies, and exemplify the library's mission.

Library Web Pages

The Virtual YA Index at http://yahelp.suffolk.lib.ny.us/virtual.html is an excellent source for examples of young adult-oriented public library Web pages. The following are samples of useful library Web pages for teens:

- The Central Rappahannock Regional Library system's Teenspoint, at www.teenspoint.org, does not fit a standard mold, with its appealing layout and organization.

- New York Public Library's site, at http://www2.nypl.org/home/branch/ teen/index.cfm, is organized and colorful.

- The King County Library System's teen Web page, located at www.kcls. org/newya/ya.cfm, is extremely eye-catching and teen-friendly.

Web Page Content Appealing to Older Teens

What type of Web pages do teens enjoy? Following is a sampling of great sites for older teens:

- Downloadable music or spoken word programs that may be listened to at the computer or burned to compact disc are found at www.audible.com.

- Conduct a college search with Princeton Review's http://www.embark. com/.

- Teenage angst books are presented at http://www.grouchy.com/angst/.

- Creative writing opportunities abound on the Internet. *Teen Ink* is a print and online magazine at www.teenink.com that publishes students' own writing for others to read.

- Teens may network with their peers at The Student Center, located at http://www.studentcenter.org/teenmap.php.

- A very popular entertainment site is www.shockwave.com, which includes games, greeting cards, cool downloads, digital films, music, and video mixers.

- Find the "most interesting sites on the Internet" on www.bored.com.

- Link to local school Websites and ask them to reciprocate by including the public library on their pages.

- Introduce teens to online journaling (Ryan 2002).

- Music lovers can share files on Kazaa.com, a peer-to-peer Web site that allows users to download free files, primarily songs.

- The High School Hub at www.highschoolhub.org is a noncommercial portal to free online academic resources for high school students. It features learning activities; an ongoing teen poetry contest; a reference collection; college information; and subject guides for English, mathematics, science, social studies, world languages, arts, health, and technology.

- College-bound high school students who want to crash online classes for AP tests should visit www.cramcentral.com.

- Tips for new drivers are listed on http://www.teendriving.com/.

- Explore anime at http://www.animerica-mag.com/.

- A one-stop source for newspapers worldwide is http://www.thepaperboy.com/.

- The Internet Public Library has created a virtual space for teens at http://www.ipl.org/cgi-bin/teen/teen.db.out.pl?id=bw2000.

- Many authors have created their own fan pages. Rob Thomas's page at http://www.hieran.com/rob/index2.html and Chris Crutcher's page at www.aboutcrutcher.com are just two examples.

CHAT ROOMS

Chat and instant messaging (IM) are near-standard communication tools for today's young adults. IM is a character-based substitute for the telephone, used for making plans and gossiping. Just read *Romiette and Julio* (Draper 1999) to discover how teens are using chat rooms, which are like giant conference calls. Whoever is on the line can jump in at any time with their views and express themselves by typing rather than speaking. Many chat rooms have been designed for teen use. Some have specific topics, such as those offered by online specialty magazines. Current popular chat rooms include the following:

Virtual chat and three-dimensional environments at www.worlds.com/.

America Online, www.aol.com.

Chat 101, www.ker95.com/chat101/index.html.

Have a fantastical online experience at www.furcadia.com.

Yahoo! Chat, chat.yahoo.com.

Chat for writers, chat.iuniverse.com.

Search the Internet for more teen chat rooms that will appeal to your library patrons.

ELECTRONIC DATABASES

Information literacy has been explored recently in the library field, especially relating to high school and college students. Joyce Valenza, high school media specialist, is featured in the November 2002 issue of *School Library Journal*. Valenza has taught students to rely on not only the Internet for research purposes but reference databases as well. Whereas students were previously accustomed to primarily using Internet search engines, now they are accessing primary documents, among other resources (Whelan and Minkel 2002, p. 48). Public librarians should also be prepared to give teens access to electronic databases, especially if they are used to using these resources at the school library. Teens with access to well-funded, technologically savvy school media centers may expect the same type of resources from public libraries. Otherwise, public libraries may lose their older teen audiences. Since information on the Internet is not always reliable, librarians should be prepared to direct teens to other electronic resources that are authentic—magazine and newspaper databases fill this void. In many states, the state library has been responsible for maintaining access to electronic databases and has given names to these groups of products. The following are suggested electronic databases for older teenagers:

- *Critical Companions to Popular Contemporary Writers*: Analysis of best-selling fiction.

- *Electric Library*: Full-text collection of magazines, newspapers, radio and TV transcripts, and more.

- *Ethnic News Watch*: Full-text collection of newspapers and journals representing the ethnic minority.

- *Grolier Online*: Multimedia encyclopedia.

- *Historic Events of the 20th Century*: Allows researchers to learn about history; includes lesson plans for teachers.

- *InfoTrac Student Edition*: Magazine articles, newspapers, and excerpts from reference books about current events, science, arts, popular culture, and more.
- *Lit Finder*: Full-text access to essays, poems, and short stories.
- *Mitchell's Online Repair Guides*: Repair manuals for many types of vehicles.
- *netlibrary*: Provider of electronic books.
- *NoveList*: Readers' advisory service including booktalks and summaries for young adult novels.
- *Proquest*: Full text and back issues of newspapers.
- *SIRS Knowledge Source*: Topic-based research with articles from hundreds of newspapers and magazines; especially useful for social issues research.
- *Test Preparation Program*: Immediate scoring and complete answer explanations for a variety of tests. One sample is LearnATest.com, providing tests relating to topics including academics and GED preparation; tests for firefighters, EMS workers, and law enforcement officials; military tests; real estate tests; and civil service tests.
- *What Do I Read Next?* Reader's advisory tool for fiction and nonfiction.

RECORDED BOOKS

Recorded books are often picked up by older teens for educational use. With their busy lifestyles, listening to a book that has been assigned or is on a college-prep reading list may be much more convenient for teens than finding the time to sit down and read the text. More young adult novels are being produced on tape or compact disc and, properly marketed, may find great appeal among a leisure-reading audience. With the variety of learning styles that exist in children, teens, and adults, the library's offering of recorded books caters to those auditory learners. Recorded books are particularly valuable for reluctant readers and those who wish to visually follow the print text while listening to the audio version. Based on patron demands, libraries will need to determine policy on purchasing abridged, unabridged, or a mixture of both versions, depending on particular titles or genres. Recorded books are also useful to teens who are learning English as a second language. Read "How Audiobooks Helped Us to Listen, Speak, and Earn a Cool Trip" in the December 2001 issue of *Voice of Youth Advocates* to lean first-hand how recorded books have helped teens.

Cassette Tapes Versus Compact Discs

Most teenagers are not familiar with record albums, and in a few years they probably will not be too familiar with cassette tapes, either. Compact discs scratch more easily than cassette tapes, but tapes can also become mangled in players. The three-minute tracks on compact discs are very convenient for jumping around the text. The sound quality of compact discs is better than cassette tapes. As new vehicles come equipped with compact disc players, and some car dealerships charge extra to install a cassette player in a vehicle that already has a compact disc player, this format caters to a modern audience. Those who do not consider themselves modern, and who rely on cassette tapes, will find more circumstances in which it is necessary to conform to becoming modern. Many teens own a portable compact disc player that enables them to listen to books while exercising or commuting. Compact discs are a bit more expensive than cassette tapes, and not all titles are available in that format.

Recorded Book Selection Tools

How do you select the best recorded books? Try these suggestions:

- One method of selection is to meet with local high school teachers and obtain copies of their reading lists. Inevitably, many of the "classics" will already be found on adult recorded books shelves.

- Run system reports to determine high circulation statistics of literature of interest to teens. If the print copy is leaving the shelves, it's likely that the audio counterpart will also find an audience.

- YALSA's Audio Books and Media Exploration Committee creates an annual list of selected recorded books.

- Pam Spencer Holley's "Audiobooks It Is!" appears in the February and August issues of *Voice of Youth Advocates*, reviewing recorded books for teens.

- *Audiofile Magazine,* at www.audiofilemagazine.com, is a good source for recorded books.

- Kliatt, at http://hometown.aol.com/kliatt/index.html, reviews more than 100 recorded books in each issue.

- Read "The Emergence of Spoken Word Recordings for YA Audiences," in the Winter 2003 issue of *Young Adult Library Services*. Goldsmith gives practical information about selected recorded works. There is also a thorough list of audio magazines and publishers of recorded books.

- Some publisher Web sites, such as Random House at www.randomhouse.com and Books On Tape at www.booksontape.com, include downloadable audio samples to hear the product before purchase.

For all patrons, the modern public library offers much more than books. Audiovisual media not only enhance recreational and educational topics but are sometimes the preferred source for imparting information. Acquiring nonprint items can be a lot of fun, since it delves into nontraditional methods of collection development. Librarians who take the time to make themselves aware of teen interests and technology will greatly enhance their communication with these library users who need to be hooked.

REFERENCES AND SUGGESTED READINGS

Berry, John. 1999. "We 'Protect' Free Expression." *Library Journal* 24, no. 16 (October 1): 6.

Birkey, Kathleen. 2001. "E-Books—The Future of Reading." *Voice of Youth Advocates* 24, no. 1 (April): 28–30.

Caisse, Josephine. 2003. "YALSA's Selected DVDs and Videos for Young Adults." *Young Adult Library Services* 1, no. 2 (Winter): 41.

Crowley, Stephen J. 2003. " 'We Gave the World New Ways to Dream': Thoughts on Selected Films for Young Adults." *Young Adult Library Services* 1, no. 2 (Winter): 44–45.

Draper, Sharon M. 1999. *Romiette and Julio*. New York: Simon & Schuster.

Flowers, Sarah. 2003. "Teen Screen: Potluck." *Voice of Youth Advocates* 26, no. 1 (April): 34–35.

Gallant, Jennifer Jung. 2003. "The Mole People Revisited: Report from the Selected Films for Young Adults Committee." *Young Adult Library Services* 1, no. 2 (Winter): 42–43.

Goldsmith, Francisca. 2003. "The Emergence of Spoken Word Recordings for YA Audiences." *Young Adult Library Services* 1, no. 2 (Winter): 23–26.

Howe, Neil, and William Strauss. 2000. *Millennials Rising*. New York: Vintage Books.

Mardikian, Lucy, Fatima Shah, and Saima Shah. 2001. "How Audiobooks Helped Us to Listen, Speak, and Earn a Cool Trip." *Voice of Youth Advocates* 24, no. 5 (December): 345.

Meulen, Kathleen. 2002. "Electronic Eye: Streaming Video On-Demand." *Voice of Youth Advocates* 25, no. 5 (December): 364–365.

Myers, Elaine. 2001. "The Road to Coolness: Youth Rock the Public Library" *American Libraries* 32, no. 2 (February): 46.

Ryan, Sara. 2002. "Tag Team Tech: Not Under the Mattress: Revelations From Online Journals." *Voice of Youth Advocates* 25, no. 2 (June): 103.

Stuessey, Joe. 1994. "When the Music Teacher Meets Metallica." *Music Educators Journal* 80, no. 4 (January): 28–32.

Teasley, Alan B., and Ann Wilder. 2003. "Connections: Recent Films for Young Adults." *Young Adult Library Services* 1, no. 2 (Spring): 35–39.

Whelan, Debra Lau, and Walter Minkel. 2002. "Making Research Count." *School Library Journal* 48, no. 11 (November): 48.

White-Sax, Barbara. 2002. "With Time and Money, Teenagers Represent a Sought–After Market" *Drug Store News* 23, no. 8 (June 25): 68.

Index

209

My Father's Scar, 116
My Perfect Life, 147
My Sister's Bones, 143
My Sisters' Voices: Teenage Girls of Color Speak Out, 42
Myers, Elaine, 189
Myers, Walter Dean, 81, 122, 129, 142, 156
Myers Briggs Type Indicator test, 56
Myracle, Lauren, 148
Mystery/suspense genre authors, 169, 176

Na, An, 81
Nabokov, Vladimir, 120, 123
Nadler, Burton Jay, 52
Naked Lunch, 119, 123
Nash, Ogden, 65
National Center for Education Statistics, 10, 87
National Film Registry, 196
National Institute of Child Health and Human Development, 67
National Library Week, 101
National Vital Statistics Reports (NVSR), 9
Naythons, Matthew, 55
Necessary Noise: Stories About Our Families As They Really Are, 144
Necessary Roughness, 155
Nelson, Blake, 146
netlibrary, 205
Neuromancer, 123
New Moon Network, 67
New Rules of High School, 146
New York Public Library, 202
New York Times, 130
New York Times Best Seller's list, 121
New Yorker, The, 65
Newspapers, 203
Nichols, Mary Anne, 101
Nickel and Dimed, 165
Nicols, Janet, 82
Night I Disappeared, The, 152
Night the Heads Came, The, 169

Night Train, 143
Nikkah, John, 43
9/11 attack, 79
911: The Book of Help, 165
1984, 107, 123
Nintendo Game Cube, 201
Nintendo Power, 201
Nist, Sherrie, 40
No Child Left Behind Act, 54
Nodelman, Perry, 146
Nolan, Han, 122, 151
Nomad, Lake, 164
Nomad, Skye, 164
Nonfiction, promotion of, 164–68. *See also* Booktalking
  finding titles, 166
  informational nonfiction, 164
    how-to, 164
    inspiration, 164
    self-help, 164
  personal interest nonfiction, 164
    hobbies, 164
    interests, 164
    pastimes, 164
    personal care, 164
  school-related nonfiction, 165
    biography, 165
    cultural studies, 165
    current events, 165
    current issues, 165
    history, 165
    social studies, 165
  science, 166
Nonfiction materials, importance of, 28–31
Nonfiction resources, suggestions, 33–83
Nonprint materials for older teens, 189–208
  chat rooms, 203–4
  computer hardware, 201–2
  computer software, 200–1
  displaying materials, 193
  DVDs, 193–96
  electronic databases, 204–5

About the Editor and Contributors

Amy Alessio is the Teen Coordinator at the Schaumburg Township District Library in Illinois. For YALSA, she has served on the Board of Directors, the Membership/Division Promotion Committee, the Teen Read Week Work Group, the Local Arrangements Committee, and the President's Program Committee. She is the co-author of *Teen Read Week: A Manual for Participation,* published by the American Library Association in 2002. She is a YALSA Serving the Underserved (SUS) Trainer.

Sheila B. Anderson lives at www.sheilabanderson.com and in Dover, Delaware, where she is Director of the Dover Public Library. In 2003 she was elected to ALA Council-at-Large. For YALSA, she has served on the Board of Directors, the Selected DVDs and Videos for Young Adults Committee, the Professional Development Committee, and the Best of the Best Books for Young Adults Preconference Committee. She is a YALSA Serving the Underserved (SUS) Trainer. She is a recipient of the Frances Henne/YALSA/VOYA Research Grant and the Baker & Taylor/YALSA Conference Grant.

Patrick Jones runs connectingya.com, a consulting firm dedicated to assisting libraries in providing robust services to youth. He has written over fifty articles and several books, including *A Core Collection for Young Adults* (2003). For YALSA, he has served on the Board of Directors, Quick Picks for Reluctant Readers Committee, Teen Hoopla

Committee, Publications Committee, and the Professional Development Committee. He is a recipient of the Frances Henne/YALSA/VOYA Research Grant, and he is a YALSA Serving the Underserved (SUS) Trainer.

Robyn Lupa is the Head of Children's Services at the Arvada Library of the Jefferson County Public Library in Colorado. She also worked for the Queens Borough Public Library. She served on YALSA's Selected DVDs and Videos for Young Adults Committee and the Teen Web Site Advisory Committee. She also served on SRRT's Gay, Lesbian, Bisexual & Transgendered Book Award Committee and ALSC's Preschool Services and Parent Education Committee.

Kristine Mahood is the Young Adult Librarian for Timberland Regional Library, comprising twenty-seven libraries in five counties in southwest Washington state, where she performs booktalks for teens. She presented "Get Real: Booktalking Nonfiction to Teens" at the Washington Library Media Association Conference in 2000 and "Booktalking Psych-Up Tricks and Program Models" at the Public Library Association National Conference in 2000. In 2001, as part of the YALSA's "Power Up with Print" preconference at the AASL Annual Conference, she presented "Be a Performing Body, Not a Talking Head: Blueprints for Booktalk Programs." She is the co-author of "The Inner Game of Booktalking," published in the June 2001 issue of *Voice of Youth Advocates*.